GRANDMA, IS THAT YOU IN MY CLOSET?

Night Terrors, Shadows, Voices, Visitations, Secret Friends

DAN LANGENFELD

GRANDMA, IS THAT YOU IN MY CLOSET?
Copyright © 2015 by Dan Langenfeld

Published by:

Peak Publishing • A Division of Healthy Life Press
6700 Wadsworth Blvd., Apt. 101 • Arvada, CO 80003
www.healthylifepress.com • info@healthylifepress.com

Author: Dan Langenfeld
Designer: Judy Johnson

Printed in the United States of America

No part of this publication may be reproduced, stored in a retrieval system, or transmitted in any form or by any means—for example, electronic, photocopy, recording—without the prior written permission of the author, except for brief quotations in printed reviews.

Library of Congress Cataloging-in-Publication Data
Langenfeld, Dan

ISBN 978-1-939267-17-7
1. REL100000 RELIGION/Demonology & Satanism;
2. REL 067010 RELIGION/Christian Theology/Angelology & Demonology

Undesignated Bible quotations are from the Holy Bible, New International Version®, NIV® Copyright ©1973, 1978, 1984, 2011 by Biblica, Inc.® Used by permission. All rights reserved worldwide. Bible quotations marked NKJV are from the New King James Version®. Copyright © 1982 by Thomas Nelson. Used by permission. All rights reserved. Bible quotations marked KJV are from the King James Version, which is in the public domain. Capitalization of pronouns referring to deity follows the style of the translation being cited, or the authority being quoted. The Peak Press Style follows the Zondervan *Christian Writer's Manual of Style*.

This book is available through booksellers worldwide, in printed and electronic form. It is also available direct from the publisher, with free shipping and discounts available for combination purchases of printed and electronic formats, and for purchases of ten or more copies at one time. For more information contact: peakpublishinginfo@gmail.com.

Acknowledgements

A SPECIAL THANKS TO MY WIFE, MICHELLE, AND MY SONS who never gave up on me throughout this endeavor. Their unconditional love and support is something I will never forget.

A SPECIAL THANKS TO MY CLOSE FAMILY AND EXTENDED FAMILY for putting up with me as I did the necessary research for this book.

A SPECIAL THANKS TO THE MANY PEOPLE IN THE COMMUNITY who opened up their homes and lives for me as I researched for this book.

LAST, I'D LIKE TO THANK GOD FOR HIS LOVE, mercy, guidance, and faithfulness.

Table of Contents

INTRODUCTION

CHAPTER 1 1
Family Fun • Big Wheels • Talking to Casper • Innocence Taken Away

CHAPTER 2 9
Knock Knock, Who's There? • Not Of This World • Fear Factor • Alluring Subject • They're Here • Open The Floodgates • Ransacked Bedroom • Is This All Random? • Elusive Spirits • Tearing This All Apart

CHAPTER 3 25
It Must Be Haunted • A Lot To Consider • Here Kitty Kitty • Hi Grandpa • Mike Is Back • Haunted Houses • Loving Spirits • Are They Everywhere? • Contact Is Common

CHAPTER 4 39
Bloody Barn • Not Just The Barn • Shadows In The Night • The Number Three And Mirrors • Obscure Numbers • Variables Are Many • A Different Perspective • Oldest Book Out There • Angels • Evil Spirits

CHAPTER 5 55
Common Sense Is Good Sense • World Jumping Forbidden • We Can't Return • Unchained Melody • Good Or Bad Angels • Hard Pill To Swallow • Fallen Angels • My Own Sister • Misery Enjoys Company

CHAPTER 6 75
Phone Home, E.T. • Close Encounters • Mom And E.T. • Demonic Deception • It's All In The Name • Closely Related • Hard To Deny Similarities

CHAPTER 7 87
Wrestling With Demons • Realm Of Responsibility • Being Gulped Up • Not Of This World Struggles • Our Struggles • Ed And Lorraine Warren • Bedroom Captivity

CHAPTER 8 103
*Attacks On Women • Bull's-Eye On Women • Orphans And Widows •
Jeanie • Sexual Abuse • Terry • Hit List From Hell •
Weapon Of Isolation*

CHAPTER 9 117
*Seeds Of Confusion • Coping With Evil • Smells Like Aqua Net •
The Gift • Helping Strangers • Death Bed Confessions •
Sir Isaac Newton • Glimpse Of The Future •
Someone Is Better Than No One*

CHAPTER 10 135
*Attacks Early In Life • New House Same Story •
Unwanted Houseguests • Right Next To Us •
Aaron's Story • Possessive Spirits •
House Possession*

CHAPTER 11 149
*Life-Long Attachments • Thirty Years Of Evil Around •
Doors That Won't Shut • Simple Candles • Pacing Spirit •
Tentacles Of Evil • Grandkids As Well •
Mindy's Sister • Generational Pull*

CHAPTER 12 163
*Entire Families Consumed • Husband Number Two • My Own Family •
Opposites Don't Attract • Growling In The Crawlspace •
My Floating Mother • Fifty Years Of Encounters •
The Next Generation • Beth*

CHAPTER 13 183
*Reading Us Like A Book • Temptation Times Five • Brenda •
Brenda's Home Life • Heaviest Kind Of Guilt •
Kids All Over • Finding A Feeding Trough*

CHAPTER 14 197
*The Big Three • Numbers Don't Lie • Almost Big Four •
Little Kids • Break It Down • Demonic Motives*

CHAPTER 15 211
*Bumpy Ride • Direct Retaliation • Demonic Scare Tactics •
Ray • Breanna • Angelina • Monica •
Power Of The Enemy • Recap Of Their Power*

CHAPTER 16 227
*What God Do You Worship • The Difference Should Be Christ •
Satan's Crown Of Deception • Dorothy • Angelic Protection •
God's Word Uncovers Darkness • The More The Merrier*

CHAPTER 17 239
*Kicking Them Out • Levitating Chairs •
Alicia • Sleepwalking • My Own Life*

CHAPTER 18 247
*Final Nudge • Made For TV • Simple Dream •
Spirit Meter • Wicked Meter*

CHAPTER 19 257
*All I Know • Some Day We Will Know It All •
Don't Jump On Bandwagons • My Dad •
Lack Of Hope • Our Hope • The Invite*

RESOURCES 270

ENDNOTES 272

ABOUT THE AUTHOR 274

ABOUT PEAK PUBLISHING 275

Introduction

Sitting in Jillian's kitchen, with the rest of her family, listening to story after story, was the most eye-opening experience I have ever had. Her family's encounters were not as evil in nature as a few I've come across, but what was eye-opening was how often the spirits made their presence known to this family. Most other people I've talked with about this describe an occasional, seemingly random run-in with spirits. But with Jillian's family it was different, much different. They had to put up with it night after night. They told me that very rarely did a day go by without something strange happening in the house, with most of these events occurring between 2:30-3:30 in the morning.

Jillian and Darren bought their house in 2004, because of its many bedrooms, enough for their family of six to live in comfortably. The house, built in 1978, was originally designed to house mentally and physically handicapped adults. For twenty years this house was used primarily as a foster home for these disabled adults. It didn't take long after they moved in before the family was introduced to one of the deceased, former occupants of this house, his name was Jimmy.

Jillian started noticing that her five-year-old son, Dave, was talking to someone when obviously no one else was around. Dave told his mom he was talking to his friend, Jimmy. Most of the time these conversations occurred at the bottom of their staircase.

Of all the places in this house, Jillian wondered, *what is so special about this staircase?* A few months later, she happened to run into a former caretaker who used to work with these disabled adults. This caretaker informed Jillian that one resident, Jimmy, died in the home while she worked there. Jillian promptly asked the caretaker, "Where exactly in the house did he die?" The caretaker told her he fell down the stairs and passed away at the bottom of the staircase.

The family has lived in this house for ten years and unfortunately, none of them are spared from encounters and sounds that plague this old adult foster care home, including cupboard doors opening on their own, family pets looking into corners of rooms growling at nothing, light switches being turned on and off. Darren even rewired one particular light switch thinking he would solve the problem. But the light still turned on and off by itself. The family even refuses to be in their own house without the lights on.

Jillian simply told me that they have learned to put up with things due to her feelings that their unwanted guests seem harmless, despite the fact that some members of Jillian's family have been physically contacted by these spirits, several of them sharing with me that for some strange reason these spirits love sitting on their legs while they are trying to go to sleep at night. Darren told me that it is almost a nightly experience for him to feel some invisible spirit sit down on his legs as he lies in bed. If the lighting is right, he can actually see the bed sink down as this spirit takes a seat.

This spirit, or spirits, have a nightly ritual the family has to put up with, which is the main reason why their encounters are almost a daily occurrence. They parade up and down the staircase usually between 2:30-3:30 every morning. Then, once upstairs, they go from room to room almost as though they are checking in on everyone. Jillian's daughter, Nancy, told me that every night they open her door to her bedroom. She closes her door on purpose when she goes to bed, out of fear of seeing this spirit approach her bedroom. The option of seeing her door swing open seems better to her then seeing this spirit approach her room with the door already open.

Nancy also told me that once she is in bed she pulls the covers over her head and never looks out again till morning. She pulls the covers over her head because of a run in with a spirit at the end of her bed one night. She told me that she thinks it was her grandfather who appeared at the end of her bed. Regardless of who or what it was, it still makes her cower underneath her blankets the entire night.

Even guests who stay the night at this house have been harassed by these spirits. Jillian's sister, Kate, came to visit one weekend and got a rude awakening one of the nights she was there. Something woke her during the middle of night and she saw a blonde haired spirit standing at the foot of her bed. She yelled at the spirit saying, "Who's there?" No sooner did she say that when it vanished into thin air. Jillian informed her sister that she has seen that same spirit in the house, at the foot of her bed as well. Jillian's sister has never stayed another night in the house.

As I write these very words, someone very close to my own family is going through a rough time. Due to circumstances beyond her control, she was forced to leave her home in Escanaba, Michigan. She and her four kids are basically homeless, and are currently staying with Jillian until they can find an affordable place to stay.

Since moving in with Jillian, her oldest boy Ross has been talking to a secret friend like Dave used to, but with one noticeable difference. At times Ross seems to be afraid of this secret friend. Ross stands at the top of this same staircase and cries while pointing to something at the bottom of the stairs. When the family asks him what's wrong he points to the bottom of the stairs and says, "Him, him, him" as if someone is at the base of the staircase preventing Ross from using the stairs. Finally Ross's mother asked him who it was, and Ross said, "It's Jimmy."

I never intended to write a book on the paranormal. But as I dug into my mother's past occult practices, to hopefully understand and come to grips with things that had happened to us as kids, I began to uncover some answers to why she dabbled in things not of this world. I needed to know why we as kids had to deal with spirits day in and day out. Well, it didn't take me long to see that this project was going to be much bigger than anything I had expected. It quickly went from mere curiosity to book form based on hundreds of interviews within a matter of months.

As this took place, my conversations expanded as well. I went from talking with just my family, to interviews with extended family and close friends, and expanding to include quite a few people from within a hundred miles of my home in Upper Michigan. To my surprise, the stories started snowballing the further I dug into things, and that's when I knew that I couldn't just stop with my own family.

One set of stories involved an old farmhouse. Everything that I have heard about his old farmhouse has left me somewhat rattled—stories of growling in an attic crawlspace, kids waking up with scratch marks on their bodies, dark figures in and throughout the house, dark shadows peeking around trees, apparitions of a woman floating by family members as they watched television, and strange voices with the sounds of people walking in places where no one should be. The youngest daughter was thrown by an invisible force across the bathroom, landing in the tub and breaking her arm. Things were so bad in this house that one of the older siblings moved out before she graduated.

Another account involved a family whose son had to deal with a terrifying secret friend. This secret friend kept telling this young boy to do horrific things. The family became so concerned they started doing audio recordings in his room at night to see what exactly was going on. The voices they recorded left me speechless and made me wonder if the word "imaginary" should be thrown out completely in relation to kids with secret friends.

When our family moved from Racine, Wisconsin, in 1972, little did I know that our new start in Michigan's Upper Peninsula would also include things that are eerily similar to some of the stories I just shared with you. I was quite young when we moved, so my memory is a little hazy on things that happened before we moved to Michigan, which explains why most of what I do recall started after that move.

What started out for me as a personal research project turned into an unbelievable collection of stories from the other side. Many people whom I've known for years told me things that were astounding. Even close friends whom I thought I knew well shared things that set me back in my chair.

This project opened my eyes, as its findings will open yours. If you've read broadly in this field, you'll realize that some of the accounts are similar to those found in other books on the subject. Of course they are. Though the forces of evil can be quite creative in how they target individuals or families, their overarching purpose is the same as it has ever been.

Though I can't speak for the veracity of the accounts in other books, I promise you that all the stories included in this book are true and really happened, though every effort has been made to protect the privacy of the persons involved.

As you read, you will find significant differences between my own conclusions and the typical explanations often found in reference material on the subject. I believe that if you will read on with an open mind, you will better understand what is going on day-by-day in your own life or the lives of those you care about and long to help.

Your word is a lamp for my feet, a light on my path
(Psalm 119:105)

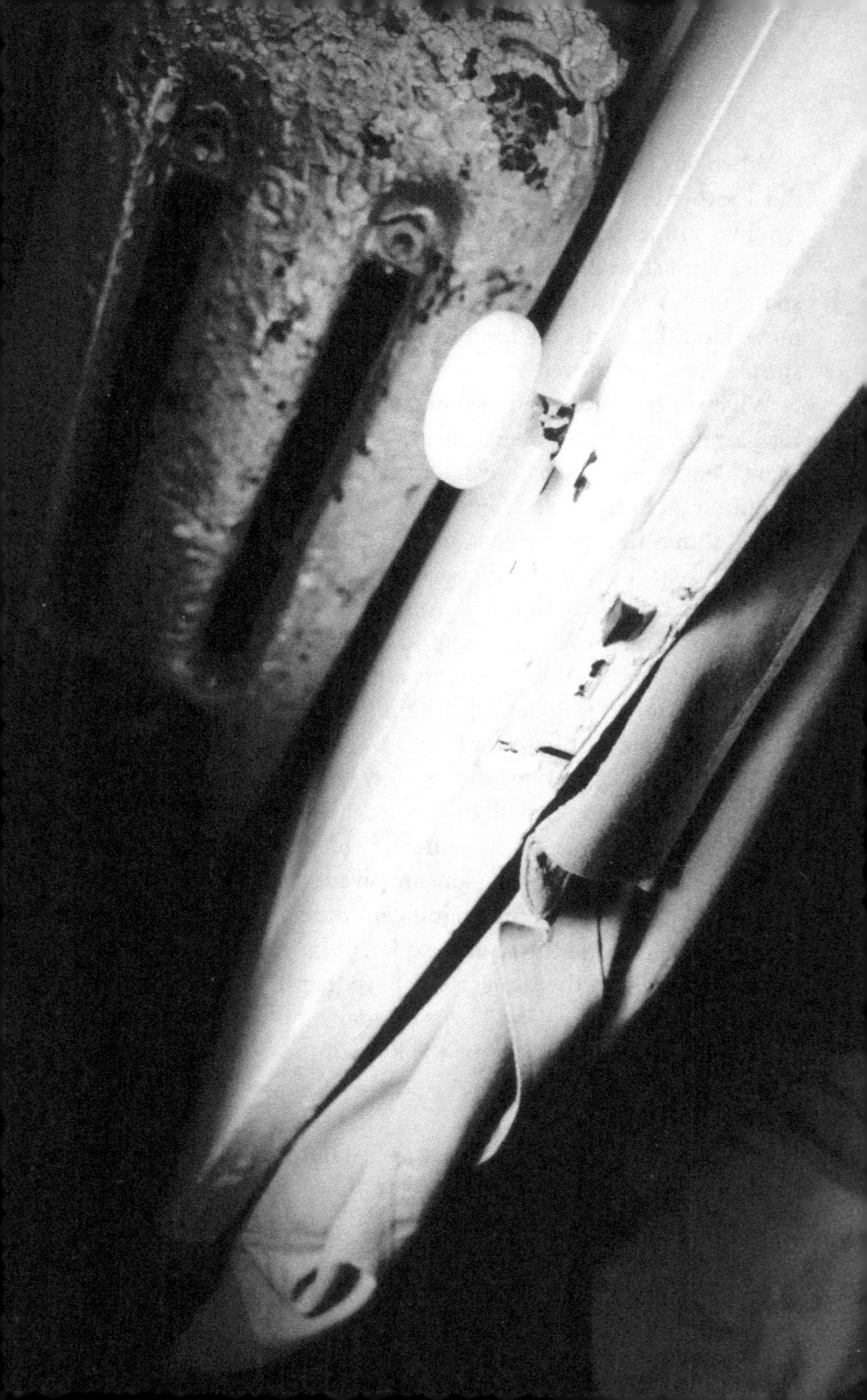

CHAPTER 1

Family Fun

Perhaps you are familiar with "Noah's Ark," in southern Wisconsin. Heralded as the country's biggest water park, this park is filled with countless water rides and hundreds of smiling faces. This is a popular vacation spot for families in the upper Midwest, even though it hardly seems like the appropriate spot for a water park when one has experienced the cold winters of the upper Midwest. The entire Wisconsin Dells area is riddled with amusement parks, go cart tracks, miniature golf courses, zip lines, and eateries.

Growing up in Southeastern Wisconsin, I lived fairly near this paradise on earth. How lucky for me to be so close to such an amazing place! You can imagine the smiles on mine and my sister's face when we got in the car and headed west toward the Dells, the land of water and fun!

My dad's Uncle Bart and Aunt Ganny lived in that area. We would stay at their house which was only minutes from this water paradise. Ahhh, life was good for this smiling five year old, as well as for my younger sister. I couldn't think of a better way for our parents to spend a few summer weekends than to take us to that part of the state, where a kid can act like a kid and have the time of his life. Life really was good for this southern Wisconsin five year old. Or was it?

Strangely, I have no memories as a five year old of sliding down a water slide. I have no memories of waves crashing into me. I am not really sure we ever set foot in any park in the Dells area. Years later as an adult, I took my family there. But I could not remember using any of the fun stuff so easily found there. I know we walked down the streets at night, that memory I do have. This probably has more to do with the fact we really had no money to spend on extras, so we would just walk around wishing we could do all those wonderful things. I really don't mind that now. It's something I just accept as a part of our life then.

But there is something I do mind now. It took over thirty years to figure out why we went there, and to see the motivation for spending the gas money to go visit our family. I knew that visiting the family was part of the reason, but something else finally came into focus that I did not like at all. Now, years later, it upsets me to have finally understand what was going on.

Big Wheels

Another early childhood memory was our frequent trips to visit my mother's sisters, who lived only a fifteen-minute drive from us. I loved going there because of all the cousins I got to hang out with. Counting our family and all my cousins, we had a small army of kids—sixteen of us. Just on the other side of my Aunt Pam's house was what I thought at the time to be a huge river.

Now I chuckle at that memory, because it was really more like a glorified ditch. But as a young kid it sure seemed a lot bigger. We would ride our bikes on the winding trails around that ditch, through the tag alders and weeds like there was no tomorrow.

There was so much to do around Aunt Pam's and Aunt Lily's house. In a way, it was another paradise for me as a kid. We all hung out and raced "Big Wheels" up and down a very long sidewalk that connected the two houses. There was a long straightaway with a sharp left turn, then a sharp right turn that ended at Aunt Pam's front steps. It felt like my own personal racetrack. That long sidewalk brings back a lot of fun memories for me. I spent many summer days on that sidewalk and no matter what we did out there, it was always fun!

On occasion, I would glance at the kitchen window of my Aunt Lily's house that faced this sidewalk that I grew up on. That is where all the adults huddled around their tall, sixteen-ounce glass bottles of Pepsi chatting the afternoon away, and of course, while being able to keep an eye on us kids, to make sure we weren't killing each other.

Sounds pretty innocent for the most part. Sounds like every day America in the late 60s, early 70s to me. But like the trips to the Dells area, these trips have also taken on a new meaning to me as I am coming to understand what was going on. Those tall bottles of Pepsis weren't the only things the adults were huddled around on that kitchen table. There was another reason we as a family went out there to visit, a less spoken of reason—something that came into focus only years later, as I became an adult.

You see, my mother had different reasons for that one hour trip to the Dells and it had nothing to do with those wonderful water slides. It had little to do with visiting family that were closer. It had nothing to do with taking the family for an exciting weekend getaway.

I do admit my mother had a beautiful voice and my father loved playing the guitar. They did go up to see Aunt Ganny and

Uncle Bart to play music with them. But there was a less spoken about reason my mother was so driven to make those visits. I have many memories of them sitting around Aunt Lily's kitchen table laughing and enjoying each other's company. I also have many memories of all of us singing. I do have many wonderful memories, that is for sure. I used to even have a cassette tape of me, as a six year old, singing, "Jeremiah was a Bullfrog," by Jim Croce. I can still picture my shyness as all the adults watched me perform.

But behind all those wonderful memories there was a more deviant, seldom talked about endeavor that I am positive at the time seemed harmless and actually fun to them. It might have been fun to them, but it produced something far more deviant for me (and others in their extended family).

Talking To Casper

My mother loved going to the Dells for one reason, so she could talk to spirits! Yes, you heard me right, she talked to spirits. When was the last time you mentioned spirits and water slides in the same conversation? Or zooming around on a big wheel while your mom was talking to Casper across the yard?

Mom and Aunt Ganny spent the weekend evenings talking to the other side, talking to beings that are normally not seen or heard. Most of my memories of those times in the Dells area are of my mother sitting at the dining room table with everyone else communicating with spirits. Years later, I would get the full story on what took place on those crazy weekends. A better way of saying that is that years later, I would feel the full impact of those "spiritual" dining room sessions.

As far as why we were at Aunt Lily's house, well, that wasn't as obvious in my five-year-old mind. My guess is that it was sheltered from us, or I am sure I would have a memory of it. I have learned from talking to family that were there, that a Ouija board sat alongside those tall Pepsi bottles on that kitchen table. For them, the board's purpose was to contact beings from another world.

A close family member told me that as they did the board at Aunt Lily's one night, something made contact with her under the table and she never participated again. So they were actually doing the same thing at Aunt Lily's house with the only difference being the method they used to contact them. They would ask the board questions and it would answer them. Her spirit contacting methods also included automatic writing. She did this and on occasion would run into the spirit of Sir Isaac Newton himself. Yes, you read that right. I will share that story later on in the book.

As I researched for this book, I got in contact with my dad's brother as well, just wanting to know a few things that he might be able to help me with. I love talking to my Uncle Dean. His facial expressions, mannerisms, and hearing his voice, remind me of my dad who has been gone now for more than twenty years. It never fails that when I contact him, he tells me a story or two about dad that I never knew before. My dad was a very reserved, quiet man. I have probably learned more about my dad from talking with others than I did from his own lips.

But this time, as I talked with my Uncle Dean about my book idea, he told me something about my mother instead. He mentioned that my mom's best friend, Elaine, had a spirit contacting habit as well. Once again, they must have done a great job hiding it because I have no memories of anything strange at Elaine's house. All I could think about when going over there was Elaine's daughter, one of my first true loves.

Reconnecting with my mom's friend Elaine was a pivotal moment as I went through the process of researching for this book. I was then able to reconnect with her daughter, Marcia, and then meet her daughter Shar as well. Shar is married with three children, and the stories she told me about her son's secret friend are remarkable. It totally changed my perspective on secret friends; you'll find her story later in the book.

Innocence Taken Away

Once I knew that Mom's best friend dabbled with the occult, it all started making more sense to me. It was as though my young childhood wasn't as innocent as I was led to believe. I hate to use the words betrayal, or lied to, but those feelings were hard to suppress as I learned more and more about what went on as I was growing up.

We really had no friends or any relatives that we went to see without the motivation to contact spirits. Granted, people generally associate with like-minded people. But it was just very revealing to me that it wasn't the simple friendship they sought out. It was that they all shared this unusual passion to make contact with beings from another world. Strangely enough, in doing research for this book, I have discovered that my mom even broke out her Ouija board with a few of my own friends when I was a teenager. I wonder what happened when she did it with them because I could only get one of them to answer me, and all she remembers was that she was scared out of her mind.

So you can see that on the outside my childhood looked and seemed pretty normal. But behind the scenes my childhood wasn't so normal or innocent. Little did I know then, but my life was being changed right before my eyes, and mostly without my knowledge or consent. Some of the roads that I hadn't traveled yet were being mapped out for my four siblings and me. I am convinced that the things my mom and those closest to her did with those spirits, had a lasting effect on everyone involved.

Since I was a very young child when all this started, I'm referring to memories of things that happened before I was five years old. I have vague memories of seeing a Ouija board. I also remember seeing tarot cards. I did have a chance to reconnect with an old friend of my mother's who told me that mom talked about us kids having issues with dark shadows in our room.

But there is one memory that does stand out in my mind and it has nothing to do with that water park. It has nothing to do with that long sidewalk we played on at Aunt Lily's house. It has nothing to do with the family we were visiting. It has nothing to do with spending quality time with those I loved the most in life. That memory is of my first encounter with something from the other side.

In the pages that follow, you will see the far-reaching effects of my mother's involvement with the occult, not only in me and my siblings but also in our extended family. Some people may think that using a Ouija board or tarot cards is harmless in itself, but by the time you finish reading the results of my interviews with over 400 people and my reflections on the significance of what I found, I am confident you will see the devastating long-lasting negative consequences of bringing these spirits into the lives of children, either through directly exposing them to the occult, or by opening the door for evil spirits to harass them because of the generational curse that will be another consequence of your own involvement.

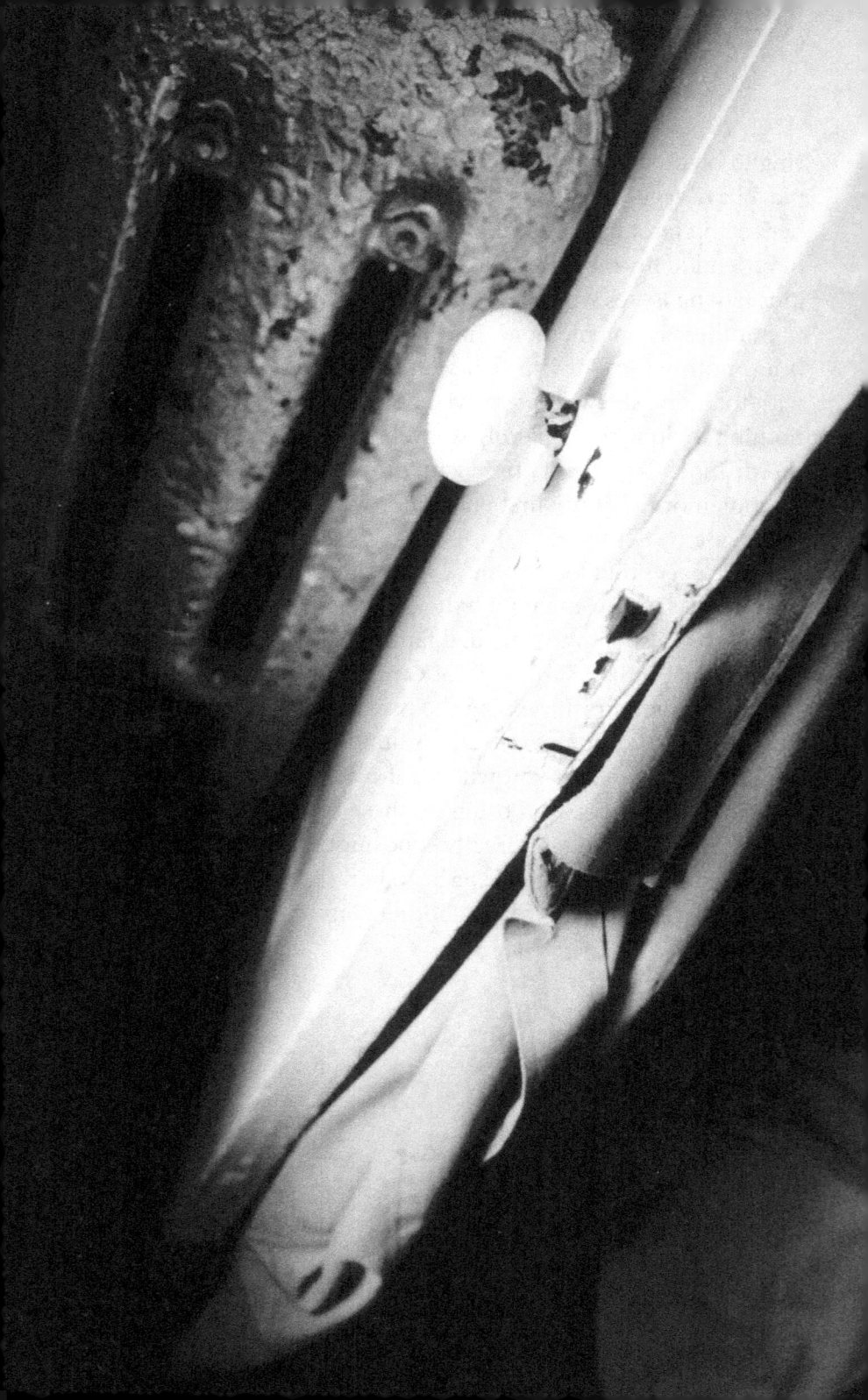

CHAPTER 2

Knock Knock, Who's There?

Out of all the memories I have as a five year old, there is one that I will never forget. That memory stems from our weekend getaways to visit relatives in the Wisconsin Dells area. This memory really can be summed up in a few simple words, one knock for yes and two knocks for no. Those words are forever etched in my mind. My mother and Aunt Ganny would literally talk to a spirit by way of knocks that could be heard throughout the house. This was as real as it gets when it comes to communication with the other side. It wasn't a muffled hard to hear knock or some faint distant sound that everyone tilted their heads to hear. These were distinct knocking sounds that seemed to be coming from upstairs.

I remember sitting at the dining room table listening to these knocks. Everyone from both families would sit there, looking up as if they were gazing at the stars, waiting for the answer to any of the questions asked. I can still picture being focused in on that staircase across the dining room, not really knowing what to expect.

I do not remember any of the questions that were asked, but there is no doubt in my mind we were interacting with beings from another world. The distinct sound of someone's knuckles hitting the floor above (or should I say, some*thing's* knuckles) was undeniable.

My mom told me about seeing a guy reading a newspaper in that same dining room, an incident that was confirmed by one of her friends who was present (a friend who refused to visit that house after what happened). One weekend Mom and a few of her friends stayed at Aunt Ganny's house. While her friends were sleeping in a bedroom adjacent to the dining room, she heard the pages of a newspaper being shuffled. She got up looked into the dining room, where she saw a newspaper and the hands holding it, as though someone were reading it. She started walking toward the individual and just as she almost reached him, the paper fell to the floor. Whoever or whatever was holding the paper vanished into thin air. I guess this spirit needed to catch up on current events before the next knocking session.

Not Of This World

Around 1966 my mother decided to start dabbling in the occult. According to my mother's good friend from back then, they all started messing with tarot cards to liven things up; evidently they were looking for an adventure of sorts.

Around this same time someone did a reading for my mother. This medium told my mother that she had a gift and should use it. This catapulted Mom into the world of the occult. One of her friends told me that my mother became obsessed with it.

Perhaps I should explain some of the practices typically associated with the occult and which my mother did so when I refer to the occult in a general sense, you will understand what that encompasses.

My mother loved to use her Ouija board and did so with quite a few people. The Ouija board is a board game used to contact spirits. The board is filled with letters and numbers. Also the words yes and no are on the board. There is a separate piece called a planchette that is generally in the shape of a heart or teardrop. This planchette has a hole near the top so you can see the appropriate letter or number through it as it slides across the board. A person places their hands on the planchette and relaxes, allowing a spirit to move the planchette and spell out the answer or number to the questions being asked. This planchette allows the individual whose hands are resting on it to converse with spirits.

Tarot cards are used more to help the recipient of the reading with life choices. The cards themselves are pictograms that include a concept on them. Someone flips the cards over and the cards reveal to the recipient what may be ahead for them, or what is revealed is supposed to help in making a life decision. Many people I have talked with during my research go see a medium on a regular basis to get their cards read. Many people rely on these cards as sort of a life compass, never going long without getting a new reading to ensure they make the right choices in life.

My mother also claimed to be able to leave her body in spirit, to go places while her body stayed behind. This is called an out of body experience. Evidently my mother did this quite a bit, as I have found out through some of her friends. My mother claimed she left her body in spirit to go to the aid of people who needed her. My sister even reminded me of a time when my mother supposedly left her to body and aided some people in finding a lost child.

She could fix broken objects by just holding them. One time I witnessed her fix a broken pocket watch. Some friends of hers brought the watch over and told her it hadn't worked in twenty years. She held it in her hands, in a cupped fashion, and fixed it.

I remember my mother's friend taking it from her and laying it on the table very fast, claiming it was too hot to hold. The power she used was undoubtedly real.

She also claimed to have extrasensory perception, premonitions, she used crystals, and she was a big believer in reincarnation. She also practiced automatic writing. My mom would lay her hand on a piece of paper while holding a pen. She would close her eyes and allow a spirit to take over her hand and write things down on this piece of paper.

I wish I knew why Mom was so fascinated with contacting the other side, and especially why she accepted it so easily and didn't look into it more in regards to what it might do to her and us. But she has passed on and I will have to wait to talk to her. For many years I blamed her start with the occult on Aunt Ganny. But while she had a lot to do with my mom's earlier experiences with the occult, my research revealed that there were others who practiced this with Mom: aunts, uncles, and quite a few of her close friends.

"Practiced" might be a poor choice of words, since she wasn't shy about breaking out the Ouija board anywhere she went. Since we kids were there, we had to tag along on these trips to the other side. These activities were disguised as trips to see friends, or a Saturday of visiting her sister. When we would go to visit someone, chances were pretty good that the Ouija board or tarot cards came along. And if these instruments of the occult accompanied us on a visit, we as kids were sure to be exposed to things not of this world.

Fear Factor

One of the few things I do remember when I was sitting at the table in Aunt Ganny's house, was that I wasn't very scared. As a five-year-old, my wheels were spinning, with all my attention on that staircase leading to the upstairs, that is for certain. I used to think that my small dose of bravery was unusual. Why wasn't I under the table cowering with shear fright? I have no memory of being scared sleeping in that very same upstairs where we could hear the knocks coming from earlier that same evening.

Think about this for a moment: Here's a five-year-old kid sitting at a table no more than ten feet from a spirit from another world —a five-year-old boy who had a crush on Ellie Mae Clampett and loved watching "Gilligan's Island"—a five-year-old not afraid of what was obviously something from another world tap dancing upstairs in one of the bedrooms he had to go sleep in later.

We can include my three-year-old sister as well. As this book progresses, you will see the full scope of how all this has affected her. I can picture grown men scattering out of that dining room hearing what we were hearing. My dad had a difficult time with all this as well, and it showed in his face. My dad even ran upstairs once to find the person who was doing all the knocking. (Or should I say he went up hoping to find a human being making the knocking sounds?) Needless to say he came down five minutes later in disbelief as he could find no one up there. So why was I so calm about it?

I think it's because my parents had no problems sending us to bed upstairs in that house. They weren't scared so why should I be? My mom simply didn't look at those spirits as some would look at them. She honestly thought they were "good" spirits. Really let this soak in for a minute: *We would sit there as kids listening to those knocks, and then promptly be told to go to bed in that same upstairs where this spirit was.*

Alluring Subject

Many books have been written about the paranormal and many more will follow. It is without a doubt a captivating subject. TV today is littered with shows like ghost hunters and celebrity ghost stories. All you have to do is click on the television and scroll through the channels and you will find something on the paranormal. Perhaps due in this explosion of focus on the paranormal, many are aware that things not of this world are closer to us than we like to admit. It could be a house everyone avoids in your town, or a cemetery that should be avoided after dark.

Twelve miles to the west of where I currently live in Carney, Michigan, is a well known haunted establishment. The Four Seasons Resort is steeped in history and allure. The notorious gangster Al Capone is rumored to have hidden out there. A river surrounds this resort and the only access to it is old bridges that seem risky at best when crossing them. Whenever I visit the resort I picture his thugs standing guard on the old wooden bridges with their "Tommy Guns" draped across their thighs. The allure of this subject can even be felt here locally as this resort offers ghost tours to the public, with tales of a ghost the locals have named "Laura" lurking around every corner.

It is an unusual subject though, as most are scared of it, yet curious at the same time. They watch some of the TV shows with one eye closed. I have talked to a few friends who walk past a supposed haunted house in a town just north of me in Nadeau, Michigan. They tell me they purposely try not to look in the direction of the haunted house as they walk by it. Then, at the last minute, when they feel they are a safe distance from it, they sneak a peek. Our curiosity definitely can overtake our fear with this alluring subject.

What I'm focusing on is far different from anything you have watched on television. It might be difficult to even find another book that will approach this in a way that I am about to cover it, because I'll be focusing more on why they (*evil*) are around specific people. Although I'm familiar with many books on this subject, my goal is to take it a bit further.

It will also be controversial because it will be an attempt to rip people away from their normal line of thinking. The last few years I have spent hours talking with real people who have real stories to tell. What happened to me and my siblings growing up in small town America, coupled with heart-wrenching stories of young kids exposed to unseen forces has compelled me to write. Let me share briefly some examples that touched my heart, why I feel I *must* write about it, and how this went from a mere curiosity, reserved for close family, to a lengthy book project within a few weeks.

They're Here

I'll start with my own family. Although I was certainly aware as I was growing up that there were some very unusual things going on under our roof, no matter where we lived, it didn't really hit close to home as an adult until a chat with my sister Danette a few months ago. Her story tore right through my heart as it hit close to home for me for the first time as an adult. I had a difficult time stopping the tears after I hung up the phone with her. I had called her to see if she had any stories from our past that might fit in this book.

I asked her if she ever had any problems sleeping at night when we were kids. Her answer floored me. "They (*evil*) used to pull the covers off me when I was trying to sleep," she said. "One time I had a tug of war with them to keep my blankets on. Sometimes I would come and get you and you would sit by my bed and protect me so I could get to sleep." I almost cried when she told me that. Imagine one young child asking another young child to protect her from unseen forces of evil that were harassing her.

What she said hit me very hard, for these reasons:
1. That my four-year-old sister was getting harassed by someone or something unseen, in a bedroom no more than fifteen feet from my own room. It hurt knowing they picked on her, and not me.
2. That I, a six-year-old kid, had to protect her. Picture her standing in the doorway to my bedroom asking me to come protect her. That image still hurts, realizing how scared she must have been.
3. That I *couldn't remember helping her*. I don't remember sitting on the floor by her bed so she could fall asleep. I can picture that little hallway, and where her bed was, but as hard as I try, I can't picture sitting by her bed protecting her.

This little girl was calling on her big brother, all six years of me, to come and protect her from an unseen entity, beings from another world. I can't even begin to tell you what is wrong with this picture. Why can't I remember? I think I blocked it out because I was scared. Wouldn't you be frightened out of your socks in a situation like that?

Open The Flood Gate

Lois, a friend of my wife's and a single mom with two kids, explained to me that she had three spirits walking around in her house at any given time. She explained to me that two of the spirits were female and the third was a male spirit. For her to tell me the different apparent genders of these spirits screams loudly of how clearly they appeared to her. According to Lois, the two female spirits walk around as though they lived there. They would open her cupboards and push down the toaster as though it was their house.

Lois went on to tell me that one of the three spirits, the male, was very mean. He would scare them occasionally by appearing in the windows to her house—a horrifying face in the window looking in at her and her family. This was even verified by some guests she had one night who also witnessed this spirit appearing in the windows.

The worst thing about this mean spirit was that it seemed to be keyed in on her young son. Lois's son was two years old when this spirit started harassing him. They lived there for five years, so from the time he was two years old through the age of seven, this spirit harassed him. No child should have to endure something like that.

Ransacked Bedroom

On many occasions Lois would hear a crash and go running to her son's bedroom. The crash was her son's dresser being knocked over and things thrown about in the bedroom. This dresser had been knocked over so many times the drawers were starting to not open properly. Remember, this was only a two-year-old toddler so there is no way he could have tipped it over.

This happened so often that she screwed the dresser into the wall to prevent it from happening anymore. That only seemed to infuriate this "mean spirit." The next night the crashing was heard again and sure enough, the room was torn apart. The screws holding this dresser against the wall didn't stop this spirit, as the dresser was once again tipped over.

This time, when Lois entered her son's room, his bed had been torn apart as well, with him in it! She said when she got to his room, he was just lying there on the mattress in the middle of the floor. I can't even begin to imagine what this poor boy went through as this spirit ransacked his room. The picture of that little boy lying on that mattress brought tears to my eyes as she told me about it, possibly because I had worked with this boy in the youth programs of our church.

When I imagine what this little child endured that terrible night, I'm left shaking my head in disbelief. Did he huddle in the corner of his bedroom doing his best to stay clear of the ransacking spirit, crawling back onto his mattress after things settled down? That image will pull at your heart strings for sure. Did he fake sleeping in a vain attempt to block out what was happening all around him while he tried to imagine in his own little mind that it wasn't real? Or did he simply ride along on the mattress as it flew across his room, landing on the floor where his mother found him? I don't know about you, but by now all of my heart strings are broken.

Is This All Random?

I believe that these encounters happen for a reason. They are not random. In almost all the cases I have studied in depth, involvement with the spirit world is generational. This was true in my family. It was true in my wife's family. And as I did my research, I found this to be one of the most common elements.

Most people I talk with about the paranormal, however, prefer to believe it to be more random than by design. They are willing to accept almost any other explanation, including that certain people are more sensitive to spirits, that some people or houses are spirit magnets, that some houses are haunted, that the spirit is of someone who has died but hasn't left this world for some reason, that the people involved live too close to a cemetery, etc, etc. As a result of hundreds of interviews, my conclusion is that it cannot be random; it's orchestrated. I will go one better. I believe encounters are orchestrated and carried out by evil spirits with an agenda.

I believe that my mom's Ouija board sessions affected me and my siblings years down the road. It has altered our lives and sent us down roads we might not otherwise have traveled.

I also believe there is a reason why certain kids get paid visits in their rooms at night by spirits. I believe there is an explanation for just about every encounter with beings not of this world. There is a reason why it doesn't happen to some people, as well. A lot of my time researching has focused on why this kid sees things, and why that kid doesn't.

As a result of my research, I began to discern patterns. I started to see distinctions in the methods used by these spirits that some folks like to call "ghosts," by which some people mean they are the spirits of the dead, especially dead relatives paying a friendly visit. These spirits leave a crumb trail that reveals anything but randomness.

There are quite a few common denominators that a high percentage of people I have talked to all have present, including broken homes, divorce, depression, drugs, abuse, and living conditions that are borderline unacceptable. I wasn't the first to recognize this pattern with these visitors, either. Authors like, Charles Kraft, Neil T. Anderson, and a few others mention these ills of life being prevalent in the lives of those who have encounters.

Even the well-known "ghost hunter" Lorraine Warren mentioned something along the same lines in the book, *Ghost Hunters*. The book is a description of Lorraine and her husband Ed's fourteen most famous paranormal cases.

Lorraine said this about homes that her and her husband get called to, "Many of the families we deal with are experiencing 'problems outside the demonic.' We find broken homes or couples on the brink of divorce or children so distraught they need to see psychiatrists. Usually you can understand how demons might settle on such families. We've learned that, in general, families who are having trouble with the supernatural run to a pattern—alcoholism, adultery or even outright child abuse—that enables the demonic to find a suitable place." What I found as I conducted my own investigation was absolutely in line with her description.

Elusive Spirits

Even though I am gaining clarity on some of the things I am uncovering, I still have some questions left unanswered. I had the opportunity to talk with Carmen Reed this past year. She was the real life mother portrayed in the movie, *The Haunting in Connecticut*. After the terrifying encounters she and her family experienced in that house, she wanted answers to why it happened to them. She has spent the past twenty or so years studying this subject and looking for answers. When I asked her to share with me one thing that she has learned from all the years of trying to understand, she said, "Every time I thought I understood something, five more questions would evolve." She was describing the complexity of this unusual subject, complexity that my own study has concluded comes because we are dealing with highly intelligent beings that don't like to be pursued or for anyone to figure out what they are up to.

They (*evil*) are real, whether or not people believe them to be real. It's similar to the fact that God exists whether or not we believe that to be true. However, this subject that is unpredictable and the answers are somewhat elusive because one encounter is not the same as the next. The encounters one family has aren't always the same as the next family. The variables that have to be taken into consideration are many. And the interpretations of what is going on in a specific case may vary from one participant to the next.

For example let's say someone has seen a dark shadow in the corner of their bedroom, and they believe it was Aunt Helga who died four years ago. The next person might say it was a demon, or maybe even an angel from heaven. I have even heard people suggest it was a beloved pet that has passed on. So while you're trying to understand what is happening, the explanations can range from Rover to Aunt Helga in matters of seconds.

There are so many possibilities and explanations it defies the mind. Let's suppose Grandpa's picture on the mantel moves all by itself since he died ten years ago. If we discuss this with several different members of the same family, all of them will give a different opinion on why it moves.

So it's easy to see how many opinions can be thrown into the mix when dealing with the other side. It really doesn't take long before you step on someone's toes or say something that sends them into a frantic rave. I recently had a lady tell me I am way off base with the direction my book was taking and she severed ties with me. She told me I better not use her story in the book, either. It is an emotionally charged subject to say the least. That's what you would expect though, because we are potentially talking about a cherished loved one who is still poking around the living room, right?

Tearing This Apart

I'd like to address the common mentality that when we see or experience something not of this world it is a loved one, or a good spirit, or that is totally random. I believe the only way to do this is to literally tear apart a specific experience or to take a much closer look at any given family. Many people I have talked to were surprised at some of the questions I asked, which I did as many common denominators started coming into focus. Most of those who shared stories with me had quite a bit in common.

My biggest struggle with all of this is that most people would love to just assume it is all good and allow these spirits to be involved in their lives. More specifically, they don't seem to care that something is visiting their young child in his or her room at night. They write it off as a passed on relative and don't look back. They would be the first to tell me that my sister must have been playing tug of war with one of our deceased loved ones. I don't know about you, but if one of my sons had ever told me some of the things others have told me, I would have gone on the warpath. I love my sons too much to just assume it was something good. Things would change abruptly if my own kids told me that something was breathing in their ear at night.

As we go, this endeavor will get complicated and tug at people's emotions. It would be my hope and prayer that you set aside your preconceptions and assumptions and really follow along with me. You might not agree with all my conclusions, but please, at least stick this out and hear it to the end, because these really are sinister forces who really do want to wreak havoc on you and your loved ones. But they really can be stopped. I'll have more to say about that toward the end.

If something is taking place in your own home, look into your child's eyes and ask yourself this question: Is there something I could do to stop these spirits from making contact with my child? What if your son had to go into his sister's room at night to protect her like I used to do with my own sister? Wouldn't that trouble you, deeply? Is that really my child's grandma checking up on her as she is sleeping or is there something menacing taking place in your child's bedroom? Wouldn't you want to dig a little and find out so you can protect your young one? If so, read on as next we take a look at some of the possible explanations for visitations like those we've been describing.

CHAPTER 3

It Must Be Haunted

Growing up with unusual and unexplainable things happening in someone's home for the most part gets explained away. Sometimes it gets ignored; that's how my dad handled it. This happens more frequently with men than with women by the way. Quite often, if something unexplainable happens under their roof they will immediately attribute it to either a good spirit or a dead family member. They prefer to take the warm and fuzzy road as opposed to a much more plausible explanation. Or perhaps they find comfort believing it is someone who used to care about them.

Another common explanation I hear quite often is that the house is haunted, usually because a deceased former resident can't let go. These spirits haven't accepted the fact that they are dead so they are still hanging around. Very few seem to entertain the thought that whatever it is might not be a good thing, or that it is there by its own choice. It's as though everyone has been programmed to believe a certain way when it comes to what most people call "ghosts." They also seem to be programmed to accept them when they are a part of their lives or take up residency in their home.

One person I knew endured five years of spirit attacks simply because she thought she was sensitive to the spirit world. She would put up with it wherever she had lived over the years. She said they would follow her anyway so why move or why fight it? When she was a young girl growing up in Illinois, she used to see a young boy spirit playing with a ball in her hallway. From her bedroom, as she lay there trying to go to sleep, she could see this spirit's back and watched him bounce a ball off the hallway wall. She said he showed up quite frequently. Since she moved to Upper Michigan she's had run-ins with native-looking spirits who have taken over her house.

Another good example of someone not dealing with things happened to me just the other night. A friend of mine, Denise, was sharing some of her childhood stories with me and went on to tell me she knew of someone else I should get in contact with. The only thing Denise told me was that her friend's two daughters see dark figures, especially in the hallway of their house. She conveyed to me that the girls were very scared to be home alone. Then Denise told me that she had better check with her friend to see if she would even talk to me.

A few nights later I got a text message from Denise that she had just been told that the woman would be willing to chat by phone. But when I texted Denise's friend, only a few minutes later, she replied that she had changed her mind. That left me with a sad feeling because I knew her daughters were being harassed by dark figures. Perhaps her husband had intervened, trying to protect the family from being labeled crazy. Or worse, perhaps something frightening had happened in that house just before we connected. I've heard several stories of people getting "spooked" by something when they are about to talk to me.

A Lot To Consider

Of course I'm aware that a child's imagination can run wild sometimes, especially with the things they are allowed to watch on television these days, or with all the games that they play, where killing zombies is the coolest thing since sliced bread. A child's mind is very easily manipulated and yes, they can come up with some pretty amazing stories.

Some kids know how to push their parents' buttons; for example, claiming they are scared so they can stay up later. This may be one reason parents choose to write off a lot of things their kids come up with. But what if some of what they say really happened? Oh my. That would definitely take most parents out of their comfort zone. It's much easier for a parent to take the road with less stress associated with it and blame it on a video game or a scary movie they watched earlier that night.

For our family, experiencing the paranormal wasn't viewed as anything bad so we all accepted it, even though my dad expressed his disapproval of it on more than one occasion. This might be the case for other families as well, who have loved ones that practice contacting the other side. If mom did it, how can it be evil or even dangerous? Or when a family has activity soon after a death in the family, it's easy to assign the activity to that loved one. Who else can they blame when you really think about it, right?

The passed on loved one theory gains support when activity picks up on the anniversary of someone's death or on a birthday. For some people, encounters are almost a given when a deceased loved one's birthday rolls around. When activity picks up on a dead relative's birthday, it has to be them, right?

What really happens after we die? Can we actually hang around after we die and move objects in our loved ones' homes? Do some people really get trapped between worlds? When you feel your bed sink down in the middle of the night and can actually smell your favorite uncle's cigar does that mean it is really him coming back to check on you? When you walk into your child's bedroom just after you cleaned it up and see all the toys piled up in the middle of the floor is this something that you should be concerned about? Is this a spirit with a sense of humor or should you all become ghost busters? I will get to those answers a little later on in the book.

Here Kitty Kitty

A young girl heard some glass items jingling on her dresser during the middle of the night. Her mom comforted her by telling the little girl that it was her dead cat. Her mom explained to me that their cat had died recently. She said it was common for the cat, when it was alive, to hop up on the dresser like that. So she told her daughter it was the cat coming back to visit her. I am sure that it comforted that young girl to think it was her pet cat and it most likely calmed her enough to help her get to sleep that particular night.

So what's wrong with that? "Nothing," you might think. "It didn't matter what caused the commotion, as long as the girl got a good night's sleep." But think it through. Consider the potential long-term negative effect of opening the door to your daughter's room to something far more sinister. For, if it was not her cat (and it surely was not her cat) then some *thing* else jingled the glass on the dresser. If a certain detective were examining this case, he might say, "Elementary, my dear Watson." Something else or something other caused the disturbance.

How would you feel if your ten-year-old daughter approached you and said, "Mom, someone was looking at me through my bedroom window last night"? Want to make this really bother you? What if she said that a man slipped through her window last night and sat on her bed next to her? Here is the worst scenario, which happens quite frequently with people who see figures in their room. Your daughter says, "Last night I was lying in bed and it felt like someone was lying on top of me." She further explains that she felt this unusual heaviness come over her. This heaviness was something I struggled with as a kid, myself. It is the most unusual feeling I have ever experienced. I would have to say that most parents would come unglued if their child told them someone was lying on top of them last night. Call the cops, lock the windows, and go on the warpath to get to the bottom of that.

So why do we knowingly blow off the same exact thing with these spiritual visits? Of course there is a difference between the physical and the spiritual. But the bottom line is that something is in their room, visiting them at night. And for the life of me, I can't understand why this kind of thing can go on without causing deep parental concern, though I can understand why kids stop sharing such things with their parents after their reports have been ignored enough times.

Hi Grandma

Darlene shared with me that when she was growing up it was common in her home for items to go missing and then magically reappear a few days later. Hearing footsteps upstairs when no one else was home was another common occurrence in their house. Darlene said those things didn't bother her too much, but what was happening in her bedroom and other private places was a different story.

It was hard for her to sleep because of the feeling she always had of being watched, even when she was in the shower. Then one particular night her feelings were confirmed as one of them (*evil*) made contact with her. This spirit sat at the end of her bed near her feet, telling her, "Everything is okay." She couldn't see this spirit's face, but for some reason she sensed that it was her deceased grandmother.

This ***"passed on relative explanation"*** came up quite a bit as I talked to people about their encounters. This is by far the most common explanation I have heard over the course of my research, and it stands to reason. It makes the person being affected feel more comfortable about what is happening to them. If it is a deceased loved one, they can't help but feel all fuzzy and warm inside, and if it is grandma standing at the end of your bed it makes it easier to roll over and go back to sleep. This mindset is quite common perhaps because we want to believe that our passed on loved ones haven't forgotten about us . . . that they stick around to help and protect us . . . that they will on occasion stop in for a visit to see how our human lives are going. After all, even though they have died, they are still with us in spirit, are they not?

Just entertaining the idea of this being something evil would no doubt scare us to death. So we prefer not to entertain thoughts of what it might be. I myself would not want to try and explain to a young child what it could potentially be, especially if the child was scared enough to come to your bedroom and wake you in the middle of the night. How are you going to explain to a child that it's not Grandma at the foot of their bed, but an evil spirit pretending to be Grandma. Beyond that, how are you going to deal with that possibility yourself?

Mike Is Back

I was amazed with how often people had activity pick up in their home when there was *"a tragic death"* close to the family, especially if there was a suicide. This is even more devastating if it was a young teen, which happens more times than we want to talk about.

I was talking with someone from the area whose husband killed himself years ago and got a glimpse of what some go through when someone close takes their own life. On the anniversary of their wedding, she would wake up and find his wedding band lying on the pillow next to her. She told me that she always kept it in her jewelry box. So there was no way it should have been near her bed, so naturally she assumed it had to be her passed on husband. Who else could it be?

After my cousin Marty killed himself, there were many reports that Marty was behind the sudden, strange activity that some of my extended family were experiencing. The assumption was that he was letting everyone know he was okay. One cousin told about toys moving in her kids' bedroom shortly after he died. She naturally thought it must be Marty. Marty was the playful type and full of mischief, so it must be him. Some relatives told me that appliances and light switches would turn on by themselves in the house shortly after Marty passed as well. Considering how traumatic a suicide can be, it is natural for close loved ones to attribute any activity to the passed on family member. It provides comfort to them. It replaces the word scary in their minds eye with the commonly heard words, "Awe, it must be Marty."

Friends of mine had this happen to them when a local youngster committed suicide about seven years ago. The young man was very close to this family and actually lived with them for a short time. Shortly after the suicide, a tall dark figure appeared to one of the girls in this family. She was home alone brushing her hair in front of the mirror when it happened. She personally told me that she could feel the temperature in the room getting colder. She was overwhelmed with the feeling that she was no longer alone. Then it made contact with her. It felt as though someone had brushed against her, and at the same time she felt a breeze. She turned around to see a tall, dark figure moving away from her, which disappeared down the hallway. She ran to a corner in the kitchen and hid, then picked up the phone and frantically called her mother, who was at work. Crying and hysterical, she ran outside in only a pair of shorts and a tank top, and stood there in the snow waiting for her mother to come home.

Later on that same day, the family discovered a hand print on the screen of a dusty television they weren't using anymore. I saw a picture of it; very creepy! Judging by the length of the fingers of this hand print, clearly it wasn't human. But the entire family blamed the sudden appearance of this dark figure to the recent suicide of their close friend. Even though the entire family slept together in one bedroom for the next several weeks, the thought that it was their friend made it easier to cope with it.

Another good friend of mine told me about how her mother appeared to her shortly after she passed. My friend woke up suddenly during the middle of the night, to find herself staring right at her deceased mother. Her mother was hovering right over her while she lay in bed. A few days later, my friend walked into the kitchen and immediately smelled her mother's favorite shampoo. She told me that those were the only two times that her mother appeared to her after she died. Note: She was certain that it was her passed on mother. Should I have told her that I was sure it was something else?

Haunted Houses

The **"haunted house"** is easily the next most common response I get from those who have had encounters. I've heard things like it must be the previous deceased owner of this house roaming around, or it has to be the old guy who died in the back bedroom. It's as if they are blaming the house itself because of something from its past. I have read many books on this subject and many authors give some compelling evidence that *it is the house*. I believe myself that there is some truth to what some of these authors say about haunted houses, but I don't for one minute put all the blame on the house. My research has led me to a different conclusion.

Perhaps you have heard of the movie, "The Conjuring," which is based on the true story of a haunted house in Rhode Island. This haunted house and its property were supposedly cursed by a previous owner. Roger and Carolyn Perron moved into the house and because of this curse, had to endure years of turmoil at the hands of the evil spirits. The entire family witnessed countless apparitions the whole time they lived there. Naturally the blame fell on the curse put on the property by the previous owner.

The problem with this conclusion is that the people who moved into this supposedly cursed house after the Perrons left did not have the same activity as the Perrons endured. Norma Sutcliffe and her husband moved in and only reported hearing a few strange noises here and there. They claimed to have never seen even one apparition the whole time they have lived there. If this house and its property had a curse on it, don't you think the Sutcliffe's would have experienced the same turmoil as the Perrons?

I have searched out people who moved into supposed haunted houses. Quite a few of them reported no activity once they moved in. When people tell me that, I am more inclined to believe that the occupants were more the reason, and not the house.

The house I am living in now makes this case quite well. Our house was built in 1956 and the original owners were Bible believing Christians. They lived here forty-five years and had no issues. The next owners lived here eight years and things did happen while they lived here. The granddaughter of this couple told me stories of spirit contact, hearing voices, pounding on the basement door, and one case of someone being tripped intentionally and falling down the stairs. After I heard this, I contacted the person who fell down the stairs and she told me the story was true. She said that no one else was on the stairs with her when it happened, adding that she always felt uneasy when she stayed here. The granddaughter went on to tell me that her grandmother, Susan, haunts this house.

I bought the house in 2010 and have had no run-ins with "Susan" yet. I also am a Bible-believing Christian like the original owners were. My youngest son has stayed here many nights and also had no problems. This story leans more toward blaming the occupants then it does the house. The fact that both I and the original owners were Bible-believing Christians has more significance than anything else.

Loving Spirits

The last explanation I would like to bring up is the ***"good spirit"*** mindset that I hear from some. Some have told me that they were overwhelmed with warmth when it was present, so it must have been a good spirit. Or because it didn't do any harm to them, then it must have been a good spirit. I hear quite frequently that it made them feel safe. Others have shared with me that the spirits even spoke to them, telling the individuals that everything was okay.

A woman once told me that she was lying in bed one evening and on the verge of falling asleep when she got kissed on the nose. She explained to me that the only person in the world that ever did that to her was her dad. He had passed on over twenty years earlier so she wholeheartedly believed it was him who came back to do that to her. A kiss on the nose when no one is around has to be an eye-opening experience, wow!

Another woman told me about hearing a child's laughter in and throughout the house. Her granddaughter has even given this spirit a name and hears the giggles as well. She has a difficult time believing that the sounds of a little child giggling should be reason for alarm. How could the playful sound of kids ever be a bad thing?

All these explanations seem to re-direct the responsibility for the presence of spirits from themselves to other circumstances. Evidently, it makes people feel better if they can shift the blame to someone or something other than themselves. Keep in mind that most, if not all of these explanations, are sprinkled with hope of the spirit being something friendly and that the spirits are there due to reasons out of the control of those who inhabit the house.

Are They Everywhere?

Now that we have discussed what most people believe to be the reasons behind these visits, and who is visiting them, what are the chances of you having an encounter with something not of this world? Do most of us really have to worry about this? Worry might be a strong word to use, but I would be willing to bet that it has happened to you.

Last night I was sitting at a local basketball game talking with an old friend of mine. She was sharing some of her encounters with me from when she was a child. I mentioned to her that these visits happen more frequently than most will ever imagine. I say that to quite a few people, seeing that some are a little hesitant to talk about this unusual subject.

As we chatted away that evening, something suddenly dawned on me as I was watching the game. Most of the girls playing for the opposing team that particular night had actually shared stories with me over the past few months. Eight of the nine girls had shared some type of encounter with me. The only reason I don't know about the ninth girl was that I hadn't talked to her personally. This ninth girl's mother did share with me that she had some encounters growing up, but she never got back to me with any specific stories. So chances are that her daughter had as well. So I have to believe all nine girls on this basketball team have had some type of experience over their lifetime.

Out of seven girls on the other team, I know for certain that three of them have had some type of encounter. The remaining four, in my opinion, more than likely had seen something as well. I say that with confidence due to the research patterns that were developing as I worked on this book.

One of those research patterns was something I like to call my "big three" theory. Later on in the book I will share my "big three" theory more exhaustively. It is the three most common denominators found in a family that has encounters. The "big three" are divorce, the occult, and if a family has more girls than boys in it. If these three are present in any given family, the odds are almost 100 percent that they see things. That is why, even though I am speculating on the other four girls, I can say with confidence that they more than likely have encounters. To summarize my point for now, I can confidently say that out of the sixteen girls present on the floor that night, all sixteen have probably experienced something not of this world.

Contact Is Common

I believe contact with the other side to be inevitable for most people. If I had to take a stab at how many of us have had some type of encounter, I would guess that 80 percent of us have. I base that number off of my own personal research results, not a wild guess.

I would also be willing to bet that some of those who told me they have never had an encounter, did. I say that with confidence after getting the cold shoulder from people who I considered friends. I live in a small community and people talk. So I know for a fact that many who told me "no" face-to-face, did indeed have encounters.

Those who gave me the coldest shoulder were professing Christians. That greatly puzzled me, since they of all people should know this subject better than most. Until they experience the power they have over these spirits, I can see how the subject may scare them.

Even touching base with old friends on anything they may have experienced over the years has left me speechless. A few weeks ago I chatted on the phone with someone who graduated several years after me in high school. She floored me when she told me that she can hear spirits' voices on audio recording devices. It is called EVP, short for electronic voice phenomenon. She told me that she has this "gift." She is well-known by her close friends as having this gift, so on occasion they call her to do an EVP for them. She will show up at their house and use some type of audio recorder and literally pick up voices from the other side. Her friends that call her can't record any voices on their own. They need her there, along with her supposed gift, in order for the voices to actually get recorded. I have a cousin who can pick up voices on recording devices as well. So it happens more than we might expect.

We ourselves are spiritual creatures. Not everything we experience is physical. We share a world with spiritual beings and there will be times our paths cross. But I couldn't help but wonder why it ended for me personally. Why haven't my sons had any problems? Why does one family see things all the time while the next door neighbors never seeing anything? Why would one family move into a haunted house and have problems, then the next family moves into the same house and doesn't have even one encounter? I've pursued most of these questions, and will offer my best answers in the pages to come.

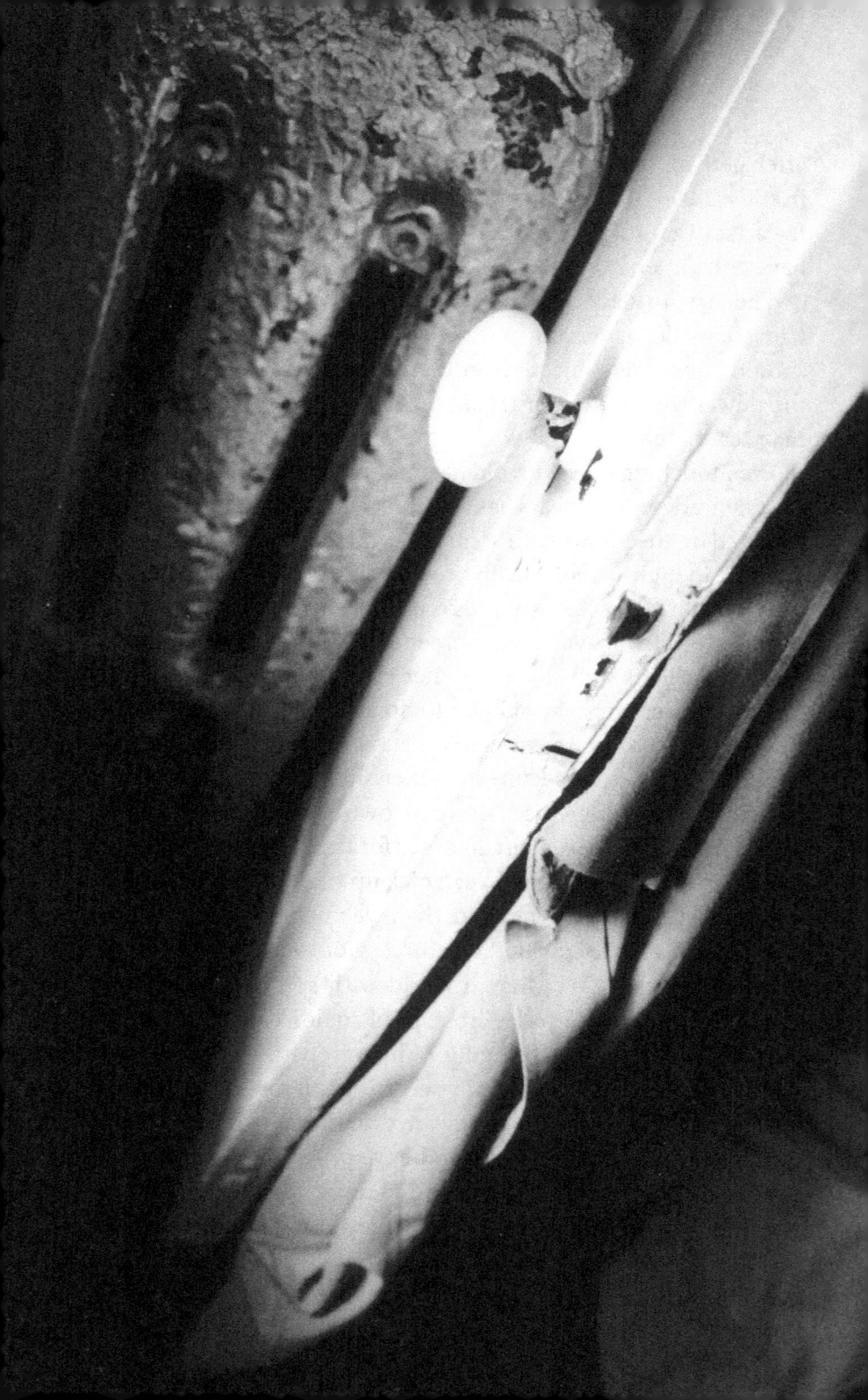

CHAPTER 4

Bloody Barn

Living on an old southern Michigan farm for Corinth was anything but normal. Her family was renting this particular farmhouse which happened to come with many out buildings. Corinth remembers when they moved in and how she instantly sensed the need to stay away from these creepy old buildings. In fact, she never once stepped foot in any of them, especially the barn. Her gut feeling on this proved to be right as time would tell.

She recalls how common it was for her to see things that most will never see. Her encounters were quite a bit different than what I was used to hearing. After talking for a short time with her, I realized she had stories that I may never come across again.

One of her early experiences involved that creepy old barn she felt uneasy about. As she was walking past the barn one day, she heard a distinct sound of something smacking one of the barn windows. She turned to see what made the sound and watched as a bloody hand slid down the glass. And as it slid, the hand made the streaking sound of something wet sliding down glass.

A few weeks later she got dropped off by the school bus at the end of her driveway. From a distance she could see through the open barn doors what looked like some people standing around. She finally made out what was going on. A man seemed to be strung up to the rafters by a rope, with his hands above his head. She remembers thinking that some kids must be playing with a rope in there. But as she focused in more she could see someone whipping the man who was strung up to the rafters. She remembers thinking that she should have heard him screaming from pain. But she couldn't. She could not hear the sound of the whip, either.

Terrified, young Corinth ran to the house and got inside as fast as she could. She peered out the kitchen window at the barn to see if the people she had seen were still there, but they had vanished.

Not Just The Barn

When Corinth was around seven years old she had a very vivid dream of her babysitter. To this day she still recalls every detail of that horrible dream. She was standing in her babysitter's bedroom, and noticed her sitting on the edge of her bed crying. Corinth was on the verge of asking what was wrong when she watched in horror as her babysitter killed herself. She slit her own wrists and there was blood everywhere. Corinth couldn't stop her and she couldn't scream for help. She just had to stand there in her dream and watch this terrible act as it played out in front of her. Two weeks later Corinth's family got the call that her babysitter had killed herself.

She also described hearing screaming in the house when no one else was home. She heard scratching sounds in her closet, and heard loud footsteps upstairs when everyone was downstairs.

When Corinth was a young child, it was common for her and her siblings to sleep together. Many nights something would scare her siblings, and they would find comfort sharing a bed together. She recalled waking up one of those nights and sitting up in her bed. As she looked around the room, a small child came out of her closet. This child spirit walked toward Corinth's bed with her arms stretched out as if she was reaching for her.

Corinth remembers being on the verge of screaming when the spirit turned and walked out the bedroom door. Just as she felt somewhat relieved, a taller shadowy looking figure came out of her closet. This figure was much taller than the child spirit. The figure followed the child spirit out of bedroom into the hallway and vanished.

As of this writing, Corinth's own children are now having experiences. This generational involvement is quite common, as you will see. Wondering about this, I contacted Corinth's mother, who told me politely that she would rather not talk about those days on that old southern Michigan farm.

Shadows In The Night

Of the 404 encounters people have shared with me, 250 of them have seen something that resembled a human being. Many different descriptions of these spirits came up in my research. From tall shadowy figures, normal size people, kids, and even toddlers. I have even heard stories of entire "ghost" families being seen at one time. One fellow said that they circled his kitchen table as if they were seeing what was for supper.

What I found very interesting was that if someone described a dark figure in their room, it seemed to be keyed in on the bed of that person. Sometimes these spirits stood at the head of their bed looking down at them as they lay in bed. But for some strange reason the foot of the bed is popular with spirits. I get the image of a doctor coming into a patient's room and grabbing the medical chart off the end of the bed, reading it while looking down at the individual as if they are accessing the situation.

A young woman told me that she sprinkled flour around her bed to get tracks of these spirits that harassed her during the night, pulling on her toes and fingers. Her parents didn't believe her so she wanted proof they were real. The next morning, sure enough, she discovered tracks in the flour. The tracks stopped at the head of her bed, like they were standing over her looking down at her face as she slept.

I've heard many accounts where the dark mass or figure hovered over a person as they lay in bed. One sixteen-year-old girl said that a red-eyed creature stayed up by the ceiling as it looked down at her. A woman told me that she got the feeling they were examining her. Many others have told me the same thing, even going as far as to say they felt violated. In some of these accounts their blankets even moved, like they were being fondled. They (*evil*) seem to have a curiosity about us as we lie in bed, like they are on a reconnaissance mission gathering data.

I've heard described a figure in a trench coat with some sort of hat on. Most that were similar were described as being tall, as high as a doorframe. Interestingly enough, the style of clothes they wore was from the turn of the century; more times than not it was a woman dressed in a long dress that went all the way down to her ankles. Some of the little girl spirits wore bonnets like you would see around the turn of the century.

Other figures were described as being more like a black, formless mass. Some of the more odd descriptions were of a figure with horns and small midget-like figures. Many different colored eyes were described as well. I've heard many stories of young children running through someone's house when no children should have been around. Voices of children was another common occurrence heard by many. Many younger kids described dark child-size figures with long hair.

The Number 3 And Mirrors

The number three was something very common with people when they had encounters. The most common time of the day for encounters was about three in the morning. If it was knocking or banging, it was usually in threes. Some of these spirits made contact with people by scratching them, and yes, it was usually in threes. I have seen scratch marks on people, on doors, on walls, and on floors—all in threes.

Mirrors were involved in many sightings. One girl told me she had to take all the mirrors out of her bedroom to stop seeing "them." Many others shared with me that they don't like mirrors, either.

It was common to hear of objects moving on their own. One girl told me that the spirits in her house like to throw her salt and pepper shakers around the kitchen. One time when she had company over the salt and pepper shakers flew at her guests.

Another common occurrence was items being lost or misplaced—keys and wallets being the items of choice by these sneaky spirits. Some people said that they would eventually find their lost items a few days later in a spot they never would have put them in.

These spirits also seem to enjoy messing around with children's toys. They love switching the TV channels on people, and love to mess with the lights. One lady shared with me that many times she has come home to find her light bulb in the upstairs hallway unscrewed and laying on the floor. I even heard of smoke alarms with no batteries in them going off.

Here is a breakdown of some of the common things I came across during my interviews of 404 people:

- 250 of these 404 people said that what they saw was human in form. More times than not it was black in color.
- In 89 cases people used a Ouija board, or were present when someone else was using one.
- 29 individuals had ties to the occult, personally, or through a past family member.
- In 56 cases, people were physically contacted by these spirits; 17 of them were scratched.
- 44 kids had a secret friend in the house—someone or something that they would talk to while alone in their bedroom.
- 58 people felt like something was lying on them or pressing them down while in bed. It is hard to describe this unusual heaviness (I know because it happened to me). It is like your entire body is buried in the sand. Many people woke up feeling like their chest has been compressed and they are out of breath.

Obscure Numbers

Many of the things I've just described are found in other books on the paranormal. But now we're going to take an unusual turn as I list certain facts that were common among people who have had encounters with the other side:

- Out of the 404 individuals who shared some type of encounter with me, 310 of them were women.
- Of the 163 families involved in my interviewing, 125 of those families were made up of more girls than boys.

- Of the 404 individuals, 261 of them came from a broken home or were currently in a broken home. [I consider a broken home any home that doesn't have the traditional biological mother and father in it; or any addition to the family. Obviously that includes step-fathers or step-mothers, adopted kids, foster kids, or a live-in boyfriend or girlfriend.]
- Of the 404 individuals, 147 had experienced some form of sexual deviance. [By this I mean any type of sexual misconduct that steers away from the normal sexual relationships. That includes rape and/or sexual abuse. But I also include things like spouse swapping, peeping Toms, and even strange things like a husband letting his friends watch. So the 147 total involves many variances, but the prevalence is important nonetheless.
- Of this group, 55 individuals told me they experienced some form of physical abuse growing up. [I realize that everyone has a different opinion on what is physical abuse. My dad used to smack me around when I was younger, but I don't consider that abuse. I am quite sure I deserved it. Abuse is when the person being abused doesn't deserve it.]
- Depression was a symptom for 93 people; 44 people shared with me that they have anxiety attacks as well. I believe these two are closely related and major contributors to those who see things. So far, I've interviewed 32 people who suffer with bipolar disorder. Of course this is not the same as depression or anxiety, but the emotional disorientation involved may leave such folks at risk.
- Suicidal thoughts were common; 37 individuals told me they had, or still have, such thoughts. I have a story later on in the book that sheds some light on this subject.
- Sleepwalking, sleep paralysis, or very vivid dreams were experienced by 55 people in the group. I lump them together because I personally feel they are all related.

Variables Are Many

As you can see from this information, people can see just about anything in regards to spirits. One person might see a dog run through the house, even though they don't own a dog. The next person sees spider-like creatures crawling on their walls. Seeing such things is confusing enough by itself, but when you add in the opinions of others trying to explain it all to you, the confusion snowballs.

Before I proceed, let me add a disclaimer: I am well aware of other contributing factors for those who claim to see things. I am well aware that some who talked with me could be lying; that is something I can't control. I've not used some stories because I detected they weren't true.

I also realize that some suffer from disorders of various kinds, and some just crave attention. There's really no point in listing all the possibilities of mental illness and how they may affect what a person sees or says. The medical community says one thing, but I keep in mind that they presuppose that the other side does not exist; therefore, they seek a label (or have made them up) to describe what they consider to be delusions of one sort or another. The best I can do is to include in our conversation certain questions that will help me determine the validity of someone's story.

Bottom line is I have to take anything anyone tells me at face value and go with it. I can't administer a psych test to everyone or know for sure if they are lying to me. I wish I knew the mindset of everyone I have talked to, but I simply can't pull that off. The answers and stories people do share with me seem easy enough for me to decipher with confidence.

A Different Perspective

I plugged into some social networks and joined a few paranormal sites for educational reasons, and to get as much information for my research as I could find. At first, I thought this would shed some light or give my own research more support, by hearing some people I'd not interviewed share their paranormal encounters. There were a few times this was helpful, but poring through these sites actually did more harm to my fact-seeking mission than it helped. If you want confusion about what and who these visitors are, spend some time surfing Internet paranormal sites. I couldn't believe all the different answers they can come up with when trying to explain something not of this world.

The list of descriptions used to identify these spirits is long and out of control: angels, ancient aliens, demons, poltergeists, deceased relatives, earth giants, gnomes, ghosts, aliens, vampires, and lost spirits is a short list.

This name game could go on forever, along with the descriptions that follow close behind. I believe it's a true indication that people will just simply make things up to scratch their own itching ears. If what they saw was slender with large eyes, it had to be an alien. If what they saw was white or glowing, it was a good spirit. If it was dark with piercing eyes, it had to of been a demon.

When I do the math on the endless list of names and descriptions, I come up with two words: mass confusion. When you type the words "paranormal books" into one of the search engines on your computer, you'll come up with as many as 20 million hits. How could anyone possibly come away with any certainty if there are so many books and opinions on this vast subject?

Another thing that is troubling is that you can consult ten books on the paranormal and find five different answers on the meaning of seeing a child spirit. Also problematic is that most of the legitimate reference material on this subject is no more than fifty years old. What reference material did someone around the turn of the century have on these visitors, or where did they get their advice 400 years ago? I think I know the answer to that question.

Oldest Book There Is

To get away from all this confusion, and the many different opinions voiced, I decided to try something very seldom done these days. I decided to bounce everything I was coming across against the Bible. Before you question this approach ask yourself this: What seems to happen at the end of most horror movies that are based off of true events? What happens at the end of most TV shows based off of real life hauntings? Most of these shows bring in a priest with his Bible in hand to rid the home of these evil spirits. Some of these shows end with a demonologist saying the Lord's Prayer to expel the unwanted spirits.

I find it very interesting that most people won't go to God's Word for any explanation about these spirits. But when the time comes to get rid of them, God's Word comes in pretty handy. If God plays a part in chasing away spirits, why not look into his Word to see what he says about them. Let's do that:

Unlike paranormal books, and the many stories someone can easily dig up, the Bible has never changed over the years. As I proceeded with this investigation, it was very important to me to know I had a book in front of me that has stayed the same. I knew if I didn't find something with clout to bounce all of this off of, I was just going to add to the confusion.

When I bring this up, some people try to deflect me, saying that with all the Bible translations around, who really knows what the Bible says? But that's just an excuse for not believing the Bible that we have today is more authentic than ANY other document of antiquity.

A great discovery was made in a cave near the Dead Sea in 1946 and it included scrolls from as far back as 300 B.C. Included in these scrolls was a complete book from the Bible, called the Isaiah Scroll. When they took this Isaiah scroll and compared it to today's Bible, they found that it has not changed at all, it was spot on. That gave me something to sink my teeth into; knowing God has preserved his Word through all these years. All that has changed is human language, so the ongoing task for translators is to produce translations that say what the original meant, in words that make sense to an average reader.

The Bible is the oldest and most reliable source we can use and go to with confidence, not having to worry about the integrity of the author like many of the newer books. I checked into angelic visits, and focused on any passages that dealt with evil spirits. My assumption was that, since God created these spirits, there had to be some answers in the Bible to the questions I have about them.

A good place to start is Colossians 1:16:

> **For in him all things were created: things in heaven and on earth, visible and invisible, whether thrones or powers or rulers or authorities; all things were created by him and for him.**

Clearly, God created the invisible as well as the visible. He created things not seen with the natural eye. Could it be that one of these invisible, created beings is standing in the corner watching your kids as they sleep?

Angels

Before we look at the verses that deal with evil spirits and angels, I want to point out something. There is no mention of vampires, gnomes, gargoyles, aliens, or child spirits anywhere in the Bible. There is no hint of spirits who get caught in this world, unable to move on to the next; no mention of a spirit haunting a house. But verses dealing with angels, good or bad, are found throughout the Word of God.

In all fairness, I want to point out that there are no references at all to the common things that seem to be plaguing people who have encounters. There is nothing in the Bible about piercing eyes seen in a young child's closet, no stories of items moving on their own in anyone's house, and no mention of dark shadows in and throughout anyone's house's either. But there is no doubt that God mentions evil spirits, and his Word mentions angels as well. This is where we have to start, to get anywhere in diagnosing what people are seeing in their homes.

In the New Testament alone the word angel is used nearly 100 times. That is excluding the book of Revelation, which is a book on future events that have yet to be fulfilled. Forty of those 100 references to angels can be found in the first four books of the New Testament, the gospels. When I say references, these are uses of the word "angel," not individual encounters. I want to also make note that the gospels are repetitive (in other words, two or more of the gospels may contain the same story), so some of these angelic references are duplicated. Taking the duplication into consideration, angelic references in the gospels are not very numerous. Most of those encounters were angels delivering messages about the coming of Christ, or angels carrying out something God dispatched them to do.

When we consider the angel encounters dealing with the coming of Jesus Christ, there are very few angelic visits dealing directly with humans. Most references to angels are done in a general sense, but they are mentioned enough times to convey to us they are around and active in the lives of believers. Another invisible creation of God was the demon. I am making reference to a demon this way, knowing full well that demons were at one time good angels. For argument's sake I am referring to demons as creations of God to distinguish between the two.

Evil Spirits

The words Satan, devil, demon, or evil spirits can be found twice as many times as references to good angels in the New Testament; specifically, almost 200 times. Quite a few times New Testament writers used other names to describe Satan. Words like serpent, tempter, and deceiver were used in reference to him.

So, God thought it was important for us to be aware of the presence of evil more than he thought we should hear about good angels. This is consistent with their very nature. God's ministering angels are not attention-getters like demons are. They love working behind the scenes, rarely bringing attention to themselves.

This lopsided number of references (demons vs. good angels) cannot be accidental. God obviously knew that evil would be active and present in the lives of those he created. And evidently he felt it was important to warn us of the existence of evil. He knew that evil would go after us and he wanted to make sure we were well-prepared to accept and handle it. By "accept" I mean "accept it as a reality in our lives" vs. denying it or pretending it's not real. God wanted man to know that evil is a literal force to be wary of.

When I was in the Marines, I was put in charge of keeping all of our operating and field combat manuals up to date for our company of tanks. We had manuals on everything from tank maintenance to tactical combat maneuvers. Every type of field manual had to be kept updated and on hand for use by anyone within the company. Most of these manuals helped us to prepare for the enemy, from how to defensively maneuver our tanks against them to how to attack them. These manuals helped us as a unit to be prepared in every situation. They were there in our library to ensure that our tanks were combat ready.

We didn't have many manuals on the good guys; only tank recognition slides. These were obviously important for us to view occasionally, so we didn't fire on any tanks from our NATO allies if we ever went to war. With the exception of those slides, we had very little references on the good guys. Most of our manuals were on how to engage the enemy.

This seems to hold true with God's Word. God knew, when he inspired men to write the Bible, that passages needed to be in there so that we could recognize and identify evil when faced with it, and be able to stand up to it. He purposely included many of Jesus' encounters with demons as well, showing us how to deal with evil. He included many references of how Satan and his minions operate as well.

The bottom line is this: With God's Word as a solid reference tool, we can easily see that when it comes to things created, that have the ability to enter our homes or child's bedroom at night, we really are down to two choices. **A not-of-this-world being must be some type of angelic being; further, they must be a good angel or a fallen angel (a demon).** I believe the key to knowing which is involved in a given instance is to apply common sense in terms of how the being is interacting with us.

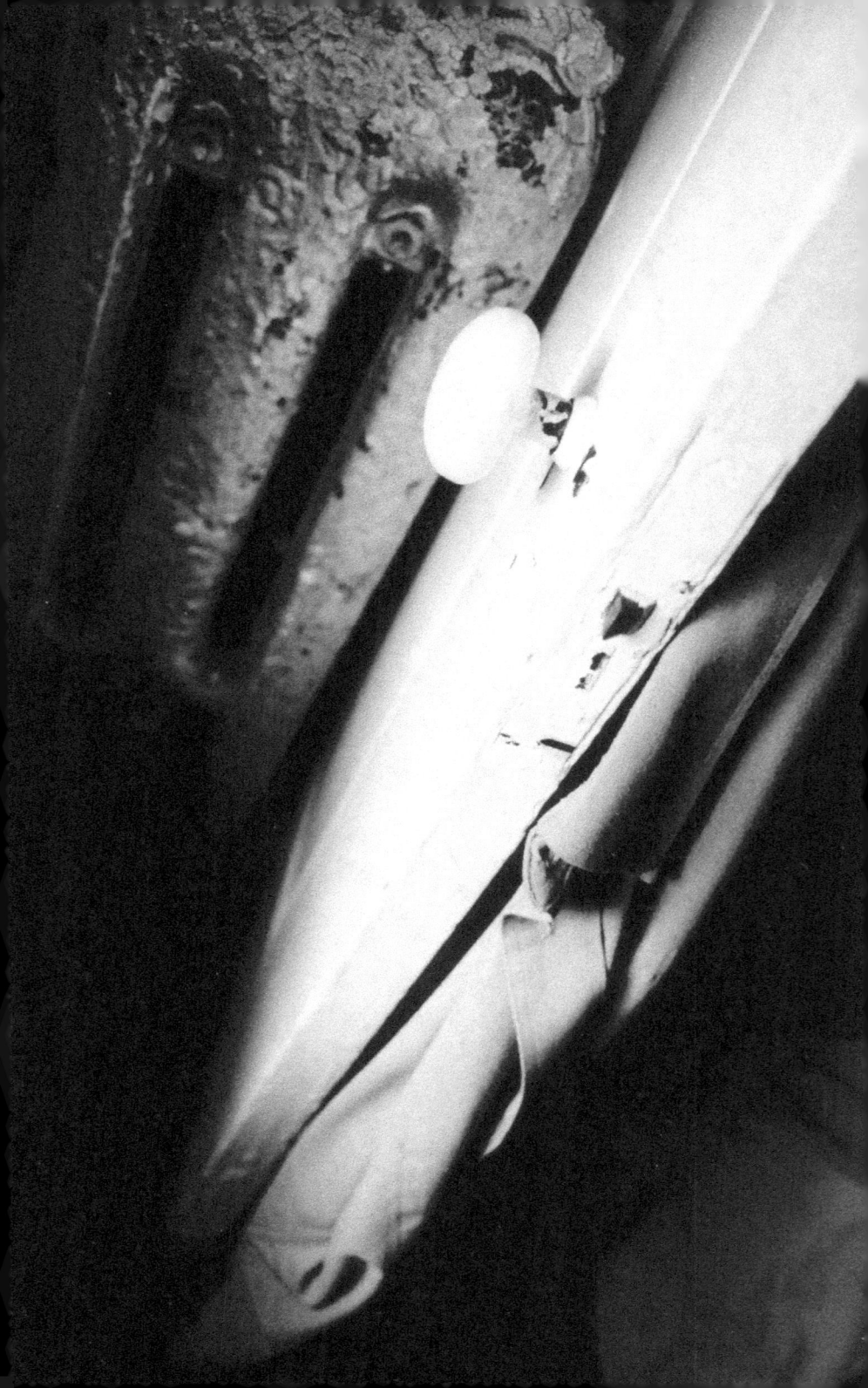

CHAPTER 5

Common Sense Is Good Sense

Some nights, Chelsea has to watch dark shadows jump back and forth from her two children's bedrooms. Her couch faces the hallway where her children's bedrooms are, and she can literally see dark, shadowy figures cross from bedroom to bedroom, going from one child's room to the other.

Chris and Cindy are sisters who share a bedroom. Chris told me that they have to put up with dark shadows in their room. These beings mostly just stand there in the corner by their closet, almost like they are trying to figure the girls out.

Understand, these girls are not having hallucinations. [Two people cannot have the same hallucination.] Chris watched her sister's blanket get yanked off of her as she slept. She just pulled her own blanket up over her head and prayed that they wouldn't come over to her and do the same thing.

Amber has to deal with a human-looking man in her room at night. This spirit stands in the corner of her room, looking straight at her as she tries to sleep. He only shows up on occasion according to her. Her mom tells her that it is the previous owner of their house and he is just checking things out.

Now, let's focus for a moment on any child who is alone in their room at night. Many kids are typically scared of the dark to begin with. Why would a mysterious spirit visit this youngster? If you're a skeptic about these nightly visitors, please, for a moment pretend that this really happens.

The most common explanation I hear is that it has to be a deceased relative. Apply common sense: If a deceased loved one had the ability to visit this child in their dark room, and they are motivated by good intentions, why would they do so in a way that will scare their pajamas off? If you want to scare a young child, the best way to do it is in a dark room. We have all hid somewhere in our houses as kids and jumped out at one of our siblings. It made them jump out of our socks. I don't know about you but the grandparents I know are not in the business of frightening their grandchildren to death.

I am actually a new grandpa and I can't ever picture myself doing anything that would scare him. If I have that kind of power when I am gone, I know for sure that I won't be showing up in my grandson's room in the dark of night. I can't picture a bazillion deceased loved ones, floating around earth saying, "I think it's time to go appear out of nowhere in junior's room." I can't imagine them saying, "I think I'll sit down on the end of the bed, causing it to sink down so they know a body-less spirit is right by their feet." Or why would a benevolent spirit sit on that bed as a dark, scary mass. That would scare most adults, let alone a small child.

I myself had one experience where I sat up in bed in a cold sweat because I thought my mom was standing at the end of my bed (she was alive at the time). I can brush that off as a realistic dream, but the point is it scared me to death. I remember my heart racing and my loss of breath. I'm an ex-Marine who was in the prime of his life when this happened and I was scared to death. I can't even imagine any deceased relative who would knowingly scare any young child by stepping across to this side.

World Jumping Forbidden

One of the few references I can even find on this matter is found in the Bible. By references I mean anything that touches on the subject of humans being able to come back to earth after they die—more specifically, being able to leave where they have gone after they die. It is found in Luke 16:19-26 and it really sheds a lot of light on the matter we are discussing:

> *There was a rich man who was dressed in purple and fine linen and lived in luxury every day. At his gate was laid a beggar named Lazarus, covered with sores and longing to eat what fell from the rich man's table. Even the dogs came and licked his sores. The time came when the beggar died and the angels carried him to Abraham's side. The rich man also died and was buried. In hell, where he was in torment, he looked up and saw Abraham far away, with Lazarus by his side. So he called to him, "Father Abraham, have pity on me and send Lazarus to dip the tip of his finger in water and cool my tongue, because I am in agony in this fire." But Abraham replied, "Son, remember that in your lifetime you received your good things, but now he is comforted here and you are in agony. And besides all this, between us and you a great chasm has been fixed, so that those who want to go from here to you cannot, nor can anyone cross over from there to us."*

In this passage, Jesus is explaining to all of us that there is a fixed barrier between worlds. I always take into consideration that God made sure a passage like this was included in his Word. He wanted us to know that bouncing around between worlds was forbidden. They could not go to him and he could not go to them. It is obvious to me that there are unseen barriers preventing world jumping. There is no chance to bounce around between worlds. Grandma and Grandpa don't have an all-access pass to your child's bedroom. It doesn't appear that we will have any of these world jumping abilities when we pass on.

When the rich man realizes that Lazarus is not allowed to come to him, he begs Abraham to send Lazarus to his father's house to warn them. The rich man is asking for Lazarus, a dead man, to go to earth to warn his family to turn to God so they won't end up in hell. Continuing on, let's see what Luke 16:27-31 says:

"He answered, 'Then I beg you, father, send Lazarus to my father's house, for I have five brothers. Let him warn them, so that they will not also come to this place of torment.'"

Abraham replied, "They have Moses and the Prophets; let them listen to them."

"No, father Abraham," he said, "but if someone from the dead goes to them, they will repent."

He said to him, "If they do not listen to Moses and the Prophets, they will not be convinced even if someone rises from the dead."

To add to the previous passage of not being able to jump from heaven to hell, Abraham went on to say to the rich man in hell that it would be of no use for someone to rise from the dead to warn his family. It wasn't as simple as, "I won't allow it." The message was, "It can't happen." The beggar would have to rise from the dead. The pivotal word is "rise." Abraham is telling the rich man that in order for someone to leave heaven and go warn his family, that they would have to rise from the dead. The beggar's spirit would have to be reunited with his body, which was still in the grave.

There is a pre-determined time in the future when God will raise people from their graves; it is called the resurrection. Until that time, no one can just float down and visit. They would have to be reunited with their resurrected bodies to come to earth. This passage suggests a spiritual law that forbids the dead from returning to earth. In order for that to happen, God would have to raise them from the grave before the appointed time.

We Can't Return

In the book of Job, which some think to be the first written book of the Bible, we find more proof that we are not allowed to come back. Job 7:8-10 says:

> *The eye that now sees me will see me no longer; you will look for me, but I will be no more. As the cloud vanishes and is gone, so he who goes down to the grave does not return. He will never come to his house again; his place will know him no more.*

When you read those three words, **does not return**, nothing could be clearer. The words "never come to his house again" say that we cannot come around visiting our earthly family after we've died. So here are two clear and concise Scriptures—one from the

Old Testament and one from the New Testament—that tell us plainly that this type of travel is not allowed. I believe that God included these passages for our benefit. You can dig around all you want trying to find support for, or evidence that points to, dead relatives being able to come back and visit us, but this idea is simply not supported by the Scriptures.

One more reference I want to use, that is seldom brought up when talking about the ability to go to heaven and then come back, is John 3:12-13:

> *I have spoken to you of earthly things and you do not believe; how then will you believe if I speak of heavenly things? No one has ever gone into heaven except the one who came from heaven—the Son of Man.*

Jesus is in a discussion with Nicodemus, a teacher of the Law, trying to explain to him the concept of being "born again." Nicodemus is having a difficult time understanding Jesus' words. Jesus simply says to him, you will never understand heavenly things if you can't even understand our discussion on earthly things.

Jesus then goes on to say that no man has been to heaven and came back to earth. I am reading between the lines here because the context of this discussion is about salvation. But Jesus is driving this point home with Nicodemus, and re-affirming it by saying no one has gone up and came back down except for the Son of Man. He is telling Nicodemus that earthly people have no way of understanding heavenly things when they haven't been there. Jesus is saying that Nicodemus, as well as others, have no way of understanding heaven when he is the only one who has come back from there and set his feet on earth again. This verse, as indirect as it appears, dismantles the belief held by many people that loved ones can come back to earth.

Unchained Melody

It is very easy to fall into the Patrick Swayze mentality that swayed you when you saw the blockbuster movie "Ghost." I know it really warms the heart thinking and believing that Patrick Swayze came back to help Demi Moore. That scene at the end of the movie where Swayze is glowing with brilliance along with the back drop of heavenly beings is really an amazing scene. Couple that with tears rolling down Demi's face and you have one of the most heartwarming moments in all of movie history.

The reality is that we can't come back and hold Demi Moore one more time and help track down the bad guy. It doesn't work like that. I know many people want to believe that a loved one is prancing around their house or amidst their affairs doing their best to help them out. But it simply cannot be that way, according to the Word of God. Who do you trust to get it right, Hollywood or God?

The next question would obviously be this. Who then is visiting our loved ones while they sleep? Who is sitting or standing at the end of their beds? Who was that little kid spirit that walked out of Corinth's closet? More importantly, what was that black figure that followed close behind this child that Corinth saw?

Good Or Bad Angels

The only other explanation to me is clear, it would have to be some type of angelic being showing up in the wee hours of the night. They are the only ones possible of getting in to a room undetected. On some occasions, they were seen by one family member but not the other. Angels appear to have abilities that defy logic, illustrated by a story one of my son's friends told me a few months ago.

Caine, my son's friend, told me that he was driving home one afternoon and could see up ahead that his aunt was approaching in another car. It was on a rural road so they each slowed down to chat. They rolled down their windows and his Aunt said, "Who is riding with you?" Caine said laughingly, "No one is with me." His Aunt insisted that as she approached him in her car, she could see someone sitting next to him. But when they met, no one was in the car with him. I believe some sort of angel was his co-pilot that day. Stories of guardian angels are very common. The only question with this story is, was it really a guardian angel with him that day or something else?

Stories like this one leave very little doubt that it was something with otherworldly powers and abilities. Caine's companion was seen by her but not seen by him. I wish someone could help me clear this up with another reliable explanation but I haven't heard one yet. The angel theory doesn't seem so far-fetched. His Aunt still talks about seeing someone in his car. It obviously made her wheels spin and has left a lasting impression on her to this day.

A recent foxnews.com poll showed 77 percent of Americans believe in angels. Let's do the math here on this poll. That is approximately 240 million of us who believe that angels do exist. So many people believe in angelic beings that it has to be based on something.

A while later *cnsnews.com* did a survey as well. In their survey they found that only 58 percent of people believe in a literal devil. I took the time to read over all their findings in this particular survey, and I discovered something very revealing. All of the other survey items mentioned, like a belief in heaven, God, and Jesus, were more easily believed. But when it came to evil, those numbers dropped. Seems that people don't want to accept the fact that evil is around. This lower belief in a literal devil supports the facts in my research. It is very easy for someone to tag something as good, and dismiss it as potentially being evil. We would all like to believe that these types of visitors would have to be what are commonly called guardian angels or good angels. You could easily come to that conclusion by reading Psalm 91:11 which says:

> *For he will command his angels concerning you to guard you in all your ways.*

Or you could read Matthew 18:10, where Jesus talks about angels and little children:

> *See that you do not despise one of these little ones. For I tell you that their angels in heaven always see the face of my Father in heaven.*

The following verse is probably the most important one in the context of our subject—Hebrews 1:14:

> *Are not all angels ministering spirits sent to serve those who will inherit salvation?*

There is no doubt in my mind that God sends his angels to help out with things on earth. In the book of Daniel, we find a story about how an angel was dispatched to go to Daniel with the answer to his prayers. The angel was sent to give Daniel understanding of a vision he'd had. In Daniel 10:12 the angel says:

> *Then he continued, "Do not be afraid, Daniel. Since the first day that you set your mind to gain understanding and to humble yourself before your God, your words were heard, and I have come in response to them."*

Obviously, God's angels are at least occasionally involved in the lives of people here on earth. They came for all sorts of reasons, but most visits seem to center around a message for someone. Hebrews 1:14 says that they are sent as ministering spirits to those who will inherit salvation. But sometimes they showed up to carry out God's judgment, which can be clearly seen in the last book of the Bible, Revelation.

Hard Pill To Swallow

This is the dilemma I have with thinking that the bedroom visitors people have described to me are good angels. Are we to believe that these same angels that serve a loving God would appear to our family members as dark masses, literally scaring our kids out of their beds at night? This is inconsistent with a being who allows himself to be described as a loving heavenly Father. I have no doubt that there are good angels that serve and protect us. But there is also the chance that some of these children called on God to protect them from something that scared them. Now that is something good angels might actually do. But the stories I have come across don't sound like good angels.

For example:

- A fourteen-year-old girl told me that she felt her bedroom get cold, almost like a thick haze or fogginess had engulfed the room. Then she felt an unusual weight come over her and she was frozen with fear, unable to even scream.
- A nine-year-old girl told me that something was living in her closet. Always feeling like someone or something was watching her.
- My own sister came into my room to get me so I could help

her go to sleep. She told me "they" kept pulling her blankets off of her. She was only in first grade when this was going on.
- A twenty-two-year-old woman shared how, when she was a little girl she had a secret friend that talked to her from under her bed. Would a loving God send an angel of his to hide under a child's bed? I can't imagine a caring angel doing this, or a deceased loved one for that matter.
- Another young woman told me that when she was younger, she had a secret friend who asked her once, "Do you want to come under your bed and live with me and my friends."
- A young man said he used to have a secret friend that would even follow him outside. This was a first for me—I had never heard of them leaving the house. This young man said his mom used to make him wear glasses when he was a kid and he hated wearing them. So his secret friend actually helped him bury his glasses in the back yard so his mom couldn't make him wear them anymore.
- Two teenage boys see dark figures quite frequently. They have seen these figures crawling on the walls, as though they were big black spiders. That will make the hair on your neck stand up.
- A frantic fifteen-year-old girl called her mom describing how she just watched her one-year old nephew levitate out of his playpen. Then this same fifteen-year-old girl picked up the nephew's two-year-old sister to calm her and felt something tugging at the two-year-old's legs. This two-year-old girl now hates her toes being touched and tells her mom that frogs try to get her toes at night.
- An eighteen–year-old girl told me that when she gets depressed the door to her bedroom starts opening and shutting all by itself.
- A cousin of mine said she would wake up to a tall dark figure at the end of her bed. This was shortly after she had gone through a traumatic life-altering event.

- Another woman told me that quite often she would hear a crash in her son's bedroom. She would run to his room only to find his room torn apart—dresser knocked over and items thrown about. Her son was only two years old and couldn't have moved the dresser alone.
- A woman in her forties said that she was assaulted by her own uncle when she was a teenager. Then in the weeks following the assault, a dark figure started showing up in her bedroom. She said she tucked a knife under her mattress when he started showing up. If this was a good angel do you really think it would continue to visit her, knowing that she was so scared she hid a knife under her mattress?
- Countless young kids, mostly girls, were so scared by something that was in their room that they ran to their parents' bedroom for refuge.
- A mom heard a voice come through her baby's monitor saying, "That is my fire truck." Her child was only one at the time and much too young to say something like that.
- A girl in her middle teens slept with her mom because a dark figure would stand at the foot of her bed, watching her.
- A little girl told her aunt that her secret friend pinches her on the rear end. The aunt asked her where her secret friend comes from. The little girl said, "out of my closet."
- A mom told me that her girls were gone with their father one weekend. She was home all alone and heard noises coming from one of her daughters' bedrooms. She immediately went upstairs and opened her bedroom door and found all of her daughter's toys in a pile in the middle of the floor. She had just cleaned that room an hour before that, putting all the toys away.
- A grown man told me how, in desperation, he fell to his knees in his living room one night. He had entertained the thought of selling his soul to the devil if he could get back on his feet. He was having a lot of problems and was des-

perate. He never did ask the devil for anything, but explained to me how the next night he fell asleep on the couch. He woke up and looked around the room to see what seemed like twenty dark figures staring at him. Did all of his dead relatives show up to console him? I doubt it.

I could fill many more pages with stories like this. The ones listed here are a few of the scarier ones, but it doesn't matter. Clearly, they (*evil*) are not of this world **and** they are up to something. So I think it is safe to say that these nighttime visitors are not good angels. I have over fifty stories of dark figures (or as some call them, shadow people), standing by young girls' beds. If I were a loved one coming back to see my grandchild or if I was one of God's angels, does this sound like the proper or loving way to say hi?

Fallen Angels

There is something more sinister going on with these visits, something that has "BAD" written all over it. I could add stories of girls who have told me how they felt these dark figures lying upon them, or how some of them had their hair brushed to the side. I even have stories of some being touched while taking a shower, or as they were undressing to get in the shower.

The Perron sisters, from the movie "The Conjuring," said that whenever they were in the shower they felt liked something was watching them. This does not sound like an angel God would send to visit someone. And I can't picture a deceased relative peeking at us and touching us while we are naked in the shower.

Words used by these kids (and some adults) were, suffocated, bad odor, whispered to, choked, violated, trapped, frozen, touched, threatened, and breathed on. I have even been told by three different women that this creature that lay on them felt hairy.

After all that I have heard from eyewitness accounts and more than 400 stories, I have concluded that these are fallen angels or demons. I won't argue with anyone that in some of these instances there could have been a good angel involved. But all the evidence points to the fact that these evil spirits or demons are visiting young kids. Yes, they visit adults, too; but by far, most are younger kids, and most of them are girls.

It really boils down to having some amount of common sense. The minute anyone is willing to rationalize this away as a dead relative, they are really leaving themselves and their family open to all sorts of problems. I know that when your child tells you she could smell Grandpa's cigars it might sound like an open and shut case—Grandpa paid a visit. But think about that for a minute. I mean really take the time to think that through. We are dealing with beings from another world. The apostle Paul described the capabilities of these beings in 2 Corinthians 11:14-15:

> ***And no wonder, for Satan himself masquerades as an angel of light. It is not surprising, then, if his servants masquerade as servants of righteousness. Their end will be what their actions deserve.***

According to Paul, Satan can and will pretend to be something good when he is carrying out his evil agenda, and his servants will do the same thing. I won't take this passage out of context. The servants Paul is referring to here are literal men, false apostles preaching a false message about Christ—as such, acting as servants of Satan. But the passage also is clear that Satan masquerades as an angel of light, and that his demonic army is more than capable of doing the very same thing.

Remember all the examples of what kids experience in the dark of the night while in the safety of their own homes? Remember how scared they are? If you as a parent have one ounce of love for your child, then you should take this passage to heart. Even if you are still skeptical of what is really happening with these young kids, don't you think you owe it to them to check into it a little further? For here is biblical evidence that demons can and do appear as angels of light, tricking us into believing they are of good nature. This should not surprise us, since one of Satan's most common methods is to twist God's message or his good gifts to humanity into something evil, with the expectation that people will still think of it as "good." One such gift is what Paul was talking about, God's gift of salvation by grace through faith. Another such gift would be the gift of sexual relations, to be employed within the pure bonds of marriage. Or, in the situations we are considering in this book, to twist people's thinking about the paranormal, otherworldly experiences that some, especially impressionable children, experience to the point where they can be called "good." For Satan and his minions know that if they can get people to call what is evil "good" long enough, they will come to believe that the evil in question really is a good thing.

My Own Sister

With my sister's permission, I want to share a very personal story with you. After reading this, decide for yourself if what she encountered was evil or good.

I can still remember that night as if it was yesterday. I got a call from my brother-in-law, who said that my sister had taken a gun and driven off with it in her car. Her husband was frantic as I tried to make out what was going on.

I hung up the phone and made the two mile drive from my place to theirs not knowing what to expect. My heart was racing as I drove, knowing that I may find her too late. Thankfully I found her a short distance from her house. I parked my car next to hers. I stood there pleading with her to give me the gun. Her face, covered in tears and makeup, said it all.

I luckily noticed that she hadn't loaded the gun; the cartridges were scattered all over her lap as she sat there in the front seat. So I calmed down some, but still pleaded with her to give me the gun. She was crying and telling me that she didn't want to be here anymore. She was in such a terrible state that I was starting to think she might drive off and carry through with this idea.

We went back and forth for a short time but eventually I was able to get the ammunition from her. Her mind frame was so bad that she was content with keeping the gun even after I had scooped up all the bullets.

People snap all the time and we unfortunately read about some of them in the local paper the next day. You might even sit back in your chair as you say to yourself, "I've been there," or "That could just as well be me." But often there is a side to the tragedy that you will never read about in the obituary—a side that you will never hear the police or paramedics talk about. Quite often, these things occur due to some kind of demonic influence (at least in my opinion), for we know that, as Jesus said, Satan is a thief, who comes to steal and kill and destroy (John 10:10), and he is "a murderer from the beginning . . . a liar and the father of lies" (John 8:44). One of his lies, heard by so many, is that being dead would be better than living any longer.

In my sister's case, what had happened the night before in the darkness of her home—one of the few houses I have ever been in that made my hair stand up when I entered it—was that many stressful things converged, leaving her vulnerable. She had had many encounters with them (*evil*) as a child, but now in her early 20s she was past seeing dark figures with the same frequency as she had when she was younger.

Anyway, things had been getting rocky with her and her husband. Money was always a stressor. Additionally, we had just buried our father shortly before the night in question. But this particular night she was terribly depressed and sitting in her living room when they (*evil beings*) just started appearing—not one or two dark figures, but in her own words, they were "uncountable."

Misery Enjoys Company

In this weak moment, these dark figures just started manifesting themselves before her very eyes. She told me they were scattered all around her living room, just standing there looking at her. It was almost like a cheering section from hell. She told me that the heaviness in her living room that night was indescribable.

I don't believe these beings were all of our past relatives. I don't believe these were good angels, either. I am reminded of the accounts in the Bible where the words; "angelic host" are used, where angels show up in masses to honor God. Or when they gather to sing praises. Evidently fallen angels still show up in masses, except when they show up in numbers, it is to cheer on someone at the end of their rope to use that rope to end it all.

I have been told by others that when these figures show up the air gets heavy. Some have even described a foggy haze that engulfed the room. I myself have felt the heaviness when they are present. I shared this with my mom one time when I was a kid and she hung a cross on my wall in my bedroom.

I am starting to believe that if they have the numbers, like in the case of my sister, the depressive heaviness of all of that evil concentrated in a particular place might be enough to push someone over the edge. Strength in numbers may apply here; perhaps it's a way evil can manipulate the situation to their favor. Perhaps their presence creates darkness that has actual weight to it, and a resulting adverse effect (for example, hopelessness or despair) on someone who is already at the end of their rope.

When I was in the Marine Corps we experienced some pretty intense training. One of our classes during boot camp was a simple trip to the pool. We were told to bring all of our gear with us so we knew it wasn't going to be a relaxing swim. Of course we put all that gear on—about 100 pounds worth—right there at the edge of the pool. Then we were told to jump in and swim to the middle of the pool and come back. That was without a doubt the closest I have ever come to drowning, and I am a good swimmer. But with all that weight on I could barely tread water. I felt like I was going straight to the bottom.

That is the image I get in my mind when someone describes a demonic host in their house or directly in front of them. When they are there, it gets almost hard to move. People describe a feeling of being frozen, feeling immobile, and an almost suffocating feeling. Their presence does something to an individual as well as to the surrounding environment, creating an invisible heaviness that can actually be felt.

Thus far my goal has been to establish who or what these beings are, by a biblical process of elimination. I've been trying to narrow down who or what is showing up in the dark hours of the night to visit our kids and family members. Who could possibly be moving items around in our homes? Who is tickling the toes of young kids as they try and go to sleep at night?

When I tear apart these encounters, using a very reliable source, the Bible, and apply some common sense, a pretty clear picture emerges. It is obviously something not of this world. Most would at least agree on this. Considering everything, I conclude that it is obviously something with evil intentions. Perhaps you are still holding on to the possibility that it might be a loved one or that they are harmless spirits. If so, I believe the following pages might loosen your grip on that theory.

It should be clear by now that I am adamant about who these nighttime visitors are. But I still want to address one more "possible" explanation—aliens and UFOs. One reason is that two trustworthy sources each have shared with me that they have had a legitimate encounter with what they claimed were aliens.

CHAPTER 6

Phone Home E.T.

People seem fascinated with UFOs and aliens. The truth is, I did have some that brought this possibility up as I interviewed them, saying that they remember having a feeling that they were going to be taken as they experienced an unusual encounter. One girl even said that she would wake up from sleepwalking at the front door of their house with the feeling she was meant to go somewhere. So the subject does deserve some consideration.

Let me start with a friend of mine who feels she was almost being abducted by aliens. Janet grew up in Stephenson, Michigan. She and almost all of her extended family have had many encounters over the years. Janet's sister, Ann, has seen just about every kind of spirit I have come across while researching this book. Little girls, little boys, dark figures, and she even claims her grandmother came to see her. Ann had one encounter in her kitchen where she saw a dark figure watching her. A few minutes later, the room temperature dropped and she could see her breath. That's when something made contact and touched her leg. Right after the contact, items in the kitchen started flying around all by themselves.

Janet's mother, Colleen, has had encounters of her own, as have all five of her sisters. Colleen has had run-ins with a hovering spirit over her bed. A spirit knocked her down one time. Obviously, quite a bit goes on in this family.

Janet herself tells me she can sense when spirits are around and some even talk to her. There was a time when she was younger that a tall, dark shadowy figure would stand in her bedroom doorway and just stare at her. She has awoken several times with scratches on her, always in three's.

Close Encounters

Janet described what she thought were UFO encounters. She explained that she had a dream one time, and in the dream, she was told to "Come with us." When she woke from this dream she wasn't in bed like most of us are after a dream; she was standing just outside her own front door still in her pajamas. She felt in her heart of hearts that she either had gone somewhere, or was meant to go somewhere. To be honest, she is not sure herself whether she did or not. It's easy to see how someone can conclude they might have been abducted with an experience like this.

An old friend of mine, Darrell, had an experience that still bothers him to this day. Darrel and his wife were climbing into bed one night when he noticed that the bedroom was noticeably brighter, like someone had a spotlight aimed through their window. He walked over to the bedroom window and off in the distance could see a large bright light. Darrel said it looked like the moon had drawn in close to his house. It was as large and bright as could be. He called his wife over to the window and they both peered out it into the night sky. Then what happened next neither of them can explain.

There was a very brilliant flash, like someone had snapped a picture with a huge camera flash. When they came to their senses, they were no longer standing by the window. They were fifteen feet away, clear across the bedroom embraced in each other's arms. Face to face in an embracing hug. Neither of them has any memory of walking to that side of the bedroom, or knowledge of how they got there in that position. Somehow, that flash of light carried them across their bedroom. It was as though they had been transported.

He and his wife divorced shortly after this unbelievable night. So naturally after he told me this amazing story, I contacted his ex-wife to get her side of it. She told me apologetically that she would rather not discuss what went on in that house. This response was not uncommon as I did my research, so I cannot say for certain how she experienced whatever happened. But it seems to me that when folks declined to comment, and especially when they were abrupt about it, it's safe to assume that something out of the normal did happen, because if this weren't true, all they would have to do was deny it or to make some disparaging remark about the person who had described the event to me. But when people decline to comment, I always respect their privacy.

Mom and E.T.

A few years after we moved to Michigan our family did have an encounter of sorts with something that most would call UFO in nature. We only spent a short time at the house in Wilson and ended up moving to Spalding, Michigan. Then, a few years later, we moved south of there to the little town of Nadeau, Michigan, where incidentally, most of my stories that fill this book come from. Nadeau seems to be a hotbed for activity.

Our family was traveling down the highway on our way back to Nadeau this particular night when out of nowhere my mom yells out, "Stop the car! Something is above the car." So my dad pulled the car over on the shoulder of the highway and we all climbed out to see what she was talking about.

Sure enough, as we looked up into the night sky, there they were—two lights moving toward each other as if they were going to collide head on. These two lights stopped right next to each other, as though it was a planned meeting. Only a few seconds went by and they zoomed off in opposite directions. What was amazing about their departure was their speed as they departed. It was not of this world. I have witnessed many military planes in action while serving in the military, and this was not of this world, trust me.

Another thing that I will always remember is how my mother knew they were up there. Who told her to yell at dad to stop the car? These lights were very high in the sky and there is no way she could have seen them, since we were inside a moving car. They seemed to be straight above the car and miles from earth. I am convinced something or someone told her they were up there.

I will admit that God may have created other worlds of which we are unaware. But I don't do well with assuming something of this importance. The universe is so vast and unexplored that many people assume there must be other forms of civilizations out there, somewhere. But if God created other civilizations, he hasn't revealed that to us. From what he has revealed in Scriptures, I'm convinced that there are no other forms of life. I believe that this assumption is another deception of Satan—a cleverly mastered scheme that undermines what God has revealed to us. For, if Satan can get people to believe there are other life forms out there, instead of what God has told us he created, people will rely less on the Bible as truth, while accepting UFO and alien reports that seem to come from all over the globe. After all, how can God's word be accurate (and trustworthy) if these aliens and UFOs are all over the place, with no mention of them in Scripture?

Demonic Deception

I believe that belief in aliens is demonically orchestrated (as are ideas like parallel universes and any other construct of reality that diminishes the idea of God and a need for a Savior). My conclusion on this was proven right in my eyes when I stumbled across a seminar video on this very subject. After I finished the 100 minute video, I realized that many of these experiences of alien abductions I had heard described in this video sounded like the stories of some of the people I had interviewed for this book. I had finally come across a source that supported what my gut had been telling me all these years.

The video, which you can find on "YouTube," is called "Unholy Communion—Aliens are Demons of the Bible!" Trust me when I say that this video will rattle your way of thinking. If you watch it, be prepared for your jaw to drop and a feeling of betrayal as the truth is revealed about aliens in a way you have never heard before.

The narrator of the video is Joe Jordan. In 1992 he joined the world's largest UFO investigating organization, the Mutual UFO Network. He became a field investigator for them, gathering information about alien abductions and sightings. As time went on he realized that it was pointless for him to chase around these supposed sightings of UFOs. Naturally by the time he got to a site and interviewed the eyewitness the spacecraft was gone. So in effect they really were not gathering much reliable information to support the whole UFO phenomenon. They were also wasting money and resources chasing these stories. That's when Joe decided to switch gears.

They decided to start up some town hall meetings in the Orlando, Florida area, to interact with the local community. They let the stories come to them instead of chasing them. A lot of people showed up at these meetings. One of them was Bill, who told a story of how he had actually stopped an alien abduction. That caught Joe's attention and he started to key in on stories similar to Bill's.

Bill recalled how back in 1976 he had seen some strange lights on the horizon near his home. He described how his dogs would not stop barking that night. They had never barked like that before so he knew something wasn't right. He couldn't figure out what the lights might be so, along with his wife, Bill decided to call it a night. However, while he was lying there in bed, all of a sudden the room started getting misty or foggy. He couldn't help but feel as though someone was in the room with them. He could just sense someone staring at him. Out of nowhere he started to levitate out of his bed. It felt as though someone had inserted a pole into his rectum and was holding him up above his bed. He couldn't believe that his wife was still sound asleep during this ordeal. He then said that he remembers feeling helpless, like he had some form of paralysis. All he could think to say was, "Jesus, Jesus, Jesus!" After saying that, he recalls crashing back down on to the bed with enough force to wake up his wife. She then pointedly asked him why in the world he was jumping on the bed.

It's All In The Name

This testimony grabbed Joe's attention. He finally had an eyewitness to an attempted alien abduction who was able to stop it. This testimony catapulted Joe into a whole different direction in regards to investigating alien abductions. He decided to start gathering more like-minded accounts in an attempt to see if others had somehow stopped apparent abductions. As of now, he has well over 400 documented testimonies of people who were able to end attempted alien abductions. They all had one thing in common. They said the name of Jesus during their ordeal, and the alleged abduction abruptly ended for them.

For years I would share with others that I always believed that demons were behind the whole alien phenomenon. I remember quite a few discussions with friends over the years who thought aliens were real. Joe Jordan's research has shut the door on aliens as far as I'm concerned. Just as they (*evil*) masquerade as deceased loved ones, they also have many duped into thinking that aliens are real. Satan is the master of deception and it has been proven once again that he has no boundaries.

Something else Joe said in this video caught my attention as well. He stated that as they started coming across all these testimonies from those who stopped the abductions, they started asking the people involved why they felt they were targeted in the first place. Joe stated that they found a pattern. Practically all of the abductees or attempted abductees fell under one of three categories:

> The first group of abductees explained to Joe that they simply asked for it. They were curious about aliens and actually wanted to be abducted. These people literally invited this to happen.
> The second group told Joe that someone in their family had also been abducted. This was actually a generational problem where others have been abducted in the past.
> The third group had ties with the occult. This reminded me of my mother's ties to the occult and how she knew those lights were above our car that night. I should mention that my mother also claimed to have seen UFOs on other occa-

sions as well. My sister as well said she had seen one, herself, late one night.

Closely Related

When I was in fourth grade I was plagued with recurring nightmares. The twist to these nightmares was that they seemed very real to me, closely resembling an examination. For a span of several weeks, I had the same dream every night. I was on some sort of hospital gurney and remember feeling like there were people around me. I do not remember being able to see anyone's faces though. I do remember a lot of electricity all around and being worried I was going to get shocked. This type of dream or encounter of being examined follows closely what supposed "abductees" go through.

The similarities between alien abduction stories and those who have seen dark figures are remarkable. It is obvious to me that Satan is involved in both phenomena. For example:

- How can two people be lying in the same bed and only one reports anything happening? It is as though they both (aliens and demons) have the ability to manifest to one specific person while the other one is oblivious to what is happening.
- How both aliens and demons seem to be fascinated with appearing at the foot of the bed, as if they are looking down at the person in an examining fashion, and both entities not being restrained by walls and doors.
- People described how they felt as though they were being examined by both demons and aliens. Granted that alien abduction stories carry more details of this, it is still eerily similar. Some alien abduction stories include sexual exam-

inations by their abductors. This parallels those I have interviewed who felt as though they were being molested in their own beds by these dark figures. In a few rare cases, women told me they were actually molested.
- Kids told me stories of spirits talking to them. In quite a few of these cases the kids shared that the spirits said, "Everything is okay." The same happens with alien abductees. They are routinely told, "You are safe," or "Everything is okay."
- Another strange similarity involves them hovering over baby's cribs. I actually had a mother mail me pictures of a dark mass over her child's crib. She heard her baby screaming and went in her room to see what was wrong. She watched the dark mass hovering over the crib and snapped a picture with her smart phone.
- Some with stories of being abducted have shared how years later their own grandkids have had encounters with these same beings. In one case the grandchild told his grandparents they are his "buddies." I have forty-two cases of little kids having secret or imaginary friends.
- Many abduction stories include the sensation of the room they are in becoming hazy or foggy, bedrooms where the air becomes "heavy." Most include the impression that someone was watching them when this occurred.
- The descriptions of the aliens and the dark figures in some cases are similar—they are tall and have a slender build; they have overly large dark eyes as well.
- In certain cases involving aliens or spirits, paralysis is a factor, freezing those involved in their beds, unable to scream or fight back. This obviously can be attributed to their being scared to death. Alien abductees sometimes claim they were taken to a ship and examined, unable to stop it due to a kind of paralysis. Those who have encounters in the confines of their own home say the same thing—they were

lying in their bed unable to move or scream to stop what was happening to them.
- A woman I know felt like someone was choking her while she lay in bed. She was alone in her room when this happened. She cried out, "Jesus, help me," and the ordeal ended abruptly. The air in the room went from hazy to clear as a bell, too.

Hard-To-Deny Similarities

It is impossible to miss the similarities between these two phenomena. Likewise, the only escape from either situation is the same—the name of Jesus. If you insist on believing in aliens, you must answer the question: Why would some highly intelligent, vastly superior being who can defy gravity and zip around the universe in a spacecraft at phenomenal speeds submit to the name of Jesus? If such beings really existed, they should be invulnerable to any belief system but their own. And why should other entities that seem to possess supernatural powers simply flee at the same Name? The only sensible answer is that, as with anything evil in nature, when they are confronted with the ultimate goodness that is in Jesus Christ, his light dispels their darkness. In reality, nighttime visitors and aliens are the same—evil spirits on a mission to deceive the human race.

I am reminded of the scene from the movie, "The Sign," starring Mel Gibson and Joaquin Phoenix where Joaquin and the two children are on the sofa watching the TV with tin foil hats on. Mel comes into the living room, and they explain to him that they are wearing the tin foil hats so the aliens can't read their minds. You can spend the rest of your life wearing a tin foil hat, believing anything you happen to hear or read about spirits or aliens, or you can believe in something with substance, with clout—God's Word, the Bible, and put your trust in his Son, Jesus Christ.

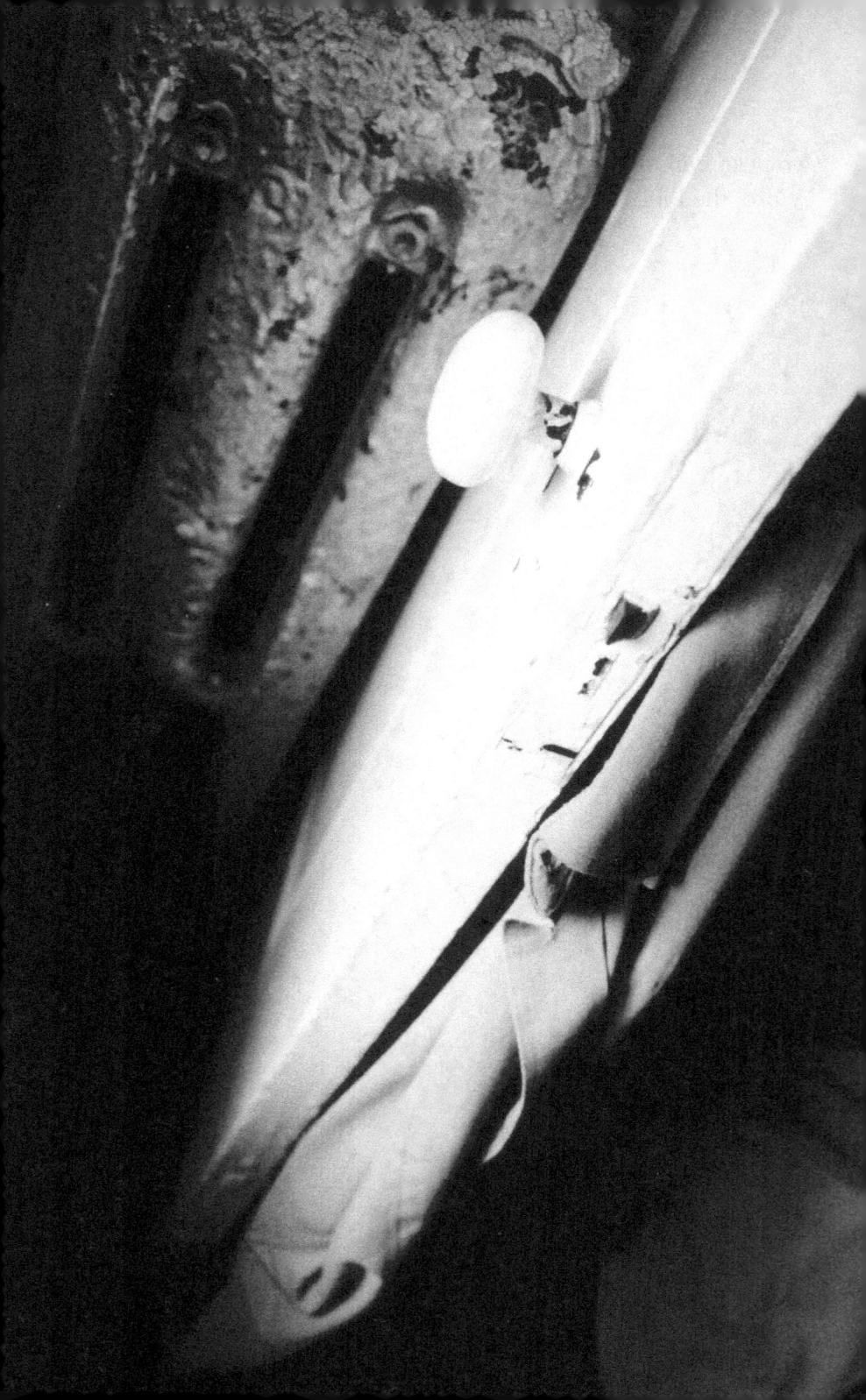

CHAPTER 7

Wrestling With Demons

Before the previous chapter on aliens, I concluded that nightly spirit visitors ("ghosts" as some call them) must be evil spirits. When the deceptive side of these visits gets exposed it leaves no doubt who these nightly visitors are. When we bounce everything off of Scripture, the darkness of these visits becomes very evident.

If all these dark figures showing up in people's houses are evil spirits, like I believe, have you ever wondered how many of them might be prowling around? Before this book endeavor, I never gave a question like that much thought. But now, I often wonder how many are at work in our lives harassing and attacking us.

No one really can put a number on how many demons Satan has at his disposal to prowl with him. But let's play the number game for a while to really put into perspective what we are up against with these nightly visitors—to understand a little bit better why there are so many people seeing them. The best we can do is an educated guess on why so many people see them. We do know from the book of Matthew, that Jesus spoke of having twelve legions of angels at his disposal, which would be approximately 72,000 angels. I believe this is a direct reference to how many could have come to aid him if he chose to call them. In Revelation 5:11 we find a reference to the number of angels that were created.

> ***Then I looked and heard the voice of many angels, numbering thousands upon thousands, and ten thousand times ten thousand.***

The math? There may be as many as 100 million angels. We have to factor in that one third of the angels fell, so assuming this 100 million are good angels and add the 50 million that fell and we have at minimum of 150 million created angels.

We could speculate on this all day because the exact number has never been revealed to us, so I am going to go with 50 million fallen angels; obviously there could be more. Now envision 50 million or so demons prowling the earth looking for victims to devour—50 million demons whose sole purpose is to harass, oppress, deceive, and cause havoc on earth.

A recent estimate of our own military, which is considered the strongest military in the world, was 2.3 million strong—active and reserve units combined. Imagine what Satan can do with 50 million active duty demons at his disposal who have superior intelligence and power, whose sole purpose is to oppress us human beings.

So many people are familiar with the common stories of good angels and how they are sent as ministering agents to help carry out God's will, but we tend to overlook one aspect of God's army. It is that they are *a literal army*. C. Fred Dickason is the author of one of the best reference books on angels called, *Angels Elect and Evil*. In chapter five he is discussing angels' names and classifications. He says this about the term "host" in reference to angels:

"Host pictures God's heavenly angels as His army, and is the translation of the Hebrew *sava*. In Psalm 103:20-21, angels are called upon to bless the Lord. In these verses, angels termed *malakim* and *mishrathim* are also termed *sava* (v.21, cf. Psalm 148:2). This term encompasses the whole array of God's heavenly army and sees them employed as a military force to accomplish His will and do His battles."

So if the good angels are a part of God's army, then it stands to reason that the fallen angels, demons, have a military structure as well. Satan has an army just as God has an army, and if Satan has an army 50 million strong, it seems likely that he has drawn up some battle plans for them. The Bible calls these plans "schemes" in the book of James. My guess is that those plans of attack have single mom families in it, and those who are loaded down with some of life's biggest ills.

Realm Of Responsibility

I did a little math regarding what demons' realm of responsibility might be. This may give you a better understanding of how easy 50 million demons can keep tabs on us and oppress us. The total surface area of the earth is 197 million square miles. If you take away the square mileage of all the oceans, that leaves roughly 55 million square miles of land. Then if you add together the area of places like Siberia, deserts, high mountain ranges, the Amazon rain forest, and other remote areas that are more or less uninhabited, the land area that demons have to operate over might be as low as 30 million square miles.

Assuming there are 50 million demons, they each have less than a one square mile area of responsibility. Remember, we are speculating on how many angels fell and became demons. The actual number could be higher. The point? They are closer than you think and hold a tight grip on this planet along with all the inhabitants.

You may recall that I don't put much credence in the idea of "haunted houses." I believe that demons are assigned to areas, not just to houses. It may be a town, or a certain area of that town. Obviously there can be a vast difference between Chicago and the town I live in that has one caution light, Carney, Michigan. The Bible suggests that they are restricted to certain areas. Daniel 10:12-13 says:

> **Then he continued, "Do not be afraid, Daniel. Since the first day that you set your mind to gain understanding and to humble yourself before God, your words were heard, and I have come in response of them. But the prince of the Persian kingdom resisted me twenty-one days. Then Michael, one of the chief princes, came to help me, because I was detained there with the king of Persia."**

This text reveals: An angel sent out by God to help Daniel was detained by "the prince of Persia," a demon (fallen angel). This demon is described by the good angel as "the prince of the Persian kingdom." He had more than likely been assigned to that area by Satan. If the higher up, more powerful demons have assigned areas it makes sense that the lower demons are assigned areas as well.

I also believe this due to a story a woman told me about a boy spirit that harassed her. She lived in Chicago and it was common for her to see a child spirit bouncing a ball against a wall in their apartment. They moved a short distance from this apartment to a new apartment and the spirit followed them. It did the same thing in her new apartment. But when she moved to Upper Michigan that spirit boy never showed up again. A few miles didn't prevent it from following her, but hundreds of miles did. I don't believe it didn't have the power or ability to follow her to

Michigan, I believe this demon was assigned to the area in which she had lived previously. Thus, when she moved out of its area, the demon stayed put. Once again this is just a theory of mine based on someone's testimony, but it does make sense in light of the passage quoted from the book of Daniel.

Being Gulped Up

If you ask someone what good angels do day in and day out, chances are you will receive an answer similar to this from most people: They help us or protect us . . . working behind the scenes, unnoticed; lifting cars off accident victims, sitting on church steeples protecting God's people.

But what kind of response would you expect if you asked someone what 50 million demons are doing day in and day out in relation to human beings? Now there's a question seldom asked or rarely talked about. Why? Because people don't have a clue about how to answer it.

In Job 1:6-7 we find an interesting account of what Satan does, and more than likely what his demonic army does as well:

> *One day the angels came to present themselves before the Lord, and Satan also came with them. The Lord said to Satan, "Where have you come from?" Satan answered the Lord, "From roaming through the earth and going back and forth on it."*

1 Peter 5:8 describes what Satan does as he roams the earth:

> *Be self-controlled and alert. Your enemy the devil prowls around like a roaring lion looking for someone to devour.*

Add 2 Corinthians 11:14 in relation to "nightly visitors":

And no wonder, for Satan himself masquerades as an angel of light.

Combine these three verses and you have a clear biblical view of what they are doing behind the scenes. Satan roams, prowls, and masquerades as an angel of light. You really can't paint a better picture as far as what he does on a daily basis. Really let these verses sink in! He is roaming and prowling, looking for victims. They (*evil*) are looking for their next victim to gulp up and it is very unlikely that Satan alone does all the prowling. He also is masquerading as an angel of light, projecting the illusion of being good.

Being able to understand the above verses from the Bible will take away from anyone's confusion as to who these unwanted guests are. Just because your mom told you that you are sensitive to the spirit world, doesn't mean she is right. If you were told the spirit in your house is a dead relative, it doesn't mean it is.

Lack of biblical knowledge will sow seeds of confusion and make people more susceptible to believing that these evil spirits are good. The Bible calls Satan a liar, and for good reason. Everything he does is deceptive; everything he says is deceiving. If he can plant seeds of confusion in the minds of those he is harassing, he will not have to worry about his scheme being unraveled.

Now that we know what we are up against, let's focus on 1 Peter 5:8. The Greek word that is translated "devour" is literally to gulp up! Satan not only wants to harass and oppress us. His end goal is to totally gulp us up. Satan does not quit until his prey is completely consumed.

He won't settle for harassing us occasionally. He isn't interested in being a thorn in our side once in a while, though the mild harassing does happen for some. But just as God wants us to love him and be totally his, Satan wants to devour us so we are totally his. The reason it's been so easy for me to find true stories and accounts of these night visiting spirits is that there could be as many as 50 million of them at work in the lives of people on earth, and if they are even remotely like the description presented in Scripture of Satan, they are prowling all over the place. That means they could very well be in your child's bedroom at night, with the goal of gulping them completely up.

Not Of This World Struggles

If someone were to ask me what evil spirits exactly do day in and day out, I would direct them to Ephesians 6: 11-12:

> **Put on the full armor of God, so that you can take your stand against the devil's schemes. For our struggle is not against flesh and blood, but against the rulers, against the authorities, against the powers of this dark world and against the spiritual forces of evil in the heavenly realms.**

Through the years of being a believer and reading Ephesians 6 quite a few times, it wasn't until this past year that I really understood the importance of this chapter in relation to my research into the paranormal.

Ephesians 6 lined up perfectly with how most of those I was interviewing with stories of paranormal experiences were going through some of life's biggest struggles. Scripture identified this a few thousand years ago and I was seeing it firsthand. That is what I love about Scripture—the more you read the same passages, the more things come to light.

Letting this passage in Ephesians sink in will be a major step for anyone toward understanding the battle we are engaged in and who we are up against. The word "battle" might seem strong, but that is what is really going on if you have evil spirits running loose in your home. The Bible sheds so much light on who these nighttime visitors are, and why they do come around. The apostle Paul makes it very clear that the things we war against in this world should not be fought "in the flesh," i.e. in our own human strength and wisdom.

First, he tells us to beware of the devil's schemes. A scheme is a large scale systematic plan. Think about that for a minute. These evil spirits are carrying out a well thought out, intentional plan that is directed at us. Paul knew it and warned us about it.

Second, he informs us that our struggles are not against the flesh, but against spiritual forces. When we have enough insight into this and turn our thinking away from the normal and the physical, we will recognize these evil schemes.

Third, he tells us that we are up against the powers of this dark world and the spiritual forces of evil in the heavenly realms. If you're going to win a battle, you must know your opponent. Otherwise you will direct your attention in the wrong direction.

Satan has most people tricked into believing his schemes. That's why Paul warned us to beware of them. When you read anything on the paranormal, chances are pretty good that it is a cleverly mastered scheme, an underhanded attempt by Satan to trick people into buying his lies, leading them away from the truth so he can gulp them up any time he wants.

Our Struggles

Paul says that *our* struggles are not against flesh and blood (not that *some* struggles are not against flesh and blood). He says our struggles are because Satan will use any and all situations to enter into our lives to harass us. Satan and his minions are continually looking for who their next prey will be. They look for those who are struggling with the ills of life, and they use the opportunity to move in and make camp. This truth became very clear as I researched and interviewed hundreds of people. Broken homes, abuse, and depression were common among those who were dealing with encounters.

Ron Phillips supports my research results in regards to those who seem to be the preferred recipients of evil encounters. In his book, *Everyone's Guide to Demons and Spiritual Warfare*, he says, "A curse is when difficulties, distress, illness, shortage, or other negative issues rest continually on an individual or family." He goes on to say this as well, "The spirit of poverty operates by using unexpected shortages to generate fear. This fear will often bring tormenting spirits, including depression, lack of motivation, quarrelling and despair."

We are in an all-out war with evil, even if most people can't see what is happening. When a person believes that a dead relative is visiting their family instead of some sinister demonic being, they have no idea of the battle being waged, and through their own lack of vigilance they are tricked into thinking some of the spirits in their home are good, so they put up with it instead of resisting or respecting it for what it really is. This scheme has the appearance of being a physical issue—since spirits are being "seen" or otherwise sensed. But it is not a physical battle. Paul states unequivocally this battle with evil is on the inside, a battle for the soul and mind of every person involved.

If you think that it's just Grandpa paying a visit from the other side, then Satan has no problem advancing forward, unhindered. You won't be concerned about it and there will be little chance of your doing anything about it. Those talons are so deep that you won't ever try to stop it from continuing. Even though those talons are not drawing blood, they are drawing out your quality of life, unbeknownst to you or your loved ones.

Satan and his army from hell feed off of our struggles, our fears, and our problems. That can be the entry point for them to move into your life. Once they sniff out that you are going through some type of life struggle, they take action and start nosing around in your home. They want to discover how far they can take you so they amplify your struggles. This, in my opinion, is why someone's house is "haunted." This is why a child gets paid a visit in her room at night. Something allowed them (*evil*) in and now they are scoping it out to see how far they can go with it.

Ed and Lorraine Warren

A cousin of mine explained to me how the dark shadows he and his family continually see in his apartment are always peeking around corners and doorframes. This is a perfect example of their true nature, a brief glimpse of what they do behind the scenes. They are acting like Navy Seals on a reconnaissance mission. These spirits love to be hidden and concealed, not allowing those they are menacing to really see them. I have heard numerous accounts of them just turning away as people catch sight of them. Their goal is to stay hidden, operating behind the scenes.

Merrill Unger, a very well-known and respected theologian, couldn't have stated it any simpler in his book, *What Demons Can do to Saints*. He said, "Satan's chief tactic is to hide his identity and his assaults." I love the last part of that quote, "hides his assaults." Unger is saying that we won't even be able to recognize the assault itself on some occasions. Just like those who are plagued by spirit encounters, they have bought into the lie that it is all well and good. As your child walks to the bus stop, no evil spirit is going to jump out from behind the bushes to attack them, they are going to attack quietly and from behind the scenes. They are going to wage the war in your home quietly, doing their best to stay undetected.

This is pivotal in understanding why so many believe that these unwanted spirits in your home are good. They (*evil*) need you to believe that so they can carry out their agenda, and especially so you don't take action to get rid of them. If they have you duped into believing they are good or that they are passed-on relatives, they can carry out their mission **to a T**.

Ed Warren, easily the most recognized name in paranormal investigating, stated that there are five levels of demonic activity that he and his wife run into when they are called to someone's home. The first one is encroachment, then comes infestation, then oppression, then possession, and finally death. The first two on this list are what I have come across the most in my many talks with those who have spirits around.

The first level of activity, encroachment, is an intrusion on a person's territory. He feels they do this as a form of reconnaissance, scoping things out in any given home. This describes what is happening in my cousin's house. It also lines up with the many children who have dark figures in their rooms at night, just staring at them like they are scoping them out. This is why so many young girls explain to me the constant feeling of being watched in their rooms at night. It might even explain why so many kids can't sleep through the night because they are so scared to be in their own rooms alone. It explains why a young girl I know well has problems when she is depressed. She has explained to me that her bedroom door opens and shuts by itself on the nights she is feeling depressed.

When I tie together Ed's theory of evil spirits scoping things out, and Paul's passage from Ephesians, it helps me understand why a friend of mine never saw a dark figure in her room until after she was raped. Her feelings of worthlessness and despair caused by her assault invited this dark figure into her bedroom at night. Her struggles were not against flesh and blood. Once evil recognized her vulnerability due to what had just happened to her, the reconnaissance began. She shared with me how this figure stayed around for quite some time, until she got a little older . . .

as if this evil spirit was there just checking her out, but never really bothering her physically.

The second of Ed's levels of activity, infestation, is defined as to spread or swarm in or over in a troublesome manner. Demons start causing problems in the life of the one they have keyed in on. Evil decides to take their assault on someone to the next level and insert their talons into someone a little deeper. During this infestation period, evil also isolates its victim, singling them out as its primary target within the family. This isolation of certain victims is where my research really took off. It became a common denominator in what I was coming across as I talked to many different people.

In my family growing up, all five of us kids had stories to share. What I could never fully understand years ago was how they seemed to concentrate on my sister the most. Since then, after studying the subject more, Ed Warren's theory of how they single out someone in the family made more sense to me. This second phase of his, infestation, along with his isolation comment, made the light bulb go on in regards to my sister. Now, with others sharing stories with me, I can see how that is being played out all over our rural area of northern Michigan.

Bedroom Captivity

It is always my hope that as I get the chance to talk to someone or a family, that they trust me enough to be as open as they possibly can be. That was the case with a family I know from Pembine, Wisconsin. The mother, Carol, was the focus of my attention as we started conversing about her family's experiences. Carol had her own stories to share, but it didn't take long before that attention switched to her daughter, Jenna.

Carol explained how Jenna was an outgoing young lady most of her life. There was absolutely nothing that was happening in Jenna's life that was a cause for alarm in her mother's eyes. She had decent grades and seemed to never have a problem making or keeping friends. When Jenna was in her early teens she met a boy who started hanging out with her. Carol told me that in a very short time the two became inseparable. That is when things took a turn for the worst.

The two of them were watching a movie in Jenna's room one night and she fell asleep during the movie. When she woke up her pants were unzipped and his hands were up inside her shirt. She told her mom she has no idea how long she was asleep. Carol explained to me that her daughter changed after that incident. It wasn't long after that when the dark figures started showing up.

Jenna started staying in her room all the time. She had absolutely no friends that came over anymore. Her life went from as normal as a teen could be, to one of total isolation. By the time Carol realized enough was enough and confronted her, it was too late. The dark figures had set up camp in Jenna's room. Jenna told her mom that the dark figures darted around her room all night, making it hard for her to sleep. The kicker to this story was that Jenna told her mom that "they" don't like it when she leaves her room. She openly admitted to her mom that she felt like a prisoner in her own bedroom.

I have an almost identical story of other young woman who shared with her mom that she hates leaving her room. She comes home from school and heads right up to her bedroom, rarely to be seen the rest of the evening. Her mother also said enough is enough after her daughter started dressing in dark clothes. She told her daughter that they needed to talk and her daughter asked her mom if they could go outside to talk so "they" couldn't overhear what they were talking about.

This young teen was worried that the spirits in her room would know what they were talking about. How revealing. This girl was being held hostage in her own room like the girl in the previous story. The captivity of this young girl was also accompanied with fears of retaliation. How sad to be in your own home or bedroom living with that type of fear.

I have a nephew whose life played out just like the previous two stories. His mother endured many years of spirit oppression. He turned into a recluse of sorts and now dresses completely in black. He even told his mother he hates her and has severed ties with her. He refused to talk with me. But his sister has shared stories with me of seeing dark masses in her room, so I am confident that he endured things as well growing up.

Level two of demonic activity seems to have been a factor in these stories. They invaded someone's life and isolated them from everything they used to hold on dearly to. This isolation was evident as more and more people shared stories with me. But it didn't end with just individual isolation. In some cases the isolation seemed to affect more than just one family member. What came into clear focus for me, in regards to multiple members of a given family being attacked, was that it seemed to be the girls of the families who were the recipients more times than not. If there were boys in the family, they were not seeing anything, while the girls of the same family couldn't escape the encounters.

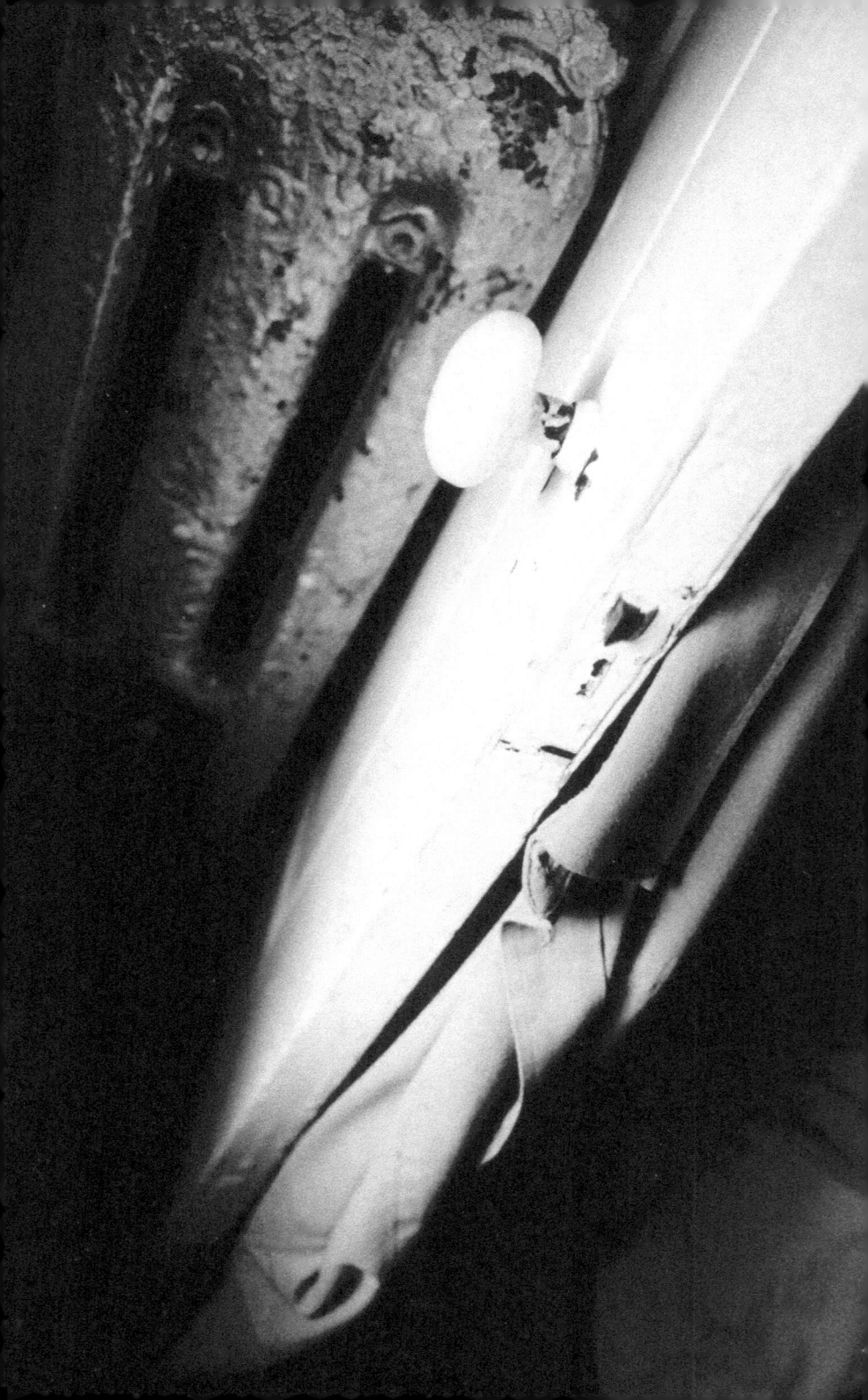

CHAPTER 8

Attacks On Women

Like we find on any traditional battlefield, the enemy will attack the weakest fronts to gain the most ground quickly. Who are the most vulnerable on this spiritual battlefield? There is no doubt that young women and kids are the most vulnerable. Some women may be insulted by me saying that and for that I am sorry. But as you will see it has some truth to it. With kids it is easy to see why evil would go after their young, impressionable minds. As far as women, that was more of a shocker to me. I have had numerous talks with families where for some reason, the girls see things but the boys don't. So there has to be an explanation to this motive used by evil.

Earlier in chapter three I mentioned the movie "The Conjuring." I had the chance to go see the movie shortly after it was released. I happen to see the trailer for the movie and knew I had to see it. I instantly thought about my sister when I seen the trailer and knew I needed to check it out.

There are very few horror movies that I will even consider sitting down and watching. My guess was right with this one. It was as close to the real deal as I have ever seen. It brought back memories of what my sister endured growing up. When I compare this movie to some of my cases, it lines up perfectly to what evil does to a family. And I really had no idea how close to home this movie was going to be for me until months later, after talking to numerous people in the area.

Like I mentioned earlier, the movie is based off of true life events that happened to the Perron family in Burrillville, Rhode Island. Roger and Carolyn Perron, along with their five daughters, moved into this 18th century farmhouse in 1971 and immediately starting seeing things. The day they moved in they started seeing full body apparitions. Andrea Perron was unloading boxes as they were moving in and recalls seeing a man standing in their kitchen. There was also a scene in the movie where one of the girls was laying in bed and had a evil spirit tugging on her leg. It reminded me of my sisters struggles with bedtime attacks when we were growing up.

The movie depicts the mom, Carolyn, as receiving the brunt of the attacks by the unwanted house guests. This setup supports Ed Warren's belief that evil singles out someone within a family and attacks them with more intensity. But I also want to talk about the five girls that lived in that house. Like I have stated earlier, most of my personal research has found a distinct pattern of these spirits to key in on women.

If anyone is familiar with this story, the father in this family was always in a state of disbelief. All the women of the house were having problems and the father ignored it all at first. Leaving these women out on an island all alone with spirit problems, isolated and living in fear.

As much as the movie as a whole solidified my own research, the movie itself didn't reveal all the intricate details of their experiences in the house. After reading several of Andrea's books and listening to some of her interviews I heard her say something that caught my eye. Andrea made a comment in an interview she did one time where she said, "Let's just say there was a very bad male spirit in the house and five little girls." I wanted to know more about that quote so I messaged her privately and this is what she told me.

"Dan, I have no idea where to look for that, hon. I've given literally thousands of interviews. I was referring to the spirit who we all sensed staring at us intruding on our privacy. We never used the bathroom alone or took a bath or a shower without having our mother or a sister in there with us as a form of protection. We never saw him but we all sensed his presence and did our best to avoid him in the house. I hope that helps. You can use that quotation directly from me without referencing another source. I've spoken that statement or something akin to it on numerous occasions."

I was very grateful for that message and how it cleared up that quote for me. I was also quite amazed on how their experiences over 1,000 miles away in Rhode Island were matching up very closely with many of the stories I was coming across here in upper Michigan.

Bull's-Eye On Women

A sixteen-year-old girl, Nancy, from the Wallace, Michigan area, had a strange shower incident just this past year. Nancy's mom told me that her daughter remembers feeling like someone was actually in the shower with her as she faced the shower head. She slowly turned around and as she did, she caught a glimpse of a human figure behind her. Then it vanished. It was so unnerving to her that she had a hard time telling her mom about what had happened. Incidentally, Nancy's sister sleeps with the head of her bed literally inside a walk-in closet. She wants to keep her own head in the closet so she can't see the hallway during the night. The reason she does this is because "they" walk the hallways at night.

There seems to be a bull's-eye on any family if they have more girls than boys in it. This falls in line with Ed Warren's theory that evil spirits will isolate certain people within any given family. I don't accept that the house the Perrons lived in, or the history of that particular property, was the only reason why they all saw things. I think the driving force behind the activity had more to do with a vulnerable group of girls that evil recognized.

When we get caught up in house history, for example that someone died in that house so that is the driving force behind the activity, we lose sight of the real reasons. It is a way evil leads us off course. Remember, Satan is called the father of lies. Evil would much rather have you believe their presence is due to some other reason than to reveal why they are really around.

I recently watched a show on TV called "The Haunted." I sometimes watch paranormal shows in hope of learning a few things, though I only watch the ones that are based on true life experiences and not those where they are literally ghost hunting. The families on these shows all share things they have endured in their homes at the hands of unwelcome spirits.

The first episode began with a lady saying, "I am a single mom with two girls." The next episode I watched started out the same way. The key people in this episode were women. *Another single mom and her daughter*, I thought to myself after watching these first two shows. *They are basically supporting my research that women get attacked more.*

In the twenty episodes of this particular TV show I watched, seventeen had families with more girls than boys. A few of those seventeen shows included extending family that swayed the numbers to more girls than boys, but most families did literally have more girls in them.

I am not the only one who believes evil focuses more on women then they do men. Well-known scholar in spiritual warfare and professor at Fuller Theological Seminary, Dr. Charles Kraft agrees. On April 26, 2013, he said, "It's as if women have a bull's-eye on their backs."

Evil seems to focus on women rather than men. I think the full scope of why evil attacks this way may never be understood, but the fact still remains that is does. Here are the results of my own research:

- Out of 163 families I've talked to with activity, 125 of the families had more females than males.
- I've talked to 404 individuals who have had encounters; 310 of them are female.

It is hard to ignore the numbers when they are as lopsided as these are. Regardless of why you think this might happen it is obvious that evil has women in their sights.

Orphans And Widows

The fact that women have far more encounters than men has to be addressed and evil has to have a motive as well. This is one of those "schemes" we can recognize with our "spiritual eyes." James 1:27 says:

> *Religion that God our Father accepts as pure and faultless is this: to look after orphans and widows in their distress and to keep oneself from being polluted by the world.*

This passage highlights that orphans and widows are in greater need than most people. On top of that, I also believe God is letting us know that orphans and widows will be attacked with more intensity. They are weighed down with more of the struggles mentioned by the apostle Paul in the book of Ephesians. They are vulnerable, today as much as they were in the first century. And we as believers are to key in on helping them as best we can; that hasn't changed either.

Let's take the application of this verse one step further. With divorce rates skyrocketing today, we have a new class of orphans and widows—fatherless kids who seldom see their dads, and women thrust into the world basically on their own. Evil has jumped all over this. We have to recognize this and help these mothers out, because evil is going after them with amazing intensity. I am reminded of that intensity with something that just happened with a young woman whom I know very well.

Jeanie

Jeanie was divorced and out on her own with three young girls. The divorce was something she couldn't avoid due to some personal private issues that threatened her kids. Fearing for her children's well-being, she moved into her parents' home near Bark River, Michigan.

After spending some time at her parents', putting aside money for her own place, she and the girls were finally able to get out on their own. That is when evil moved in quickly, going right after her and her girls. [Interestingly, nothing happened while she and her daughters were living with her parents.]

Within several weeks of moving into their new house, two of the three girls shared with their mother that they had been pushed as they walked down the stairs. Something or someone unseen had shoved each of them as they used the staircase. One of the girls was pushed so hard that she was hurt by a resulting fall. The girls all started holding on to the railing with both hands whenever they used the stairs.

Jeanie was angry at first. She thought the girls were all messing with each other, and she was worried that they might hurt each other ... until her daughter, Katherine, told her that she is seeing people in her room at night. Katherine said she would see an older man and woman walking around in her room, usually right before she would fall asleep. That's when Jeanie checked with her other daughters to see if they were encountering anything strange.

All her daughters told her that they felt like someone was watching them all the time. Two of them shared that as they took a shower they could hear steps above them in the attic. Two of them were also having reoccurring dreams, these affecting one of them so much that she hated going to sleep because she knew what was to come. The oldest daughter said that her bedroom door would open and shut by itself as she tried to go to sleep. As the four of them talked, it became obvious that it was affecting the entire family.

Jeanie and her family moved from this house, but they (*evil*) followed them to the next place, where things actually became worse. This was when I first visited with them; a visit I will never forget because it included my first experience with immediate demonic retaliation during a prayer with the family. I'll have more to say about their retaliation later.

These visits are not happening by chance. In many other cases, following a divorce the activity picks up immediately. I for one am unwilling to pretend that these attacks on women and kids are not happening. Just the opposite: I am convinced that they (*evil*) have a reason for attacking this way. This is a coordinated attack on women and children, especially girls; a sinister scheme of the devil. 2 Timothy 3:6-7 says:

> *They are the kind who worm their way into homes and gain control over gullible women, who are loaded down with sins and are swayed by all kinds of evil desires, always learning but never able to acknowledge the truth.*

I am well aware that this passage is describing how men worm their way into the lives of women who are burdened down, but it is interesting that evil follows the same sinister path in how they work in the lives of women. When I see a divorced mom out on her own, who is loaded down with stress, hopelessness, and despair, the image of shooting fish in a barrel comes to mind.

Sexual Abuse

When I started this manuscript, I never imagined that I would have to address sexual abuse. But the worst cases of evil activity that I have come across involve some type of sexual abuse. Some of them involved the worst type of sexual crime, incest.

There is no doubt in anyone's mind that when a woman gets raped or sexually assaulted, she is forever changed. Women who have been traumatized in this way experience stress, depression, low self-esteem; in many cases, they become promiscuous. If you want to break a woman down emotionally this is the quickest way to do it; evil knows this as well, and takes advantage of these poor women.

Of the 310 women I have talked to who see things, 149 of them admitted to having experienced some type of sexual assault or sexually deviant behavior—that is nearly 50 percent, much higher than any national statistics I have come across. My instincts tell me that the number is actually higher.

So, not only do we have burdened-down women who are out

on their own with kids to raise, some of them also have the emotional burden of having been sexual assaulted. This is how evil operates, attacking and taking advantage of the weak, discouraged, and depressed.

And it's a strategy that in many cases compounds the confusion and chaos. For example, women who have experienced this type of assault more times than not become promiscuous. The end result of that is that these women have a very difficult time forming any kind of normal relationship. They get divorced quicker, have more children out of wedlock, and go on to live very unstable lives. The chances of them bringing home a boyfriend and having him eventually move in is high as well, increasing the chances of some type of abuse on their daughters.

Terry

Terry, a fifteen-year-old girl, sees dark figures quite frequently in her room at night. She seems to have had no choice in the matter—evil jumped at the chance to harass her due to something a loved one did.

She told me that mirrors were her enemy, because they (*evil*) always appeared behind her as she used a mirror to get ready for school. Even when lying in bed doing her homework she would sometimes see flashes of an image in the mirror on the wall across the room.

Nights were the worst for her; they seemed to wait until she was on the verge of going to sleep and then they would start in on her. Pulling her toes, tugging on her blankets, and stroking her hair were nightly rituals in the dark of her room. This happened so regularly that for several years she had never felt alone in her own room.

Terry's mother was date-raped by several guys when she was a teenager. All she remembers from the assault is being carried to the upstairs of the house by several guys at a party she had gone to, then waking up completely naked the next morning.

Terry's mother was also sexually abused by her first steady boyfriend she moved in with. This fellow did things to her that I can't even repeat in writing. I'm not blaming her, just noting that what happened to her set up a terrible road that her daughter would also travel. I've seen it many times: A woman's choices in life affect her young daughter. Evil moves in, ensnaring the mom and then following up with her child or children, especially the girls.

Her mother's assault(s) opened an evil door for Terry's encounters with these dark figures. Despair and depression invite evil. Evil feeds off of trauma, and it can affect the kids of the family as well. This is a case of innocent bystanders paying the price for what has happened to their parents.

Another woman told me she was sexually assaulted by her uncle when she was in her teens. This uncle was visiting for a family reunion and, finding her in her bedroom alone, attacked her in her own bed. Shortly after the assault a tall, dark figure started showing up in the girl's bedroom at night. This dark figure scared her so much that she kept a knife under her mattress for protection. She politely asked me to stop contacting her about her experiences, for fear of it coming back. She was open enough to share with me though, that after this assault, she became very promiscuous.

These women struggling with this type of despair are not terrible people, they have just been through a devastating life-altering event. Evil wastes no time moving in and keeping its grip on them because they now have a foothold provided by the assault. This is a formula from hell: demoralize a woman with the effects of rape and sexual abuse, then slip right in and work her over like a boxer who is on the ropes; and after her, pummel her children as well.

Hit List From Hell

Evil starts panting at the prospect of snagging any woman so it can gain a foothold with her and then eventually her kids. I believe that is priority one on Satan's to do list—attack weak family situations and gain footholds within that family. By gaining a foothold in any family the chances of his agenda continuing multiply by the number of kids in that family. A single mom with let's say, four daughters, has a lot of potential in their eyes, since these daughters might have ten kids collectively. Those ten kids might have twenty-five more kids down the road, and so on.

This strategy makes sense when you look at the big picture. Hypothetically speaking, if I were an evil spirit whose job was to harass as many people as I possibly could, would I focus on an old man living all alone over a single mom with three kids? An evil spirit will see more dividends with the single parent family, especially if there are more girls.

I know this is speculation on my part, but it is hard to see another reason why these things are showing up and oppressing these poor families. Remember, evil is not biased and they attack anyone they can. But if I could produce a hit list from the pits of hell, the weak and vulnerable would be at the top of that list, with the words "single mom" circled with a bright red marker.

God created us and loves us. We were even created in his image. God wants us in return to love him back and to be in fellowship with him. Satan on the other hand, will do everything in his power to stop this and derail this hope of God. So Satan wants to take as many away from God as he can. That may be why vulnerable families are his number one priority. He wants to infiltrate the lives of people and keep them from loving God. I see Satan taking full advantage of a situation we find so common today: women on their own raising vulnerable kids alone. If Satan can gain a foothold in their lives, this increases the likelihood that future generations will follow blindly down the path that leads them to a life similar to the path their parents took.

The battle is being fought inside the heads of struggling women. They become susceptible to many of life's ills when they are alone and in despair. It seems as though Satan has recognized this and moves in for the kill. Then the kids are the next in line. If Satan can snatch them up at an early age his foothold becomes very difficult to break as these kids mature. If you step inside these little people's minds and see what they are going through because of divorce and losing dad, you could easily understand why Satan would exploit that and take full advantage of their vulnerable state.

Weapon Of Isolation

In the movie, "The Conjuring," the husband worked on the road, leaving a house with six women in it, and him gone most of the time. This, in my opinion, put a bull's eye on that family. What I mean is that if the right conditions are present, evil will waste no time moving in to try and get a foothold established in any family. And for some reason the absence of a male, fatherly figure seems to open up some type of door or avenue for attacks to start. Regardless if it is a single mother household or an absent father who is gone working a lot, that is by far the most common denominator I have come across—the absence of a male, fatherly figure seems to come up on evil's radar.

Another pattern also revealed itself in my conversations. I sometimes heard of families experiencing visits even with a traditional father present in the home. By that I mean he had a normal 9 to 5 job and came home every night. The common denominator with these families was that the men were skeptical of the things going on in their home—they simply did not believe their wives.

The reason women and children are being attacked is more of a psychological one. Like Ephesians 6 says, our battle is not with flesh and blood. It is a mind attack and they go well out of their way to assault kids and women. What better way to do this than to make the women and kids appear crazy in the eyes of the men of the family, thus isolating them from those who might be able to protect them.

I've heard mothers say that when the father refuses to believe them, they feel as though they are on an island, alone. The mother has no one to confide in and ask for help. She is thrust into the same predicament as are single moms, all alone with what is happening to her and her kids. That gives evil the same environment as a broken home, and freedom to prey on them and their minds in any way they want.

One time a family left their oven door open to help heat the house. The dad was in the kitchen while his wife and daughter were in the living room. All of a sudden the oven door slammed shut with a load bang as if someone had thrust it upward. The daughter said that her dad just shook his head and walked out of the kitchen and never talked about it again. This was his way of denying it had happened. If this is how a man acts, like it never happened, then evil can work unimpeded with the rest of the family. With the protector of the family neutralized, they (*evil*) are freed to gulp up whomever they can.

In her book, *House of Darkness House of Light*, Andrea Perron mentions how her father didn't believe her mother when she would tell him of the strange occurrences. Andrea was the real-life oldest daughter that the movie "The Conjuring" was based upon. Andrea said that it got to the point where her mother stopped telling her dad about things that happened, because she knew he wouldn't believe her anyway. How demoralizing.

Satan exploits everyone's weaknesses. There is no doubt that Satan has many battle fronts, but it is very hard to deny that evil seems to be attacking women and kids the most. Evil also seems to be isolating women, even if a male figure is around. This is by design, not by chance.

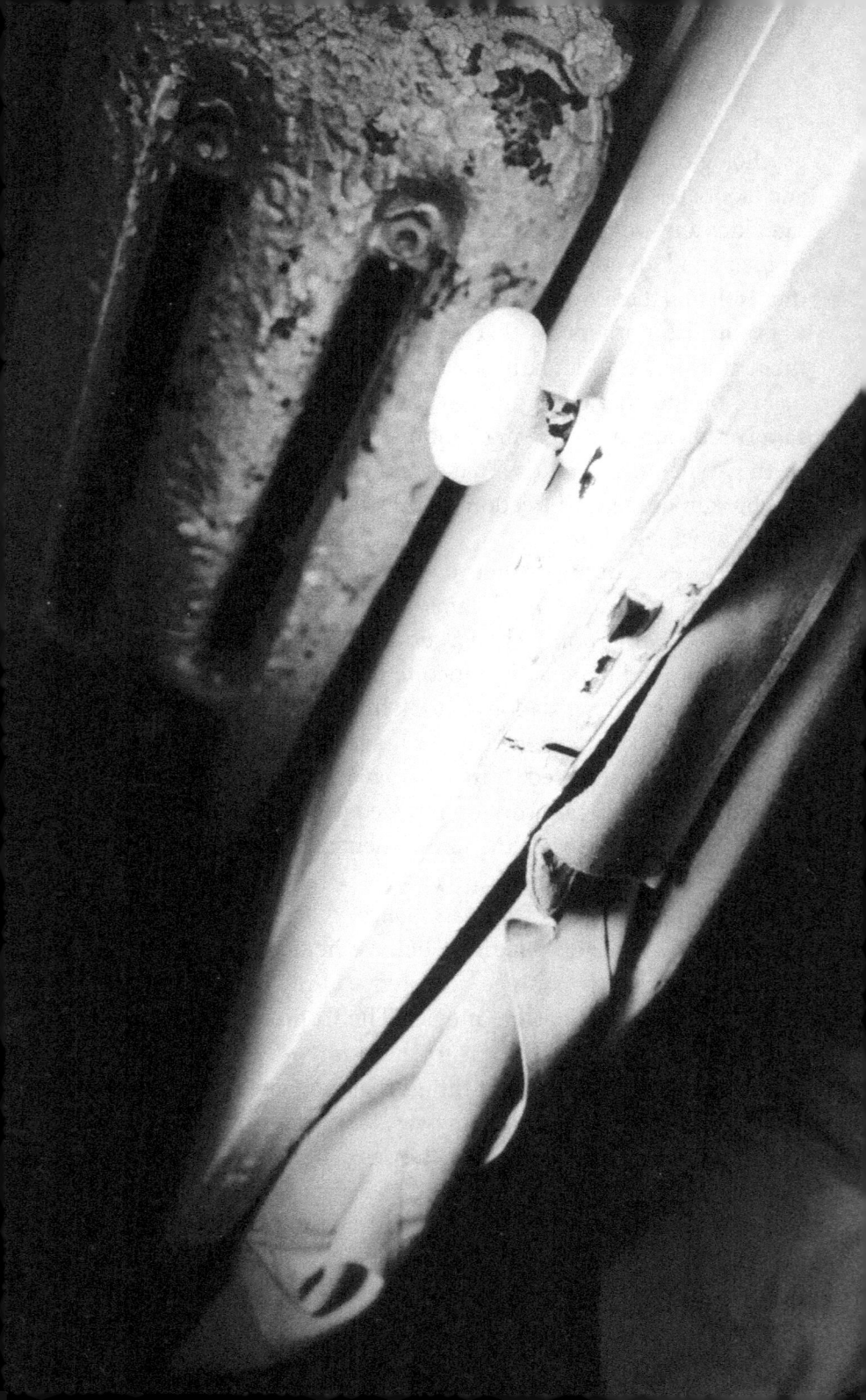

CHAPTER 9

Seeds Of Confusion

I was introduced to a teenage girl named Clarissa by her grandmother, Dee, and their stories really woke me up to how easily people become confused by all that is happening around them. Clarissa is originally from the Powers, Michigan area, but moved to Wisconsin a few years ago. She occasionally comes up to visit her Grandmother Dee and when she does, things get interesting at Dee's house.

Clarissa and her younger sister have a very difficult time sleeping at their house in Wisconsin. Dark figures dart all over their bedrooms at night, preventing them from ever getting a good night's rest. The girls on occasion wake up with scratch marks on their bodies as well. The terrible part of this is that their parents don't believe them when they talk about the encounters. Clarissa told me that she doesn't even tell her parents anymore when something happens to her. Even when Clarissa's younger sister gets spooked out of her room, she doesn't go to her parents' room for refuge; she sleeps on the couch instead. She finds it a little safer on the couch she said, because there she can see them coming.

You would think that Clarissa and her sister would enjoy the change of scenery when they come to visit Dee, but unfortunately they don't. Dee told me that when they come to visit, activity in her house takes off. According to Dee, there is a child spirit that roams the house and Clarissa has even named it Mary, due to the frequency of its visits. Dee believes this is a good spirit because it is a child spirit. Dee also told me that there are white and dark spirits in her own house even when her grandkids are not around.

Dee believes that she can determine if they are good or bad spirits by their color, or that because a spirit looks like a child it has to be harmless. When Dee comes home from work many times light bulbs are unscrewed from their sockets, lying on the floor unbroken. She believes this to be the work of a good spirit with a sense of humor.

There is real danger in associating who they are and what their intent is by their color or by the deeds they perform. That would be like telling your child they can accept rides from strangers if they are wearing a suit and smiled nicely. The root of most people's confusion is believing that a spirit's intent can be gauged by its appearance or actions. This is how demons convince you to let them be, and that there is no reason to get rid of them. It is a cleverly disguised scheme of Satan that seems to be working to perfection with many people.

Carolyn is one of many I know who can't sleep through the night. She has shared many different stories with me, anything from paintings flying off the wall in her home to music playing that seems to be coming from the her attic. Carolyn has what some in the medical field call sleep paralysis. She said that she can count on one hand the number of times she has slept through an entire night. The reason she can't sleep is because of her constant visions of human-like figures who walk around in her room at night. When they appear, all she can make out is their flesh hanging off of their bodies. She feels frozen in her bed, unable to move or scream. She has to simply endure it night after night. She believes what is happening is evil, even though the doctors tell her it is sleep paralysis and not real.

But just as she believes evil is behind her night problems, she also believes that the music she hears at any given time during the day is good in nature—simply because it is pretty music. This is another example of how a person can be duped, perhaps because she assumes that if the origin of the music were demonic, they would be playing some satanic rock music.

Coping With Evil

People in general tend to picture evil in some dark basement of an abandoned creepy old house, or within the confines of an old abandoned nursing home. This is another way of pretending that this type of darkness cannot be that close to our lives. Demons must be locked up in some dark dungeon somewhere in the pits of hell. Surely they cannot be active here, now.

Nothing could be farther from the truth. They are as active and present in this world as you and I are. We have to remember that at one time in history they were good angels that chose to rebel with Satan. And just as good angels are sent to us by God as ministering agents, so too, demons are sent by Satan to do his own type of evil "ministering" (service to their master). Hebrews 1:14 says:

> **Are not all angels ministering spirits sent to serve those who will inherit salvation?**

Many many scholars agree Satan does his best to duplicate

whatever God does, with an evil twist to it. So it stands to reason that if God sends good angels to assist those who are believers, Satan will try and mimic that with his host of evil agents. That is why Satan masquerades as an angel of light. He wants you to believe that what is happening to you is a good thing. You don't know how many times I have been told that a spirit was good because it was white. This is a deceptive ploy used by Satan, yet people still gulp it up as good.

I understand how people can better cope with nightly visits by brushing them off as visits from Grandpa. I can't even count how many times I have been told that an uncle just passed away, so it must be him checking in on his favorite nephew. When we as humans are face to face with anything that makes our hearts race, we are much more inclined to find a way to cope with it—to deal with it in a way that comforts us and helps us extinguish the fear. But why pass that on to your children; it's like giving up on them. Why deceive your own flesh and blood by telling them a lie just so they can sleep better at night. My heart goes out to these kids who basically have been let down by their own parents. By telling them it's a dead relative and letting the visits continue, they are passing the torch to the next generation, ultimately leaving the door wide open for evil to run unabated in their children's lives.

Smells Like Aqua Net

Earlier in this book I mentioned a woman whose son's room was torn apart by something during the middle of the night. She also told me how her friend who had died in a snowmobiling accident came to see her and her son one day.

Nancy was doing dishes in her kitchen one day while her son was in his playpen in the living room. She could hear her son quite easily, being in the room next to him. All of a sudden he started giggling if a funny way. She remembers thinking that she had never heard her son giggle that way before. As Nancy came around the corner to see what was happening, she observed the netting on her son's playpen being pushed in. It was an invisible force pushing in on the netting, as though it was reaching for her son. Fear came over her as she rushed over to her son. But that fear subsided when Nancy got to him. The fear was gone because she could smell her deceased friend's hairspray, so she concluded that it was her playing with her son.

The lengths to which evil will go to come across as a dead loved one are really quite amazing. The hairspray scent really sealed the deal for Nancy. But that wasn't the end of the shock and awe process of evil in this case. She went on to tell me that the last time she had seen her friend, before she passed away, was at a local club. Nancy and her friend had danced to a song called, "Taking Care of Business." Right after the playpen episode, Nancy and her son went to the local store for some groceries. When she got in the car and started it up, the first song to play on the radio was "Taking Care of Business."

Think about that for a minute. Satan's agents had to take the time to set this up so she was convinced it was her friend. I am not sure how they did that. If several demons were involved with this ploy I really don't know. Allow me to speculate about it, though.

Let's say this was her deceased friend pushing in on the netting of that playpen. Do you really believe that after being dead for all these years her hair still smells like Aqua Net? If her hair still gives off that aroma after being in the grave all these years, Aqua Net is on to something. Or even in a spirit form, are we going to have to worry about smells we had as humans? I use Axe body spray and I am quite sure that I won't have to stock that in my heavenly medicine cabinet.

Is anyone going to claim that this spirit needed to push in on the netting of the playpen to get to this child? Why not just reach in and touch him? Wait, if this spirit would have just reached over instead of pushing in on the netting, the mom would never have known that something was there. This spirit wanted the mom to see that it was there, and then to smell the aqua net. This whole sequence gave Nancy a false impression that we have the option of hanging around earth for a while after we die; thus discrediting the Bible. That is why Nancy was alerted to its presence. This spirit's goal was plain and obvious in my eyes. It wanted Nancy to "think" that this was her deceased friend.

Then there she was a short time later loading up the car with her two kids. Did her deceased friend zoom to the radio station and take it over to play this song at that exact moment? The distance from her house to this radio station is forty-five miles; I travel to this town every week. This song playing event gave her some extra reassurance that it was her deceased friend nosing around.

Since the Bible is very clear on where our spirits go after we die, it is impossible for this to have been her deceased friend. But something sure wanted Nancy to believe it was her. So I believe that evil orchestrated this entire sequence of events in order to convince Nancy that dead friends and family can come around for friendly visits. This can be a comforting thought for the one who experiences it. But it is an unbiblical doctrine, with its origins in hell.

Gift

Another example of the great lengths these spirits will go to trick us involves my mother. Her "gift," as some describe it, was her supposed ability to have out-of-body experiences. This was her feather in her cap. Of all the things she did that involved the occult, this was her most "gifted" area.

My mother passed away more than eight years ago now and people still tell me they are getting paid visits by her. A friend of my mother's told me that, on occasion, she can hear my mom talk to her in her house. I asked her, "How do you know it's my mom?" She stated that it was my mother's voice, without a doubt.

One story related to my mother's "gift" involves someone I have known now for almost forty years. Our families used to hang out together quite a bit back in the mid-70s. Julie and I are the same age, so naturally I got to know her the best. But she floored me when she told me that my mom used to visit them in their house. This is very difficult to swallow because at the time of the visits, my mother was twelve miles away at our house in Nadeau, Michigan.

Julie and her mother were watching television one night at their house in Wilson, Michigan. Out of nowhere, my mother appeared in the living room, floating by them almost in a parade-like fashion. My mother was supposedly wearing a long black dress as she passed between them and the couch where they were sitting and the TV. According to Julie, my mother was practicing her "gift" right in front of them. As I have talked to others from the family, it is obvious that they all thought my mother was special because of the abilities she had.

Julie's sister, Barb, described an experience that happened in the same house. She told me that my mom appeared to her in her bedroom one night, knocking over a lit candle on her dresser as she glided by. A third sister said she saw my mother in a doorway to her bedroom as well. Needless to say, these stories blew me away. Up until I did the research for this book, I had never heard accounts from other people of these kinds of things supposedly involving my mother.

Helping Strangers

My sister reminded me of how my mom left her body one night and went to the aid of some people searching for a lost child. My sister said that if it weren't for mom's ability to leave her body, these people would never have found this child. My mom claimed that she was able to help them find this kid, and then she promptly returned to her body. This led me to believe as I grew up, that this had to be good because she was helping people. Is this really a gift, or a demonically induced deception? If anything, this proves to me that Satan's evil agents are trying their best to duplicate the actions of good angels (ministering spirits) or masquerading as people we know, all under the pretense of being something incredibly wonderful.

My own brother shared with me recently that mom and dad's energy is sometimes felt by a friend of his. This friend of his has the ability to see and feel things most people can't, according to my brother. How he knows it is my parents' energy is beyond me. But he claims that it is, and they appear to him in the form of lights. He says that when my brothers are struggling with something emotionally, he sees a blue and a white light over them. He senses these lights saying, "Tell my boys to remember all that I taught them."

For one thing, my dad didn't talk much about personal or emotional issues. My father played catch with me one time in my whole life. It just wasn't in his nature to be nurturing to us growing up. My dad kept to himself and I don't even remember him pulling me aside once in my life to teach me anything remotely close to a life lesson. My dad's idea of a life lesson was to pick me up off the floor and pin me to the wall if I did something wrong.

My dad talked cars and that was about it. My point here is that this is obviously another method of portraying something good in the form of these lights, another ploy by evil to make people think that we can come back from beyond. This is Satan's way of tricking people into believing they can come back and make contact. My mother even told me right before she passed that the things she did were wrong. So to believe that she was coming around to give my brothers messages is hard to believe. I don't believe she would confess to me, as her life was coming to a close, that her occult practicing was wrong, then act contrary to that by coming back around in the form of a light.

The passage in Hebrews tells us that God sends his angels as ministering spirits to those that will inherit salvation. So my conclusion is that the actions of demons, through my mother, were done with one thing in mind—to pretend to be a ministering spirit and thus to deceive us into believing that all is good and all is right with this. These agents of evil were masquerading as my mother; masquerading as a ministering spirit with the grand appearance as something wonderful and heaven sent. The proof that it worked is that still, more than thirty years later, those she appeared to still believe it was her. They were tricked into believing she had a gift she could use for good purposes, not that it was evil in nature.

Death Bed Confession

Isn't it interesting that my mother confessed to me during her latter years that the things she practiced were wrong and that she was sorry she had put us kids through it all! She told me this to my face with her Bible lying open in front of her. God's Word got through to her and she was very apologetic toward the end of her life. When a person knows her days are numbered and is facing eternity, there can be little doubt that she was speaking the truth from her heart.

Let's think about all of this. Why should evil do all this masquerading? What are they accomplishing by deceiving people into believing they are something they are not? What is the reasoning behind an angelic being strolling through someone's house, or peeking at someone from a hallway bedroom doorway? Why are they acting like Navy Seals? Or why are they so often seen standing at the foot of a child's bed staring down at them? Why would a demonic being need to stand here? Or why make a girl feel like something is lying on her but she can't see it? If I was an angel, why on God's green earth would I do that to some vulnerable young girl? Or why do these agents of evil spend so much time portraying anything that is right and true?

First and foremost I believe they do this masquerading to discredit the Bible. The Bible is clear that we can't come back after death. So evil portrays deceased loved ones to counter what the Bible teaches. More importantly, by masquerading as disembodied spirits, the doctrines of heaven and hell get discredited. If Grandpa is coming around, then he must have the choice of hanging around on earth. He doesn't have to go to heaven or to hell, even though the Scripture is clear: "it is appointed unto men once to die, and after this the judgment" (Heb. 9:27, KJV). Everything Satan does or tries to make humans think is always contrary to what God's Word teaches.

Secondly, if you buy into their scheme, they get to stay for as long as they want. They have unlimited access to your family. They have secured their spot inside your home, never having to worry about being kicked out. Trust me, they know that some have the power to make them leave, but if they are in your home it is because that power isn't present.

Sir Isaac Newton

One peculiar episode happened when I was sixteen, and it was to the best of my knowledge, the last time something that mom did affected me. My mother practiced a form of contact with spirits called automatic writing, where someone relaxes their hand on a piece of paper while holding a pen or pencil. My mom would close her eyes and the spirit would take over her hand. The writing done by these spirits always stayed between the lines even when my mom's eyes were shut. Sometimes the evil spirits who controlled her hand just chatted. Sometimes they would reveal things to my mother. Other times mom would ask questions before relinquishing the use of her hands and the spirit would take over her hand while writing down the answers to her questions. I was present for this particular session so I can attest that it really took place. I actually held on to the demonic papers that were produced, until I understood that it was wrong to do so. I promptly burnt them along with an occult book of my mom's that the papers were in.

Anyway, the first spirit took over the pen and low and behold it even gave its name. The spirit said, "Hi Sandy, Newt here." This spirit claimed that he was Sir Isaac Newton. Yes, the same Isaac Newton that was regarded as one of most influential mathematicians and physicists of the past 400 years!

It is common for people who auto-write to latch on to a dead celebrity figure. It is an amazing attraction to the one writing to be thinking they are in contact with someone famous. This also sucks in the victim to do it more, because who knows, they might have a chance to talk to Elvis someday. I also love how he made it sound so personal, like they were best friends by saying, "Newt here," as if they chatted all the time with each other.

Anyway, he proceeded to warn my mom on this paper that the paint cans in the basement were too close to the stove and needed to be moved because they were a fire hazard. The writing on the paper went something like this. "Sandy, tell Dan (my dad) to go in the basement and move the paint cans away from the stove." Now take a close look at what this spirit said to us via this paper. He knew Mom by her name and knew Dad by his name. Later another spirit would refer to me as Danny, which I was commonly called by a lot of people when I was younger.

Am I to surmise that Isaac Newton himself was hanging out at our house and knew us all personally by name? Am I also to believe that he was so close with my mom that he referred to himself as Newt? Wouldn't you think he might be hanging out with Ben Franklin and Albert Einstein instead of talking to us in Carney, Michigan? Sorry for the sarcasm, but this whole event was a hard pill for me to swallow.

Then the penmanship started getting erratic and hard to read, as if something was changing while Newton was writing. This is when a new spirit came through and started writing in a totally different penmanship. I don't recall the name of this spirit, but it was a very different style of writing on the paper. Newton's handwriting was distinct, but then a different spirit's unique handwriting took over.

This spirit made a prediction about our dog, "Yeller." It told my mom that Yeller was going to have eight puppies. Yeller had exactly eight puppies a few weeks later. I still remember looking down at Yeller on the floor next to the dining room table, wondering if this prediction would come true. Unlike Newt's fire hazard warning, this spirit made a prediction that came true. It's not hard to understand how alluring it is for the one engaged in this form of demonic activity when the demon relays through the person holding the pen something that no one else could possibly know. I would like to add a note to this puppy prophecy. Do you really believe that God, sitting on his throne in heaven, dispatched an angel to tell my mom about Yeller's puppy count? Because if you do, I have some ocean front property in Arizona that I'd like to offer you.

Glimpse Of The Future

There was one more spirit that came through that day, and this one said something about me. This particular prediction really makes my wheels spin. The third spirit wrote down on the paper, "Danny is a good boy and he will go on to become a pastor someday." Now, I have never attended a Bible college to prepare for ministry, but I have preached on several occasions from the pulpit at our church when our pastor suddenly became ill. I have taught Sunday school and a few adult Bible studies. So I guess I could be considered a pastor in that sense. I do have the heart of a pastor and somehow these spirits saw that in me when I was just a youngster.

In truth, this prediction is quite amazing. Out of the many professions out there how could they possibly know what I "might" do later in life? Did these spirits have an ability to see the future? I ask that hesitantly. Or did they sense something in me that would cause them to say that? Are there some unseen spiritual laws that we are unaware of as humans that define our destinies? I really don't know. And to be honest, this one really throws me for a loop. It suggests that they have certain abilities that are far above ours. If so, would it not make their deceptive ways even harder to discern?

These three examples of automatic writing are quite caring in nature. What these spirits "said" seemed to originate in genuine concern for our family. But perhaps this is how Satan masquerades as an angel of light. His minions can come across to the one engaged with them as good spirits, meaning no harm to that particular person, deceiving the person into thinking it can't be a harmful spirit. After all, if it were evil, why would it want to help us?

I believe that this type of deception paves the way for them (*evil*) to stay attached to a particular family, which is of the utmost importance to them. There is already a foothold or they wouldn't be there in the first place. But they do need to stay if their agenda is to be carried out. What better way might there be to achieve that kind of ongoing welcome than to appear as helpful, caring house guests? Then they won't get the boot. When parents, especially, doubt that any of this is wrong it gives evil the continuing foothold they need to affect future generations. When agents of darkness masquerade as angels of light, and their trickery is accepted, only evil can come of it, long term.

I have to believe that some people deep down, know something is wrong with this form of contact. These feelings have to surface simply due to the fact they are engaged with beings not of this world. But so many just deal with it and move on with life. In Andrea Perron's trilogy, *House of Darkness—House of Light*, her family just accepted it after so many years and lived with it, almost as if it wasn't worth fighting with anymore. After all, it's a lot less hassle to just live our lives with an air of acceptance and avoid the headaches.

Someone Is Better Than No One

I think the 1993 movie "Sommersby," with Richard Gere and Jodi Foster, illustrates well what is happening to most people who see things in their homes. If you haven't seen the movie I suggest you go out and rent it. I am actually a big Richard Gere fan, so if you're like me, you will enjoy this movie.

Jack Sommersby (Richard Gere) leaves his farm to go off and fight in the Civil War. After six years of being gone from the farm he is presumed dead. His supposed widow Laurel (Jodie Foster) decides to start moving on and makes plans to re-marry. Out of nowhere Jack returns to the farm. Amid much disbelief from several people who knew him, he takes back control of the farm and continues in the roles he had before he left for the war—husband, father and farming—his homestead. It doesn't take long before his wife and several others realize this isn't the same Jack who left the farm six years earlier. The new Jack is loving, caring, and considerate of others. The old Jack wasn't like that at all. The first time he made love to his supposed wife was when she really knew it wasn't him.

The truth was, he was an imposter. He had shared a jail cell with the real Jack Sommersby and had an uncanny resemblance to the real Jack. The imposter spent that time in the jail cell getting to know the real Jack, hearing story after story of the real Jack's life back on the farm. After soaking up all the information he could about life back on the farm with Laurel, he was released from jail and made his way back to Laurel in an attempt to worm his way into the real Jack's life.

Eventually Laurel figured out that this man wasn't her real husband. However, she still decided to go with it. The new Jack was kind and loving to her. She simply decided that having the new Jack around was better than no Jack. She decided that she would rather live her life with the imposter and not pursue the truth.

The comparison is easy to see from my perspective. Sometimes people would much rather assume that the evil taking place under their own roof is acceptable. I think deep down they know something isn't right but they prefer to put up with it instead of finding out the truth.

Laurel knew what she was doing was wrong, but stayed the course anyway, not wanting to do anything about the fact that an imposter was lying next to her in bed. People who are plagued by demonic activity say the same thing. By "plagued" I mean any activity, not just the terrorizing stories. *It has to be Grandpa who is sitting on the end of my bed*, they think. They feel they can deal with that and have no real inclination to do anything about it. *It isn't hurting my child or me so why worry.* They have no desire to kick the imposter out. They have no desire to explore the possibility that this could be something sinister. They have no desire to kick out the imposter(s), because it is much easier to allow things to go on and give off the impression that all is well than to make the hard choices that need to be made.

Jack Sommersby was an imposter even though he was loving, caring, and treated Laurel well. These nightly visitors that come into our homes are imposters as well. They, like Jack Sommersby, come across as caring and loving. They can take on the role of someone we loved and do a very convincing job at it. Hebrews 13:2 comes to mind when I think of any angel's ability to take on the form of a human being:

> ***Do not forget to entertain strangers, for by so doing some people have shown hospitality to angels without knowing it.***

All angels were given the ability to copycat man. When we have a clear and concise Scripture telling us angels will purposely take on the appearance of us humans, it clears up so much in my mind. If good angels can do it, fallen angels can do it, too. Genesis 18, along with Judges 6 and 13 all have stories of how men thought angels were fellow human beings, so it stands to reason then that fallen angels, or demons, can still do the same as good angels. Nowhere in Scripture does it say God stripped them of this capability once they fell. And like I mentioned earlier, Satan tries his hardest to duplicate anything that God does. And if God sends angels as ministering spirits to us, then Satan will try and copy that by sending his evil agents to us.

So here's that question again: What do you believe evil spirits do throughout the course of a day? From Scripture we see that Satan is roaming the earth, masquerading as something good, all with the hope of devouring us—gulping us up so he can call us his. He also has the ability to appear to us as someone human, usually in the form of a dead relative. And Satan has an army of possibly as many as 50 million demons at his disposal, who roam and prowl over every square mile of this planet.

Once he has tricked you into buying into his schemes like my mother did, his plan is set in motion. He then locks onto your entire family, spreading his deceit and deception to those closest to you. No one is spared and no one is immune to him and his well-organized army.

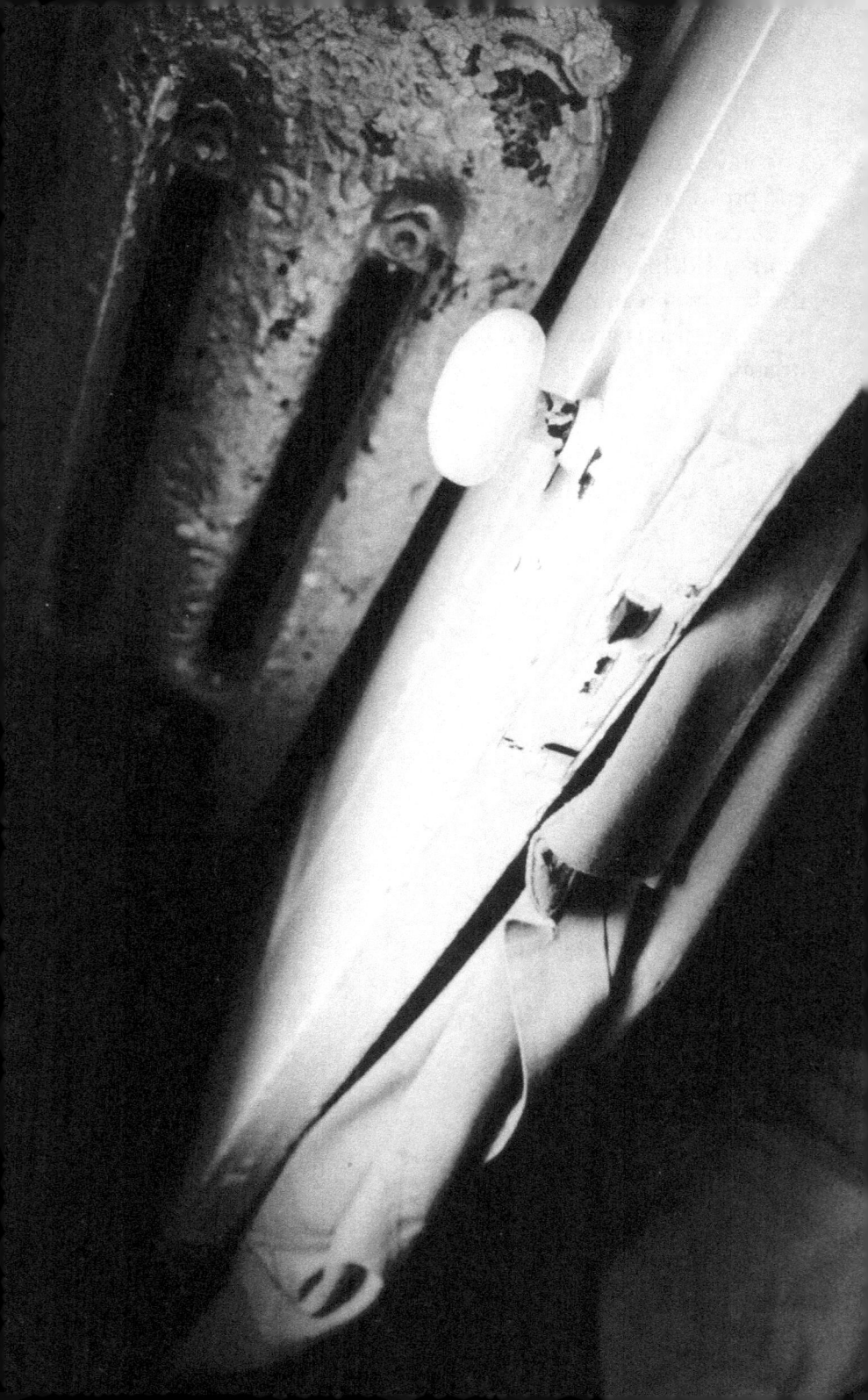

CHAPTER 10

Attack Early In Life

The following stories illustrate what can happen if these spirits are allowed to continue running unabated in anyone's home. These stories show the early signs of something evil in someone's home and what it does to a young child's mind. And yes, with these stories I am trying to scare any parent reading this book. The first story involves a young woman named Sarah, whose young children had something chasing them.

A close friend of mine told me to get in contact with Sarah because she was a single mom who had a list a mile long of failures and heartaches. That seems to be the starting point for most who see things not of this world. Evil spirits move in when they see someone down and out. It's as if evil smells fear and despair. A single mom with young kids is almost a guarantee that things go on in their home.

As I sat in Sarah's apartment I could tell her heart was huge and she loved her two kids more than anything. She wanted to talk to me because something was happening to her kids and she didn't like it. Sarah told me that her kids have never slept through the night and that they would wake up from nightmares almost nightly.

I asked Sarah about her past and it wasn't long before two red flags came up. One flag was that her mom had dabbled with the occult. Her mom had tried a few times to contact someone from the other side with the use of crystals and tarot cards. Then Sarah told me that she had tried a Ouija board herself. I concluded quite early in our talk that her claims of spirits in her apartment were real.

The apartment next to Sarah's had quite a bit of activity in it as well. A lady living next to Sarah told me about hangers flying out of her closet at her one night, so things are very active in this complex. I also came across a story from these same apartments of a spirit some little kids happened to see. They were playing in front of this apartment complex and one of their mothers came outside to check on them. She noticed they were looking up into the sky so she asked them what they are looking at. One of the kids said, "When you came out the ghost went floating up into the sky."

Sarah herself would often hear the sounds of little kids giggling even when her own kids were asleep. Occasionally she would see these little spirits dart through the apartment, though she never got a good look at them—just fleeting glimpses, as is typical of them.

Sarah reasoned that if she was catching glimpses of them, her kids must have been seeing them as well. Her oldest child, Wendy, would wake up during the night and point under her crib, saying, "Scared," to her mom. Both children suffered from night terrors. Both children, ages three and four, would come running out of their bedroom almost nightly, screaming, while looking back as if something was after them.

The final straw for Sarah was the evening her sister, Jenny, came to visit for the night. They were all sitting around in the living room watching TV. Out of nowhere Sarah's sister said, "Oh, my gosh!" Sarah's three-year-old son, Allan, was levitating right off his bed. She could see his bed from the living room where they were sitting. Sarah ran into the bedroom and took Allan out of there, while her sister picked up four-year-old Wendy, and held her close.

As they stood there in disbelief, with Jenny holding Wendy, something else very strange happened. Something was tugging at Wendy's foot as Jenny was holding her. Something invisible was holding on to Wendy's leg as Jenny tried to stop it. Wendy was crying and looking down at this invisible grip. Sarah told me that she could see her daughter's leg being pulled in a funny way and knew it was not of this world. Whatever it was it wanted Wendy, or at least wanted everyone who was standing there to know it was after her. That was all Sarah could handle and they moved shortly after this incident. Little did Sarah know that more times than not, it is not the location that brings this on, but who the spirits are after.

New House, Same Story

Sarah and her kids moved thirty miles away to Norway, Michigan. They decided to stay away from apartments for a while and found a house to rent. Sarah told me that things were pretty quiet for a short time. Then her kids started waking up from night terrors again, with an added twist this time. Her daughter, Wendy, told her mom that frogs were trying to get her feet. Whenever Sarah would hold her daughter in her arms after a night terror, she would instinctively pull her legs up, as if these frogs were still trying to get her feet. Then her son, Allan, started having frog issues.

Allan would flee his own bedroom at any time of the day while looking back and saying, "Frogs, frogs, frogs." I witnessed a frog episode while visiting Sarah at her new house. I was aware of the kids' frog issues before I went that day, so I purposely brought with me a ceramic frog, as a test of sorts. I placed it on the floor by the entertainment center shortly after I walked in, not letting Allan see me put it there. It wasn't long before he noticed it. He even walked over and touched it—not at all scared of it. The very thing he claimed to be seeing, the very thing he was petrified of, didn't seem to faze him—at least in ceramic form. Shortly after he met my frog friend, the kids were off and playing again while I sat with Sarah on her couch.

I started to wonder if what these two children were seeing wasn't frogs at all. My guess is that was the best these little kids could do when trying to describe what they were seeing. I was discussing this with Sarah when Allan came flying out of his bedroom screaming once again, "Frogs, frogs, frogs." His little faced was plastered with tears and his full attention, as he huddled on the couch with us, was focused back in the direction of his bedroom. This child was not acting or making this up. He was as scared as I have ever seen a young boy.

But Sarah and her kids' story doesn't stop there. She started noticing her young kids' language was changing. More specifically, they started using bad words that they had no way of knowing. Sarah admits she would let a curse word fly once in a while, but the words these kids were using were not ones she would ever say. Another thing she noticed was that Allan was starting to make obscene gestures and grabbing himself between his legs a lot while saying something very bad . . . something a three-year-old should have no idea about. Sarah finally asked her oldest who was telling them to say these words. Wendy told her "Sam" was telling them to say bad words. Evidently, Sam was their secret friend.

Unwanted Houseguest

Sam, in the eyes of Sarah's children, was a real and permanent fixture in their bedroom. Sarah started paying attention and sure enough, the kids were talking with someone in the confines of their bedroom. Wendy told her mom that when they played with him he was nice to them. But sometimes Sam told them to say bad words and they did what he said. Sarah believes that this Sam spirit also has taught Allan his obscene gestures that started out of nowhere. She knows Allan didn't pick it up from some TV show, because they don't have cable and the only thing the kids had been watching for the past several months was the animated movie, "Frozen."

These spirits were constantly around Wendy and Allan. For example, Sarah and her kids went to visit a friend one day. Sarah's friend, Janet, lived some twenty-five miles away, and the kids still had a run-in with something not of this world. Sarah's kids seemed to be talking to a different secret friend at Janet's house. Sarah actually confessed to me that she would have blown off this encounter at Janet's house if it weren't for Janet's comment, "That is just Mikey. He always talks to any kids that visit us." Janet added, "Mikey just likes kids, because he never talks to us." So, no matter where these poor kids went, evil was lurking, constantly harassing them.

The clincher for Sarah was when she witnessed Allan slap his sister on the backside. She asked him why he did that. He told her it was because Sam does it to her. Sarah then asked Wendy about the backside slapping problem. Wendy said, "I do it to Sam, too."

Without doubt, these children are not making up their secret friends. I've heard stories of kids telling their parents that their "secret friend" told them to hurt their own siblings. I've heard stories of kids pointing to a spot in their bedroom, even as their parents are there talking to them, saying that their friend was right there. I even heard of a young girl who told her mom that her secret friend growls at her when he is mad.

Experiences like these are some of the earliest signs of kids being harassed by evil spirits. These encounters seem to start early, and then continue as they (*evil*) attach to individuals, as well as to families, for many years down the road. Sarah's story also illustrates the generational curse of sorts that most families have to endure, because her kids weren't the first in the family to have problems.

Sarah had grown up having to deal with spirits as a young child, as did her grandmother, her great-grandmother, and maybe even some more distant ancestors.

Right Next To Us

Brice's mom, Shelly, walked past her son's room and could hear him carrying on a conversation as though someone was in there with him. Not overly concerned by this, she still opened his door and went in to check things out. Seeing Brice playing with his toys calmed Shelly down a little and she brushed it off. A few days later she heard him again and decided this time to ask Brice who he was talking to while he was playing. He told his mom, "My friend, Jill." Like most parents, she just chalked it up to his imagination.

But Shelly learned, over time, that Brice actually had two secret friends that came to see him on a regular basis. In addition to "Jill," there was also an older man that her son called "Johnny." Shelly's alarms went off when Brice told her that Jill was the mean one, and that she said bad words to him.

Amber is Brice's aunt and she spends a lot of time at Brice's house. Shelly asked Amber if she wouldn't mind talking to Brice about his secret friends and she agreed to do so. Amber told me that when she decided to talk to him, she brought a friend along as well. The two of them sat in Brice's room and recorded him talking about his secret friends. They asked Brice about what he does with his secret friends, and he said they played with his toys on the floor. Amber then asked if his friends talk to him. He said that they do talk to him. Then out of nowhere Brice pointed to the kitchen and said that Jill, one of his secret friends, was in the kitchen right now with his mom, Shelly. Though Amber and her friend looked into the kitchen, they didn't see anyone with Brice's mom.

Their next question for Brice was, "Well, where is your other secret friend, Johnny?" Brice pointed to the bed where Amber was sitting and said, "Johnny is sitting right next to you!"

Aaron's Story

This next story involving a secret friend has absolutely nothing to do with the word "friend." But it does have everything to do with scaring any parent beyond imagination. Aaron's parents, Shannon and Steve, inherited an older house from Steve's family and moved in once it was legally theirs. The house itself was over a hundred years old and came with many stories from days gone by. It had served as a bar, a gambling house, and it was even a brothel for a while. Little did they know that along with all this unfortunate history, would also come some very unwelcome house guests.

Steve described being touched quite a bit while trying to sleep and even, on occasion, having his backside pinched. He also had a run in with a very pretty spirit that appeared to him while lying on the couch one night. But as this pretty spirit neared him, it transformed into a decomposing hideous thing that he will never forget.

When Aaron was four years old, he started sharing with his parents that someone was visiting him in his room at night and talking to him. He said his visitor's name was "Sherry." Sherry told him on one occasion to "come out and play." But Sherry was also telling him things that weren't as innocent; specifically, to do bad things to himself. Naturally Shannon and Steve asked him what exactly Sherry was telling him to do. Aaron said, "To kill myself."

Because the whole family was experiencing things, they decided to place an audio recorder in Aaron's bedroom at night in hopes of capturing something. They did! And what you read next should send chills up and down your spine if you're a parent and your child has a secret friend.

The very first night they placed the recorder on Aaron's dresser they captured something as revealing as I have ever come across. Aaron was playing on his floor in his bedroom when Steve activated the recorder. At the time, Aaron was acting like he really didn't want to go to sleep. But then Aaron said to his dad, "I need to go to bed," like someone had told him to go to bed. So Steve tucked him into bed, not giving this sudden change a second thought.

The next morning Steve and Shannon listened to the recording from the previous night. What they heard sent chills up and down their spines. The recording captured a spirit saying, "Get rid of your dad." This was moments before Aaron had told his dad that he needed to go to bed. So Aaron did what this spirit said and got rid of his dad.

What followed after Steve left Aaron's bedroom caused Shannon to feel sick to her stomach. On the recording they could hear this spirit's voice as it talked to Aaron moments after Steve left the bedroom. They admit they couldn't make out the words exactly, but there was no doubt in their minds it was talking to Aaron.

After listening to this recording, Steve and Shannon hid all of the kitchen knives, because this spirit was telling Aaron to kill himself. They purposely hid the knives in their own bedroom, knowing that Aaron would not find them in there.

The next morning, Aaron came downstairs and said, "I know you hid the knives in your bedroom." Steve said, "How did you know where we hid them?" Aaron replied to them, "Sherry told me."

This story is a rare glimpse into what could possibly be happening in your child's room at night if spirits are present in your home. If your child has a secret friend, or an imaginary friend as some call it, that there is a good chance it isn't imaginary at all. There is a very real possibility that it is interacting with your young child. That should make any loving parent sick to their stomach.

Possessive Spirits

As I ventured further into the realm of the spiritual world, it became increasingly clear that these evil spirits were extremely possessive of those they felt they had control over. For example, any effort on my part to change the environment or to help some of these people was met with retaliation. Sometimes my help or advice was a simple prayer or me telling someone to read the Bible—an activity the evil beings don't want those they were harassing to have any part of.

I was invited to a family's home not too far from where I live, where I learned that they (*evil*) don't like it when you start messing with their investment. As I was talking to several members of this family about their experiences, the youngest girl doubled over with stomach pains. She left us and went to her room. Perhaps this was a coincidence, but when I talked with her privately a few days later, she confessed that she was afraid of what might happen if she talked about them. She was scared of these spirits and didn't want to provoke them.

I believe that demons keep close track of anyone they have a grasp on. If any attempt is made to alter that grasp, they respond quickly. They act like they have ownership over some people. An unusual display of that possessive attitude can easily be seen in the next story.

An extended family member of mine, who currently lives in California, has a severe problem with possessive spirits. Jordan comes from a family with ties to the occult, so her stories didn't surprise me as we talked one evening. But two things caught me off guard. First, Jordan said that she was "down to two spirits" around her at any given time. I responded, "What do you mean, down to two spirits?" She answered, "There used to be many around me when I was younger."

Then she said, "They do not like anyone else around, either." I asked, "How do you know that these spirits don't like your friends around?" Jordan responded, "They don't like my friends *or* when other spirits show up."

That was the first time I had heard that spirits were sometimes jealous of other spirits as well as human friends. As we talked I got the impression that she was a trophy to be had by these spirits—as if they were jostling for position to gulp her up.

I hated to ask the next question, but I had to. "How do you know they are jealous when others show up?" I asked. She said, "I can see it in their faces." I was speechless. Most people say that they see dark figures, but that they never quite see their faces. For Jordan it was much different. She could see their faces *and* that they were upset. Imagine having to live your young life in that type of environment day in and day out.

House Possession

Another aspect of their possessiveness can be found with houses themselves. For some reason they seem to get very active when a house has remodeling done to it. It is as if they feel ownership of some houses and get irritated when the house changes. This is one of those strange things that I really can only speculate on.

A family in the Bark River, Michigan, area on occasion will change their furniture around and it brings on activity. They have a family room and a regular living room in their home. Once in a while they flip flop them. They move all their living room furniture to the family room and vice versa. The very night they do that they tell me the spirits keep them up all night with loud banging and footsteps. There is no rhyme or reason to this. What difference can it make to a spirit if the couch is moved to another room?

This has to be one of those evil little side shows or schemes they have invented to make us think they have some emotional tie to the living room arrangement. If you buy into their scheme that they are a human spirit with ties to the house, this activity makes more sense. But since we cannot come back and reside at our old residences, this is more likely a ploy to lead you to believe they are disembodied spirits of humans who have passed on.

If I were to conjecture on this, I'd suggest that the spirits may feel that the house is theirs. They do possess other character traits such as anger, wickedness, and hatred. So maybe they are compulsively possessive toward certain houses and even the layouts within those houses.

This trait might be part of what is sometimes referred to as a "haunted house," because the spirits are reacting to something involving the house. Once again it may be just a ploy they are using to trip us up with thoughts of prior inhabitants who can't let go. In any case, there is no sure explanation for this unusual occurrence.

In this chapter, I've described how young children can be approached by these evil spirits, posing as "friends." As a relationship forms, they can become possessive to the point where they believe they own that individual. If this sounds like something your family has gone through or is currently going through, it needs to stop. NOW. For, if it doesn't end, it can become a lifelong attachment.

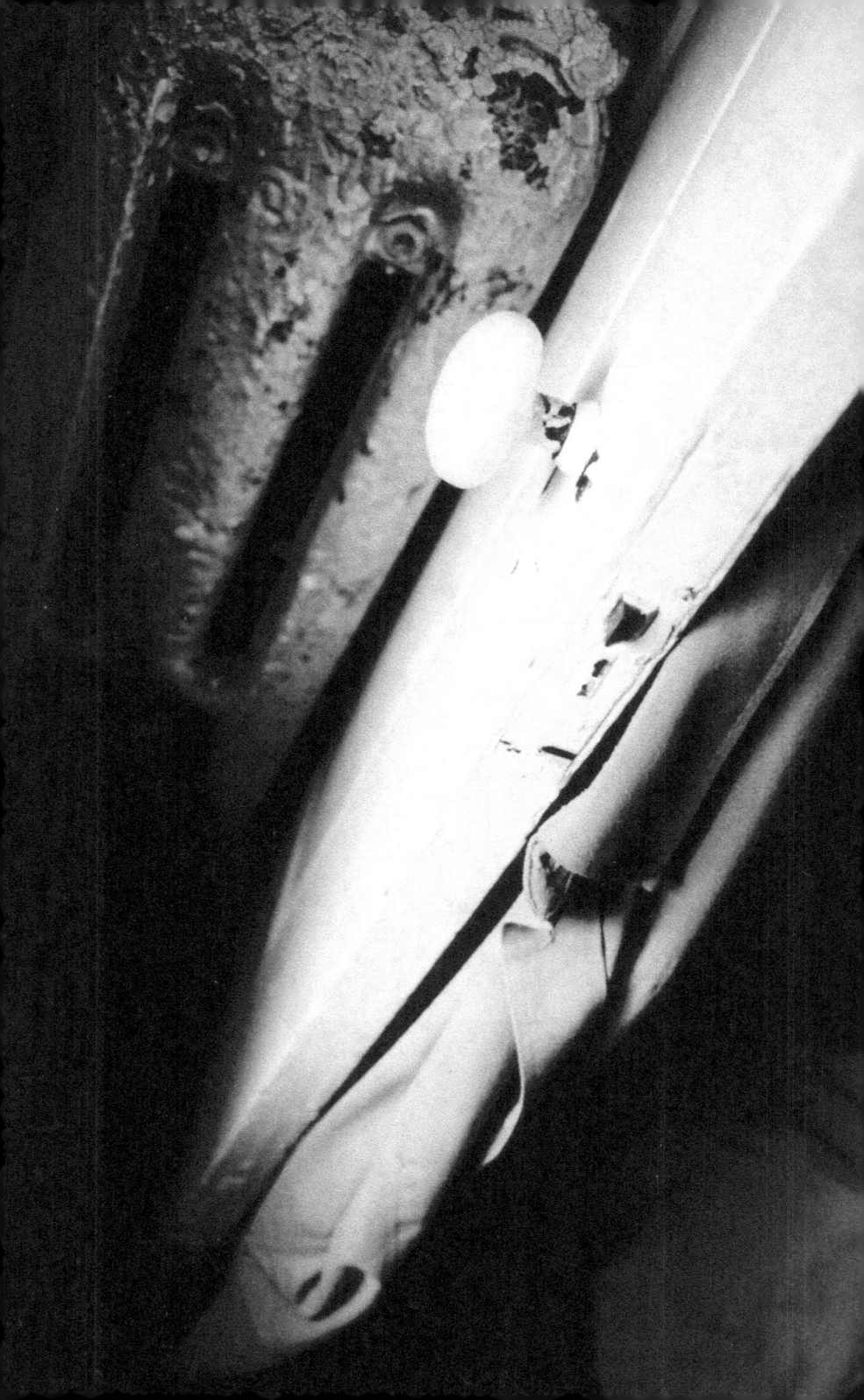

CHAPTER 11

Lifelong Attachments

I have known Carrie for about thirty-five years. I contacted her because she had suffered through a divorce and she had one child, a girl. Two of my big three requirements (discussed in Chapter 14 in more detail) were met, so I asked Carrie if she had ever seen anything weird. She responded, "What kind of weird do you want; I have seen it all."

Carrie hadn't experienced much involvement with the spirit world while growing up. It all seemed to take off for her when she met her husband, Frank. She told me that once he came into her life, a lot of things started happening—things she had never experienced before in her life.

One of the strangest stories she shared was about the night Frank brought home a Ouija board. He bought it for his stepdaughter, Amber, so she and her friends could play it at her birthday party that night. The party was also a slumber party, with two of Amber's friends staying the night.

I don't know exactly who used the board that night. But something must have scared them because Carrie told Frank to burn it. They had a bonfire going in the back yard for Amber's party so they threw it in the fire that very night. Carrie told me that she couldn't believe what happened next. She said, "That board kind of exploded, soaring a hundred feet into the air." [I should add here that I have heard other stories of Ouija boards that did strange things when an attempt was made to destroy them.]

Several friends at Amber's slumber party witnessed this explosion, also. Both of these friends refuse to talk about that evening with me. However, I did manage to get one of her friends to at least confirm it exploded. Her message to me was a simple, "Yes, it did happen."

30 Years Of Evil Around

Frank spent his entire life seeing and hearing things. Living with Carrie, he constantly saw a cat in the house that no one else could see. She said he would move about the house as if he was trying to catch it. He had moved to the Midwest from out East and brought with him the voices he constantly heard, but no one else could hear.

The part of Carrie's story that really caught my attention was Frank's own Ouija board experience. When Frank was around eleven years old, he and his brothers had played with a Ouija board. Frank told Carrie he remembers asking the board when he would die. For some reason people love asking a Ouija board that question. The board made a remarkable, startling prediction: **That Frank would die by his own hand in a basement.**

I doubt that at age eleven he comprehended this far-reaching prediction. But about thirty years later the prediction came true, showing how long evil can stay attached to an individual. I believe his encounter with the board was an entry point for him. Evil held on to him for the rest of his life, and then they (*evil*) gulped him up. The night before Frank's suicide, a spirit came to Amber's bedside and told her, "No matter what happens tomorrow, all will be okay." According to Carrie, this was Amber's guardian angel. The next day Frank killed himself in the basement of their house, just as the board had predicted and the demons had orchestrated.

Ouija boards have a way of opening the wrong doors in people's lives, often allowing spirits to gain a foothold when a person is quite young. So if you ever consider using a Ouija board, or as a parent you learn that your child is planning to be in a situation where a Ouija board will be in use, I hope you will remember this story and that you will warn them with it.

Doors That Won't Shut

When people tangle with anything not of this world it has far-reaching repercussions that aren't seen until it's too late. Numbers 14:18 declares:

> *The Lord is slow to anger, abounding in love and forgiving sin and rebellion. Yet he doesn't leave the guilty unpunished; he punishes the children for the sin of the parents to the third and fourth generation.*

I believe this verse can be fulfilled when a family member dabbles with any form of contact with the other side. When you dabble with the occult, a door is opened that is left open for generations to come. Using Ouija boards, tarot cards, and the many other forms of contacting spirits is a way of telling God he isn't enough for you—that you prefer whispers of demons over God's already revealed Word. You prefer their apparent concern and guidance to his. Most people don't realize who they are talking to when they contact the other side. And while much of this contact is done out of ignorance, it is never prudent to dance with the devil in any way, for when this happens God's "protective hedge" is removed for that person and the flood gates of evil open up wide.

Most Christian authors agree that those engaged with the occult have a very difficult time breaking out of it. The demons attached to these individuals seem to be the worst of the worst. And once a grandmother or mother "dance" with them, it is their children and their children's children who suffer down the road. As I dug into this generational pull the occult seems to have on families it became very clear to me that the tentacles of evil stretch out so much further then I could ever have imagined. Not only were certain families stuck in this unending cycle of encounters, but almost everyone close to them was affected as well.

Simple Candles

When Kristy was sixteen, she and some friends decided that they wanted to contact a spirit for fun. They had seen a show on TV that sparked their curiosity, so they all met at a friend's house one night to carry out their plan. They made a circle of candles on the bedroom floor with one candle in the middle. The outside candles were supposedly for protection, and the inside candle was there as the response candle. If the inside candle flickered after a question was asked, then that meant yes—a spirit had responded to their question. She said that she got bored because nothing was happening, so she got up and sat on the edge of the bed. That is when contact was made.

She said that if felt like an intense amount of weight came over her. [Incidentally, I had sensed this same intense heaviness as a child, so I could identify with her.] Anyway, it started at her head and worked its way down her body. It felt like she was being taken over by this weight. She got scared and tried to warn her friends, but the voice coming out of her mouth wasn't hers. It was a much deeper voice. She made three attempts to talk but each time it was a different, much deeper voice. Then, as quickly as it had taken her over, it left. She said she sat there crying while her friends tried to console her. Kristy felt as though all of her energy had been sucked out of her.

Several years went by and Kristy had two children. She moved into an apartment building with her two daughters and decided that the house was haunted—with doors slamming shut and the feeling of someone watching her all the time. Her girls constantly awoke during the night and came into her bedroom for protection. The whole time she lived there was filled with unexplainable noises and the sound of footsteps. She decided to move. However, as she moved from place to place the spirits continued to haunt *her* no matter where she went.

Today Kristy has four daughters and her life sounds like something out of a Hollywood movie on the paranormal. Her fifteen-year-old daughter woke up one morning and her bed was in the middle of the bedroom with her still in it. It scared her bad enough that she slept on the couch after that. That didn't deter the spirits from bothering her. Many nights as she reclined on the couch she could hear someone walking down the stairs. The couch faced the stairs and the whole family knew the sounds the stairs made when someone walked on them. She would lie there cowering, watching the stairs and listening to whatever it was walking up and down those steps, all without actually seeing anyone.

Her thirteen-year-old daughter has encountered the most of any of her girls, starting when she was just a toddler. When she was four she had pointed to an area in the back yard and said that a man was looking at her. No one else could see this man. It wasn't long after that when her daughter started telling Kristy that her friend Chuckie was being mean, and that Chuckie was telling her to do bad things. It was obvious her daughter had a secret friend, which is common with people who have encounters. Her daughter also complained that Chuckie used very bad words when talking with her.

As she got older, this daughter's secret friends transformed into dark figures. She told her mom that these figures would dart around her room constantly. On several occasions they even sat on her bed and said, "Hi." When Kristy can get her to talk about these dark figures, her daughter wants to go outside to do it. This suggests that she fears some type of retaliation should she be overheard.

As this girl has gotten older, she has turned into a loner. She gets home from school and heads up to her room, where she stays for most of the evening. It seems like she is being held captive in a way, as though these spirits have her imprisoned in that room. This personality change may not be the girl's choice, especially if the possessiveness of evil spirits is factored in.

Pacing Spirits

And just in case you think that Kristy and her kids were going off the deep end, one day a neighbor asked Kristy if everything was okay. He explained that the previous night he had noticed someone pacing back and forth in one of the upstairs bedroom windows. The next morning, this figure was still pacing in the same window, as if it had never stopped pacing all night. Kristy told him the girls had been at their dad's house the previous night. She explained to her neighbor that no one was upstairs the previous night or that morning. That neighbor has never talked to Kristy again.

Kristy also shared with me something else that was happening when the girls were gone on their weekends with their dad. She said it was almost like these spirits got mad when the girls were gone. She said all the typical noises were still happening, but they were amplified. The bangs were louder and the footsteps seemed heavier. If you couple that with the pacing spirit in that bedroom window, it sounds like these evil spirits didn't like their possessions leaving the house.

As far as Kristy's other daughters, she says that not much goes on with them. She did say her eight-year-old is starting to tell her about weird things, so she thinks they (*evil*) are starting in on her. Things have died down for Kristy herself now that her daughters are around. But she still has to sleep with a pillow over her head, because they like to tickle her face when she is asleep. [My own sister has this same problem.]

Kristy's story is a perfect example of someone who as a teenager tried to contact the other side. Even though it seemed harmless, and she was doing it for fun with her friends, it has had far-reaching, long-term effects. This is where the rubber meets the road. If you dabble in the occult it will jump from you to your kids. Your kids don't have any say in this because they may not even be born yet.

There are quite a few games that teenagers play that have the potential to open a door that should stay shut. These games go by the names: "Bloody Mary," "Light as a Feather, Stiff as a Board," "Candy Man," using a Ouija board, tarot cards, or participating in séances. If you're thinking of participating in these things, even as just an observer, or you know your kids are considering doing so: **STOP. DON'T think only of yourself or even just of them**, but of generations of your own family yet to come. Think of it this way: If your own daughter were pregnant with your first grandchild, would you do anything, consciously, to hurt that unborn child? Would you allow anyone else to hurt that child if you could prevent it? We're not talking here of the effects on the unborn of smoking or alcohol use, or even being able to prevent a long-term disability or disease. Of course you would try to intervene and prevent all such things that might affect your grandchild's *body*. How much more crucial it is to intervene and prevent those things that might affect your grandchild's *soul*.

Tentacles Of Evil

One vivid example of this generational curse involves a friend of mine from Bark River, Michigan. Mindy's parents were self-proclaimed witches. Her dad was a warlock and her mom was a "white witch." Both were involved with things not of this world when they were young. Mindy followed in their footsteps and flirted with the occult, not knowing the lasting effects it would have. Mindy told me that if she had known then what she knows now she would have never touched anything that involved contacting spirits. She admits to using a Ouija board, tarot cards, and crystals. She has many times been physically touched by a spirit. She claims to have seen dead relatives as well, many times.

To this day, her children are feeling the generational effects of her parents (and Mindy) contacting the other side. Her children have seen dark figures and evil spirits masquerading as little kids. One daughter said she rolled over in bed and saw a girl holding a lantern walk through her room, then vanish through a solid wall.

The list of things that happen to Mindy's children is amazing. Along with seeing full-body figures, they also sleepwalk, have vivid dreams, hear voices, hear footsteps, hear knocking, see objects fly across the room, have premonitions, had spirits lie on them, get toes tugged on while in bed, get poked, had pictures fly off the wall, mattresses shaking, and most can't sleep well through the night. All this in one generation of five kids; now let's focus in on Mindy's grandkids, the third generation from her parents.

Grandkids As Well

She has six grandkids all under the age of five. One grandchild, Dale, came out of his bedroom with a slap mark on his face. No one was in the room with him when it happened. I have seen this picture of the slap mark; it looks like three distinct finger marks on his cheek. Dale also claims that he has a secret friend named "Lewey" who visits him in his dreams. Lewey has long black hair and a dark complexion. If you ask Dale about Lewey, he gets real quiet, puts his head down, and is unwilling to talk.

Dale did tell me that his sister, Jade, gets scared at night and runs into her mom's room. Very seldom does she sleep in her own room through the entire night. I got the impression as I talked to Dale that something messes with her in her bed, just like they did to my sister when she was little.

As far as the other grandkids, it is hard to tell with them what is going on for sure. But their mothers have told me that the kids look under their cribs at something that makes them cry. One of Mindy's granddaughters said that monsters try to get her feet at night. These kids sometimes come flying out of a room looking back as though they have seen something. Two of them wake up continuously through the night, crying.

One morning Mindy's middle daughter woke up to find her own kids, all under the age of three, sitting on the kitchen floor amidst the mess of all messes—ketchup bottles emptied, butter smeared everywhere, and leftovers all over the kitchen floor. She had just bought a twelve-pack of soda the day before and each can had been punctured repeatedly with a fork. She told Mindy that there is no way the kids had enough strength to puncture those cans. A few days later, Mindy's daughter discovered a butcher's knife under the covers in her two-year-old daughter's bed.

Later that same day, the whole family heard what seemed like someone dragging something very heavy across the floor in the attic. It scared them enough that they called me. I went over and opened the attic access, which is a small access panel in one of the closets off a bedroom and found nothing upstairs. In fact there was no floor in this attic, just blown insulation everywhere. So there was no way for anything to have made the dragging sound they were claiming to hear. You might be tempted to call this an auditory hallucination, but again keep in mind that no group of people can have the same hallucination. Mass hysteria is not the same, nor does it apply in this case.

Mindy's Sister

Along with Mindy's own kids and grandkids we can add her sister, Chris, to the story as well. Chris is accustomed to seeing dark figures around her house. Chris had one experience where she was lying in bed and felt something climb on top of her and start to choke her. It felt like someone was sitting on her chest with their hands wrapped around her neck. Choking is a common occurrence with women who have encounters. She also mentioned a certain spirit in the house that is female and likes to get very close to her face. Numerous times Chris has awakened to find herself face-to-face with this spirit. Chris's daughter has shared similar stories with me about this spirit, too.

Chris has three children, all of whom see dark figures just like their mom does. One of the boys even described these dark figures as climbing up and down the walls in his bedroom. He said they remind him of big spiders crawling up and down the walls.

Chris's daughter, Jenny, talks very openly about having two dark spirits around her constantly. She told me that when she was younger there were more spirits around and she saw them regularly. She mentioned that lately one spirit has been manifesting itself above her bed at night. It stares down at her as she is lying in bed.

Because Chris has deeper ties to the occult, claiming to be a white witch, I feel her kids are suffering more than others. When a parent openly practices the occult, like my mother did, activity is at a higher level. It affects them greatly, and it will affect the next generations of that family as well.

Generational Pull

I believe that the most ignored aspect of those who see things is how it sets the next generation up to be harassed by demonic spirits. One of my primary reasons for writing this book is to shed light on the fact that we are not being visited by past relatives. We are not stuck in a haunted house. We are not dealing with a spirit who can't move on to the next world. The randomness so often assigned to encounters isn't random at all. I believe that most times we can trace our problems back to a relative who dabbled with something from the occult, just as was true with my own mother. I do have examples of that not being the case, but they are few and far between. This generational curse is well-documented by other writers and scholars. It happens, and it is very difficult to break.

That is why I believe there are so many references in the Bible warning us to stay away from such practices. God has no choice but to remove his protective hedge from that person. And even though he loves us, he will back away if a person decides to rely on doctrines of demons instead of relying on him. Leviticus 20:6 says:

> *I will set my face against anyone who turns to mediums and spiritists to prostitute themselves by following them, and I will cut them off from their people.*

This is a stern warning, yet many ignore it, so it should not surprise us at all when the person involved has serious problems. God knows the potential problems anyone will have if they dabble with this, which is why he sends such a strong warning to avoid such practices. Some people say they don't understand why some things happen to them, when all they have to do is consult the Word of God. In Leviticus 20:6, the King James Bible uses the word "wizard" instead of spiritist. When wizard is translated from the original Hebrew is means conjurer—one who summons the dead. God tells us he will set his face against those who do this. Those who try any form of contacting the other side will be cut off from God. Regardless of the word that each translation of the Bible chooses, it is describing some form of contacting the dead. We are to have nothing to do with it.

When one of our past relatives has crossed this line God has no choice but to cut them off, and this "curse" can extend to the third and fourth generations. I have not come across any other explanation for why some families get oppressed generation after generation. It cannot be coincidental, but it's not because some witch put a hex on them, either. It is not hereditary. It is simply that God has turned his back toward them for their willing disobedience. If you wonder why your little one has creepy nightly visitors, all you have to do is open God's Word to find the answer. But don't stop when you find the explanation. Keep reading to discover how this curse can be broken.

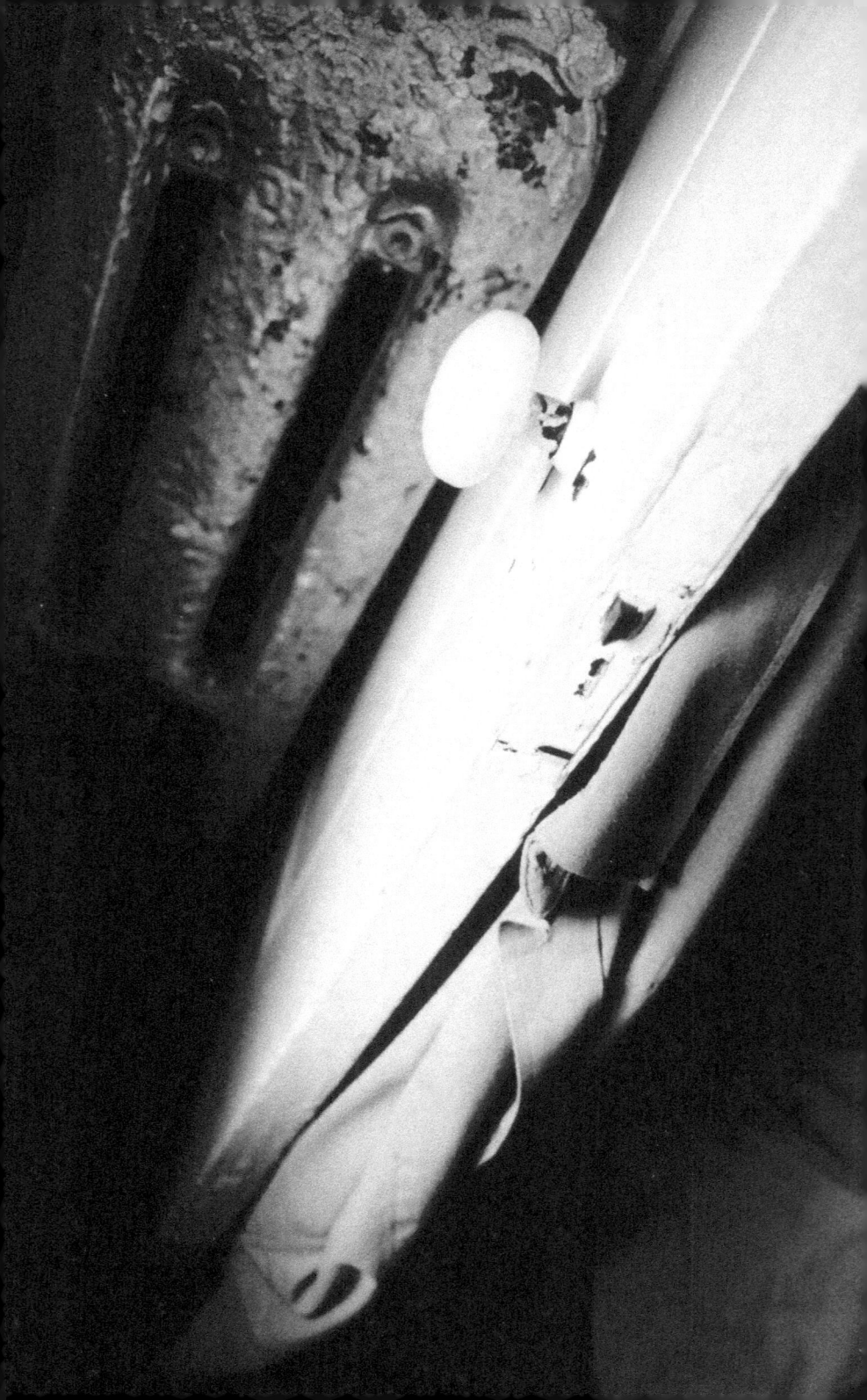

CHAPTER 12

Entire Families Consumed

What does a family look like with evil breathing down their necks day in and day out? Frankly, we really don't know. All of us stumble and we all make mistakes in life and we obviously can't blame Satan for everything that happens to us. What I can say with some confidence is that when there is an ongoing problem that affects generation upon generation it should be an evil red flag. Scholars call it a generational curse. Or it can be referred to as generational bondage. I prefer to say it is a form of bondage that the next generation can't seem to shake. The occult is the worst of these forms of bondage that gobble up each generation to come. It can exhibit as alcoholism, pornography, addictions to drugs, or something more sinister.

Debra is the perfect example for this passed-down bondage. Debra's entire life has been plagued by spirit encounters and unexplainable experiences. Those experiences, as well as her own bondage and that of her family, were passed down to her. Her unfortunate family bondage just happened to be sexual issues; specifically, the family's inability to escape deviant men. As a result the family's history is littered with sexual assault after sexual assault.

Debra has past relatives that may have been involved with deviant sexual behaviors and the occult. This heritage was a serious one-two punch against her. Debra's parents were rumored to have been into spouse swapping in the early 70s. Her father even told her about someone in their family who may have been a prostitute around the turn of the century.

Debra's mother, Jackie, fought off an attempted assault by her own uncle when she was in her early teens. Once he realized she wasn't going to give in to him he resorted to other deviant methods. He would enter her room during the wee hours of the night any time she slept over, and fondle her in her sleep. She awoke one time finding him with his hand up her shirt.

Jackie's sister was assaulted at age ten by this same deviant uncle, something that wasn't revealed until they were much older. Debra's grandma was raped when she was younger, having fought off another attempted rape a year earlier. Debra's sister was raped and her daughter was sexually assaulted as well. One of Debra's first experiences with sex happened when she was a teen. A guy simply tried to force himself on her, but she stopped it. Shortly after that she met her first husband, Chris, who seemed like Mr. Right to her. It didn't take long for Debra to see this wasn't the case. He was physically abusive and during his fits of rage, would pin her to the wall with his hands around her neck. He was deviant as well and actually allowed his friends to watch them have sex . . . without her knowledge. Chris would leave the bedroom door cracked, or leave the curtain to the window slightly open and his friends would watch. Debra told me of an episode where she caught one of her husband's friends crawling on the floor into the bedroom as they were having sex so he could sneak a peek.

Chris would crack the bathroom door open after she was already in the shower so his friends could watch her.

Chris's father was sexually twisted as well. He actually attempted to rape Debra when she was seven months pregnant. He asked her to go for a ride with him, taking her to a remote area so they could "talk." But as soon as the truck was parked, he attacked her. He got his hands down her pants before she finally stopped the assault, pleading and begging for him to stop. Chris's father also wormed his way into Jackie's room one time when she was visiting. She woke up to him sitting on her bed rubbing her shoulders. It's a very twisted father-in-law who makes sexual advances on his daughter-in-law and her mother.

Debra decided enough was enough with this family and obtained a divorce. She moved out and got her own place. After she left, Chris muscled his way into her apartment one night and raped her. The rape was violent and has left her with emotional scars more than two decades later. At present, Chris is wearing a tether for sexually assaulting a young woman. If it wasn't for his poor health, he would be in prison for this crime. This was Jackie's first husband's family. Nothing more needs to be said.

Husband Number Two

Shortly after her marriage from hell, Debra met Bruce. They dated for a while and she believed he was different than her first husband, so she gave marriage a second chance. Little did she know that Bruce was also a sex addict who continually cheated on her throughout their marriage.

It was common for Bruce to have questionable friends around the house and one of them even tried to assault Debra when he was alone with her. He grabbed her and forced his hand under her clothes. This fellow was on the national sex offender list! Ultimately, she left Bruce, who showed up after she moved out and raped her.

I don't believe any of this was a coincidence. Evil orchestrates and manipulates circumstances in favor of more evil. This may seem like speculation on my part. But it cannot be denied that these "wrong" men all had some form of sexual deviance.

Now, let's take it another step. Debra's oldest daughter's first boyfriend would assault her in the middle of the night. She would wake up and he would be on top of her. Against her will he would have sex with her. She learned after the first few times of fighting this to just let him go through with it, out of fear of upsetting him further. She feared him when he was angry so she let him do his thing. What she couldn't understand was that she was more than willing to do things with him under normal circumstances but he just seemed to enjoy taking it from her when she was asleep and when she would say no. He is currently serving time in a Wisconsin jail for having sex with a minor.

Mindy's next daughter, who has had many encounters over the years, was raped in her teens. She turned promiscuous for several years and then met a guy who was very sexually deviant. He also took sex from her when she would say no. She would wake up to him being on top of her, demanding sex. He even made attempts to convince her to invite other people into their bedroom.

This is evil operating behind the scenes *ensuring* that the "wrong" men enter the picture. There is no doubt in my mind that this was all orchestrated or manipulated to prolong the ongoing issues this family has to deal with. Both the mom and her two daughters being attracted to horribly deviant men. Still not convinced? Let's bring Mindy's sons into the story.

One of her sons is currently dating a young woman who was date-raped. She told me that she simply woke up after partying to find a guy having his way with her. It seems no coincidence that this same son's previous girlfriend was also raped. His girlfriend before that was also raped. And they all have had encounters with evil spirits.

Mindy's other son dated a girl who was raped by a former boyfriend. I also have reason to believe she was assaulted when she was younger. This young woman has told me of many encounters that would knock your socks off. She told me when she was little, a spirit used to talk to her from inside her closet.

Here we have the stories of a mother and her children, as well as some extended family. The total number of rapes, sexual assaults, and attempts to them, or people extremely close to them, is over twenty. This is a pattern, not a coincidence. Evil will always stick to what works and this seems to be the case for this poor family. Did evil make these men attack these poor women? Of course not. Did some of these women put themselves in terrible spots? Of course, yes. But there is no way this all happened by chance.

I believe the evil attached to this family has found the best way to oppress them and it is relentless. Can there be any doubt with so many "Mr. Wrongs" and "Ms. Wrongs" finding their way into their lives? Can there be any doubt that evil has latched onto this family using sex as a foothold? Sex is actually a mild word to use with this family with so much violent sex in their history.

Evil does not just lurk in dark, creepy basements. Demons are intelligent beings tasked by their master to disrupt the lives of as many people as possible. When they see an angle to use on a certain family they move in and attack that front with precision and purpose. When they see a wound they will keep pouring salt in it for as long as they can. If a family's weakness is sex, then they will exploit that to no end. If it is drugs, then they attack that front . . . and so forth and so on.

My Own Family

To further support this theory of how evil attacks a family, amplifying any sinful area present, I want to talk about my own family. In this case evil has attacked on another front, but a front nonetheless.

- My parents split up early in their relationship and talked about divorcing. Both suffered from depression their entire lives.

- One of my brothers is currently dating someone who sees dark figures on a regular basis. She informed me that they are always around her. He has also been through a divorce. He has depression issues as well.

- My next brother is currently with someone who has had many encounters. His previous girlfriend also has many stories to tell. His girlfriend before that had encounters as well. His past includes a divorce just like the last brother. He, too, has an ongoing problem with depression.

- My last brother married someone who had many encounters as a young child. So did her sister. My brother and his first wife are divorced as well. His next girlfriend had encounters to share with me but never got back to me.

To summarize, all my brothers went through a divorce. All three brothers struggle with depression. All three brothers spent time with partners who were plagued with seeing spirits.

- My sister has been divorced twice and to this day still has encounters. Her first husband had depression issues, but I don't know for certain if he ever saw anything. Her second husband was abusive in many different ways, so she divorced him after being married for only a year. She has had a terrible time with depression.

- Perhaps I should include my aunt and her two children into this equation, since they have lived with us for most of their lives. My aunt divorced her alcoholic husband when the kids were very young and always seemed to need a place to stay. Both my aunt and her daughter have been divorced. All three of them suffered with depression. Depression got to my aunt's son, who committed suicide roughly four years ago.

- Finally, there's me. My wife and her extended family have experienced more evil then anyone can imagine. I, too, have suffered through a divorce. I was afflicted with depression many years ago, but that has all but disappeared. I thank God for that.

My reason for taking you behind the scenes in these two families is to show how each family has a reoccurring issue that they can't seem to shake. Our family, like Debra's, has been under attack, just on a different front. What we share is that encounters with spirits have been a part of the past for both families, and to some extent they continue to this day. Such things are hard to accept and recognize, which makes them all the more difficult to stop.

One more similarity between the two families is that all ten (five from each family) met someone who had had encounters as well. As I write this, nine out of the ten people mentioned are still with someone who has ongoing issues with encounters. All this chaos cannot be coincidental; it is by their (*evil's*) design. They found weaknesses and exploited them, working their deceitful schemes across generations in both families.

Opposites Don't Attract

The old saying of opposites attract does not apply to those who have encounters. For some reason, we seem to be drawn to people who have encounters like we do. Or is it that Satan is trying to do the exact opposite of what God wants? Mark 10:6-9 says:

> *But at the beginning of creation God "made them male and female." "For this reason a man will leave his father and mother and be united to his wife, and the two shall become one flesh." So they are no longer two, but one flesh. What therefore God has joined together, let no man separate.*

Just like Scripture says that God brings people together, could it be that Satan does the exact opposite? Remember, Satan always tries to duplicate what God does, with an evil twist to it. If God is absent from your life, then Satan is in control of who you meet. Evil brings together those who should not be together. Does he bring them together so his job takes less effort? Or does he play a part in making sure people meet others with demonic problems to ensure they, as a couple, will self-destruct by being together? The possibilities are endless because we could speculate on this all day. But I am convinced that there has to be some method to his madness, with the result that more families are affected.

Another speculative angle on this might be that evil gathers those who have problems together to save on resources, to make it easier to oppress people. If one demonic being is harassing a certain individual, why not bring in someone with the same or similar problems? This makes it easier for one demon to oppress these two people simply because they are now in close proximity —to each other and to the demon. Whatever makes his work easier becomes his M.O. (method of operation). That is how I believe evil operates. Misery loves company, and that saying is followed closely by Satan.

To close out this chapter, I would like to describe a family history that supports my theory that once a family messes with things of the occult, it is very difficult to break the hold evil has on them. The quality of life got sucked right out of this family, and the kids and grandkids weren't spared. It just so happens that my mother was involved with this family, and the stories I have heard left my mouth hanging open. It wasn't just the stories that left me speechless; it was that my mother was a part of it.

Growling In The Crawlspace

I remember, as a kid, going over to visit this family and not really wanting to be there. I witnessed the father of this family, Jeff, hit his stepson so hard he flew back out of his lawn chair and landed on his back in the grass. I surely didn't want to be around someone that untrustworthy and violent. The stepson's name was Ralph and we used to hang together when we did visit.

I later found out the step-dad of this family, Jeff, was paranoid schizophrenic with many anger issues. He had had a very rough childhood and he took it out on everyone else. He happened to be right next to his own father when he committed suicide. How does someone even begin to understand what was going on in a person's mind after witnessing that.

The mother of this family, Sheila, was physically abusive to all of her kids as well, pulling the girls' hair and digging her fingernails into their skin quite frequently.

I mentioned earlier that we really didn't go anywhere unless contacting spirits was a part of the plans. I have since found out that this was true also with the family of Jeff and Sheila. Sheila wanted to learn the "black arts" from my mother. Somehow Sheila found out my mother was into the occult. After that they spent a lot of time together. As far as I could learn, Sheila was practicing the occult before she met my mother. But it is obvious that when the two "joined forces" and practiced together, things were quite a bit worse for everyone involved.

One of the daughters of this family, Julie, told me that everything took off when they moved from Bark River to Wilson, Michigan. This is around the same time my parents started to visit them. Julie told me that the dark figures were everywhere on this property. Sometimes they would hide behind trees spying on her. They would also stand at the foot of her bed watching her as she tried to go to sleep.

She also reported that she and her brother Ralph both used to hear growling coming from a crawlspace off of Ralph's bedroom. Many times as she walked by this crawlspace she would hear this spirit growl at her. Clearly it was something not human. She avoided going by the opening to that crawlspace as much as possible.

My Floating Mother

Shortly after our families got to know each other, something happened that to this day astounds me. Supposedly different members within this family saw an apparition of my mother floating around the house. This was while my mother was still alive. If this was all the same night or on different nights no one is certain. My mother supposedly floated by some of them as they were watching TV in their living room one night. My mother was wearing a long dark dress as she passed between them and the TV. Then she simply faded away as she neared the far wall of the living room.

Another incident involving my mother occurred in one of the bedrooms. She was seen in the doorway to the bedroom of one of the girls. She was also seen in one of the girls' bedrooms. The final encounter happened to the mother Sheila. She woke in the middle of the night to find herself face to face with my mother as she hovered over the bed. This apparition of my mother floated out the bedroom door, and Sheila followed close behind. When Sheila got to the hallway the apparition simply vanished.

I believe this demonic apparition happened because this family thought my mother had a gift. Sheila herself was trying to learn the "black arts" from my mother. I can't think of a better way to reassure her than by conducting this amazing out-of-body experience. If Sheila desired to learn the "black arts" from my mother, these demons did an outstanding job of selling it to her, drawing her into it further by using my mother as a floating salesperson.

Another of the daughters in this family, Joslin, was not spared run-ins with the other side. She went into the bathroom alone one time and locked the door behind her. Moments later, the family heard her screaming at the top of her voice. As Joslin opened the door the family rushed in and found her arm broken. Joslin claimed that she had been thrown across the bathroom, causing her to land in the bathtub. Encounters don't get much scarier.

Joslin was prone to talk to imaginary people, as well. She would have tea parties in her room, claiming there were actually people sitting with her having tea. One time she claimed it was her dead grandmother and a dead aunt sitting with her.

Many people in the area believed this young girl to be mentally unstable. But with all the other stories from other family members, I believe Joslin got a bad rap. I believe she had to find a way to cope with her evil encounters (without much support from her family) and the cumulative effect was that she got a reputation that wasn't entirely fair, since she was describing experiences that had actually happened to her.

50 Years Of Encounters

To this day, another of the daughters, Barbara, can't seem to shake the encounters. Growing up on the farm she recalls many encounters with dark figures and hearing strange noises and footsteps all throughout the house. For her, the encounters continue, even though she is in her 50s now.

For most, these types of encounters taper off with age. But Barbara told me that they still talk to her at night. They say things in three's to her. Like death, death, death. Or profane words that I won't repeat, which also come out in threes.

Barbara was harassed by a spirit one night shortly after we had spoken. They said to her, "We could hang her." She messaged me the next morning and asked me if they had contacted me as well. I told her that nothing had happened on my end. She thought that since we were talking about this stuff the previous night, they would have harassed me as well. Although some harassment of me or others has occurred due to my involvement with this research, in this case they left us alone.

Barbara also claims to have an unusual "gift;" specifically, she can sense death. By that I mean if someone is going to die and they are in her presence, she just knows that they will die soon. She tells me that there has never been a time in her life that these spirits weren't around her—that's fifty or so years of constant contact with the other side.

As far as the remaining members of this family, it has been difficult to get any of them to talk about those days. One gives me the cold shoulder and the other one tells me she has blocked it out. By that last statement I think it is fair to say that they went through hell on earth, too, and would prefer to just forget about it. Sometimes even silences says a lot.

The Next Generation

The following is a summary of how evil has expressed itself in the next generation of this family. Remember, it is always the future generations that pay for this. I have disguised this to honor the wishes of some members of this family who would prefer no one figure out who they were.

Sibling 1: Got married and went on to have two children. For the most part they haven't had any encounters. These kids were raised in a godly home, though. I used to be pretty good friends with this father and he quite possibly could be the most caring man I have ever met. I believe evil hit a brick wall with this family and the generational bondage ended. One of their children did get married to a woman from a foreign country. She practiced another religion and their young son now sees things.

Sibling 2: Got married and went on to have three children—two kids from one marriage and the third child by another man. Physical abuse and sexual abuse has affected this family. Drugs were commonplace as well. Two boys from this family are bipolar, with one of them still in prison. One of the boys from this family was known for torturing animals just for kicks. I was not able to get any of these kids to tell me if they have had any encounters with spirits.

Sibling 3: Went on to have four children, three by her husband and the last one by another man. She is bipolar, as are two of her grandkids. This sibling struggled with substance abuse addictions over the years. She has battled depression along with suicidal thoughts. She endured physical abuse from some of her partners, which led to broken bones and many trips to the hospital through the years. She was also sexually assaulted, which led to severe promiscuity that she still struggles with today. One of her children got attacked by something while in the shower, so encounters are present with these kids. Another one of her kids has premonitions and dreams that come true.

Sibling 4: Went on to have three children, two by his wife and the third child through a woman he knew. He has battled with alcohol his whole life and had bouts with drugs. One of his children confided in me that he still sees things. He was once dragged across the floor in his mom's apartment by some unseen force. He told me his own children have the gift of sight, too—meaning they see things. So with this sibling we are seeing the effects of the occult to the fourth generation.

Sibling 5: Went on to have two children—one with her husband and one with another man. Her husband and even some of her boyfriends were physically abusive with her, causing several broken bones. After she graduated from high school she had quite a few encounters away from the farm:

- She saw her own mother shortly after she passed on.
- She felt someone sit at the end of her bed while she was trying to go to sleep.
- She saw a dark figure at the top of a staircase while she was babysitting at a friend's house. (I might add here that while she was babysitting there she chanced upon a Ouija board but never touched it.)
- One of her kids is bipolar as well, having battled depression and cutting.
- Even her youngest had a run-in with a spirit. He was upstairs in his crib with a baby monitor next to the crib. She told me that out of nowhere she heard, "That is my fire truck" come across the baby monitor. She ran upstairs and witnessed her son pointing at the toy box, cry-

ing. Her son couldn't talk yet, so she knows that what she heard was a spirit.
- Shortly after the baby monitor incident she saw scratches on the inside of her child's bedroom door. She never let him sleep up there again.

Sibling 6: Went on to have three children, two with one man and the other with a different guy. I have talked to this sibling quite a bit. Because of her state of mind, due to drug addictions, I am not sure what to believe. I do know she was promiscuous. There were reports of physical abuse to her own children, resulting in her kids being taking away from her. One of her kids spent time in prison. He saw quite a lot growing up. The other child has seen so much that I could take up a whole chapter just describing her experiences. Her name is Beth.

Beth

Sibling six's daughter, Beth, to this day sees spirits on almost a daily basis. Her two children have "the gift of sight" according to her. So here is another fourth generation of kids affected by this. She told me how one of her friends was visiting with her one day and tripped coming down a flight of stairs. She said her dead grandmother was responsible. Beth also told me her dead grandma is always around her. She currently has several different spirits that wander around her home.

One of earliest memories of seeing spirits was with her father. They were crossing a bridge to go fishing. As they approached the bridge she could see many figures standing on the bridge. She asked her father if he could see them and he said no. As they crossed the bridge she was so scared of them that she crawled on her hands and knees. She did that so she could keep her eyes on the bridge and not on them.

Beth shared with me that no one would believe her when she would see something, so as she got older she tried a common trick that others have tried when dealing with spirits. She sprinkled flour all around her bed on several occasions, hoping to get some footprints of her visitors. Sure enough, she found footprints, most of them human-looking. Sometimes the human tracks would have a drag mark in between the steps. On a few occasions they looked more like a dog track. One morning when she woke up, it looked like someone had done some doodling in the flour with a stick.

She said the tracks would usually come from her bedroom door and always end at her nightstand, which was by her head. This led her to believe they were looking down at her face as she slept. One eerie thing about these tracks was that not once did they lead away from the bed. Whatever it was simply vanished with no sign of where it went.

She says she can smell them when they are around. She says she has to sleep all coiled up in the fetal position because if she doesn't, they will tug on her hands and feet during the night. She even has to cover her head or they will blow on her hair. (I'd heard accounts like this from my sister.)

Beth also told me she can't have certain people over because the spirits in her house will become agitated. Bruce is one of those friends. On the few occasions he has been there, the spirits in Beth's house became quite active. Beth, Bruce, and a few others were sitting at the kitchen table one night. Beth noticed a spirit walking toward them. As it entered the kitchen it vanished. Seconds later Bruce got pushed right off of the kitchen chair he was sitting on. She told me his face became white as snow.

Here we have a family with six siblings, and those siblings went on to have eighteen kids. From the detailed account of their lives and the ongoing problems that plague this family, it is clear that evil has never let go. In three examples there is proof that it has made its way down to the fourth generation. If others would have talked to me, I believe that list of fourth generations affected would have been longer.

I hate to say this, but I feel my mother was part of this family's ongoing issues. The bulk of the blame falls on this particular parent's head. And the fact that my mother and Sheila practiced their "art" together only made matters worse for this family.

Some observers might say that some families just get in a rut, that they can't seem to catch a break and will always have problems. I sure thought that for many years about my own family:

- Sometimes in the winter we would have to sit in front of our cooking oven warming ourselves because we had no money for fuel oil.
- Many mornings we kids had to share half a loaf of bread for cinnamon toast for breakfast.
- We moved fifteen times.
- All of us had depression.
- All five of us siblings went through divorce.
- Physical and sexual abuse was in our family's past.

All of these things I just mentioned must have been due to bad luck or poor choices, right? That's what I once thought. But now I know the bad luck explanation is just an excuse. I know the things that happened to us as kids happened in some cases due to our parents' poor choices. Evil wasn't always to blame. But I also know evil spirits were around my family constantly and they had a way of making things worse. They amplified problems. They were there for a reason and just didn't sit by idly; they played a part in some of the problems.

They (*evil*) are the underlying, well-hidden reason, why some families just never catch a break. That is one of the key points about evil spirits. We cannot blame them for everything. But a healthy understanding of how they are able to amplify many people's problems is pivotal to recognizing the truth found in Ephesians 6 where the apostle Paul says that "our struggle is not against flesh and blood, but against . . . the powers of this dark world and the spiritual forces of evil in the heavenly realms."

Based on over 400 interviews, years of research, and a lifetime of personal experience, I am convinced that evil can be generational in some cases. Evil wastes no time turning molehills into mountains for those who don't have God in their lives.

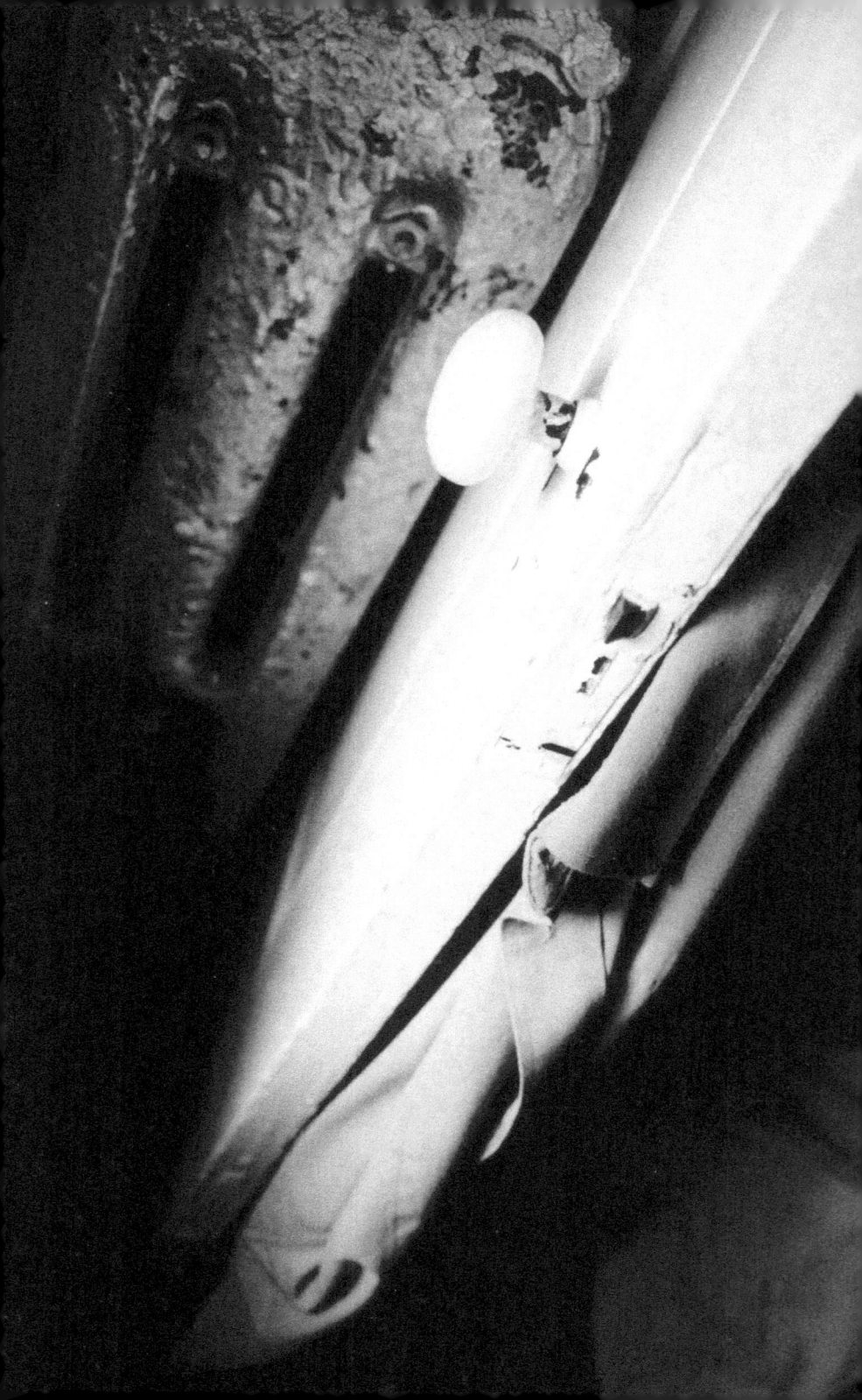

CHAPTER 13

Reading Us Like A Book

Perhaps you are familiar with the Bill Murray movie from 1993 "Ground Hog Day." Bill Murray plays Phil Connors, a reporter who is assigned to cover the annual ground hog festival in Punxsutawney, Pennsylvania. Phil is not very excited about his assignment but he and his crew head out of town to cover the story, only to run into a snowstorm, which forces them to return to town and get a room for the night.

Murray wakes up the next morning and finds its Ground Hog Day all over again. He is the only one who is aware that this has happened and it frustrates him. He goes to bed again the next night and sure enough, it's Ground Hog Day again the next morning. He hates everything to do with the day and now he has to relive it day in and day out. This continues with each waking morning until Phil finally realizes that he can take advantage of it. He realizes that the same things happen exactly at the same time and the same place each day. He is learning so much about that day that he knows what people will say before he sees them.

Phil is attracted to his news producer Rita, played by Andie MacDowell, and decides he is going to learn all he can about her to turn her apparent displeasure of him around. So every day he wakes up he makes it his goal to study her and learn all he can with the hopes of winning her over. He pushes her a little further with each passing day, learning as much as he can about her likes and dislikes. By the end of the movie he has gathered so much information about Rita that he knows her better than she knows herself.

Phil accomplishes his mission, as the end of the movie shows them intimately involved. Each repetitive day brought more information and more tidbits to use against her so she would finally fall for him. It worked like a charm.

This is similar to what Satan's evil agents have been doing since the first human sin—learning as much about human beings as will further their agenda. They are masters of knowing human weaknesses, tendencies, and habits and exploiting them to their advantage. They know us better than we know ourselves. More specifically and more personally, I believe that is why they stand at the end of kids' beds. They are studying their prey; learning all they can about each individual. This is such an integral part of their all-out attack on us as human beings that few seem to realize is taking place. In fact, even those who should know better seem oblivious to the spiritual warfare being waged.

They know our fears, our anxieties, our tripping points, and they know what the end result will be if they can manipulate our circumstances. Their job is to know us inside and out. That is why I feel they are around us all the time. That is why they are seen many times as though they are studying kids as they lie in their beds. They are not all-knowing like their Creator, so they have to be around us to gather information—like spies gather intelligence. The more they study us and know us, the better they can manipulate and attack and even use us to further their ends and fulfill their mission.

Their ultimate goal is to keep us from having a loving relationship with God. The further away from God we live, the closer evil spirits can operate around us. The longer they stay attached to any particular person, the deeper their talons dig in. What do they do with all this intimate knowledge they have mined from us? They work us over our entire lives because they know what buttons to push, just like Bill Murray knew how to get his prize – Andie MacDowell—in "Ground Hog Day."

Temptation Times Five

Ground Hog Day gets played out each and every day in every small community. No town is immune from it. Since I know the Upper Peninsula of Michigan best, it is clear to me that Carney, Nadeau, Powers, Hermansville, Stephenson, and a host of others have a Bill Murray around every corner. These information seekers are not acting; they are the real deal. They are standing in our kids' bedrooms, mining information from them so they can find a way to attach to them. Once they find a foothold, they attack and it can become a lifelong attachment that is extremely hard to break.

Once they find our weak spots they attach and life changes for us. Simple things we do every day become hard to do. Temptation goes from manageable to hard to handle, like a muscle car goes from zero to sixty in a matter of seconds. Of course, temptation comes to all humans. We have been tempted since the start of humanity, since Adam and Eve gave in to the lies of the serpent. But when a presence is continually around someone it is far different from normal temptation.

What is it like to have an evil presence in your life as compared to someone who doesn't have that same presence? I call it the "pretty girl analogy" (and I don't mean this as sexist, since this kind of temptation may exist for women, too. I'm just writing about what I know about). Imagine a normal guy walking down the sidewalk who has no evil presence in his life. Suddenly, he sees a pretty girl heading his way. She is in a short sun dress with high heels on. She is a stunningly beautiful woman. Most men will struggle right away with the temptation of looking her over as they pass her by on the sidewalk. But as she passes, within a short time, men without an attachment will forget about her. Most men won't dwell on her and her beauty once she is out of sight.

Now imagine a man who has an evil presence in his life, an evil attachment or foothold, who meets the same girl under the same circumstances. The evil foothold he struggles with is sexual thoughts, or maybe even pornography. His ability to avoid thinking about her is many times harder than the guy without the attachment. Why? Because that is how evil works us over. An attachment or foothold amplifies any and all problem areas of our lives. Demons know our weaknesses and they exploit them every chance they get. That is a tell-tale sign that is easily recognizable with those who have a demonic foothold. When they face temptation they fall harder and faster than those without such a foothold.

This is why demons need to be around people. And this is why some people and families are burdened with ongoing struggles and continuous setbacks. I may come across as blaming evil for all of our problems. Believe me, it just sounds that way. I am not naïve enough to say evil is always to blame for our wrong decisions. We can't blame evil spirits for 100 percent of our failures, but for those in whom a spirit has a foothold, they themselves can tell you how intense that feeling surfaces for them, how it seems to push them from deep inside to consistently make wrong choices even when they know what the right choice is in a given situation. They live with the burden of relentless demonic influence that some will never understand.

That's why demons need to gather up information on us and

use it to benefit their program. Then once they know our area of weakness, they come at us full tilt. That is why someone caught up in an ugly cycle of addiction or adultery has a difficult time of breaking free of it. They have the amplified pressure that others don't have. There is an evil presence with them that makes it so much harder to think, say, or do the right thing.

Yes, we all still have free will and can choose what we think or do in situations like the one just mentioned. But for those who are strapped with an evil foothold, it is almost unbearable. And this inclination toward evil may have been passed down to them through a generational curse. So they may enter life with that inclination already in their heart and never know it until they become adults. I'm not talking about "original sin" here, the inclination we all have to sin until we come to know Christ and we are empowered to choose right versus wrong. This is something even more dastardly than that.

I met Brenda several years ago. We have talked many times. By the age of nineteen, Brenda had been through more than any other woman her age I've yet to meet. Like no one I've known, evil has mastered Brenda's buttons, her "control panel." Even though all humans make mistakes and sin can lead anyone astray, there is no doubt in my mind that evil has gulped this young woman up. Evil is close by her, doing its best to keep her quality of life as low as possible.

Brenda completed a test of sorts for me. After studying this subject for many years I have compiled a list of common attachments. [You can find this list in Appendix 1.][1] Brenda has most of them. Obviously, she has a lot of issues she needs to address.

Due to Brenda's complete openness with me, plus giving me permission to do so, I will next share with you the intricate details of her life. I want to add here that I did convince her one night to pray about her circumstances, and it was met with retaliation from evil.

Brenda

Brenda's story illustrates what it is like for someone to have evil constantly around them and what that can do to a person over time. The reason I say evil was always around this young woman is from the countless stories I have from her and the rest of her family, all of whom have had encounters. The family has lived in seven houses over the years and has had to deal with encounters in all but one of those houses. The only exception was when they lived with family for a month in between moves.

Before Brenda was even born and had any say in the matter, her grandparents were self-proclaimed witches. So before she was even born she had a generational problem; some would call it a "curse." Brenda's mother and aunt dabbled in the occult as well. So from birth she had evil attached to her that was passed down from her grandparents, mother, and aunt. And she didn't even know it. Remember the ending of Numbers 14:18? He punishes the children for the sin of the parents to the third and fourth generation. While this verse is intended as a stern warning to parents, many have ignored it, to the detriment of their descendants.

Brenda's Home Life

Brenda's parent's relationship was rocky at best and the kids knew it. The family felt the effects of this with their parents separating several times before they actually divorced. Brenda's mom had caught her dad cheating several times and had left him a few times. His own kids know this about him and hang their heads when the subject is brought up. One time Brenda's mother actually found a black book with hundreds of female names and numbers in it. Some of the names in this black book had stars by them, as if he was rating them.

Brenda and her siblings grew up despising their own father. Her story is unique in that she did have a father around, whereas so many young girls don't. I had a chance to chat with a guy who knew the family from years ago. He used to be the kids' school bus driver. He said it was common for the kids to huddle near the front of the bus as they approached their own house because, he said, "They wanted to see if their dad was home before they got off the bus." If he was home, they talked as if they just wanted to stay on the bus and not get dropped off. How sad is that, to not want to see your own father?

It was also common for Brenda's dad to have questionable friends around. At one time, one of these friends of her dad's was on the local sex offender list. Brenda has told me in confidence that he never touched her, she just remembers him always picking her up and setting her on his lap. This same friend of her dad's also attacked her mom when no one was around. She fought him off. When a father allows a friend like this to be around his young family, the atmosphere for the children is less than ideal, to say the least.

In C.S. Lewis's book, *The Screwtape Letters*, he says that evil will orchestrate bringing "ideal" people into our lives. Since this book is a fictitious exchange of letters between a senior demon and its apprentice, "ideal" in this case means ideal for the promulgation of evil. This is what has happened to Brenda her whole life. The list seems endless, but the lowlights include strippers, the sexually deviant, pedophiles, drug dealers, and self-proclaimed witches.

When Brenda was eleven years old her parents finally got a divorce. The effects of divorce on any kid are traumatic enough, but in Brenda's case the "garbage" in her life seemed to snowball after this. She told me that when her mother and the kids left their dad and moved, the demonic activity in the family picked up. Specifically, she mentioned a closet in her room that she was deathly afraid of. This degree of fear generally happens shortly after a traumatic event for a child.

It was very common for the family and Brenda to see things wherever they lived. "Little ghost kids," as Brenda called them, were common sightings wherever they lived. Strange noises and objects moving on their own were so commonplace that they seemed hardly worth mentioning. No one in the family seemed overly worried about seeing or hearing strange things; it was just a common part of their life.

When Brenda was twelve years old a close friend of the family died in a four wheeler accident. The activity in the family picked up after he died, with some even recalling tall dark figures appearing. So here was Brenda, at the tender age of twelve, when her peers were immersed with mostly frivolous concerns, with much heavier matters on her mind, including numerous evil spirits roaming the house.

Then, when she was thirteen, the bottom fell out. She was at a friend's house and what may have started out as a joke turned into an assault. She was dared by her own friends to go into a bedroom alone with an older boy they all knew. She took the dare and went into the bedroom with him. Once she was in the bedroom with him, her friends held the door so she couldn't get back out. This older boy turned on her and raped her as her friends held the door and listened to the assault.

Soon after that she turned promiscuous. Then came alcohol and drug abuse. For Brenda, the next three years were a roller coaster of drugs, drinking, and sleeping with guy after guy. Her self-esteem was so low that she started to cut herself and had thoughts of suicide. She recalls constant voices in her head telling her to end her life. She described it as "a cheering section from hell" egging her on.

Heaviest Kind Of Guilt

Brenda started to settle down when she was sixteen, largely due to finding a steady boyfriend. Chuck seemed to be the answer to her problems. She started easing off the pills and her relationship had signs of actually going somewhere. Then the bottom fell out once again. Chuck confided in her that he had cheated on her and she broke it off with him. Chuck pleaded and begged for forgiveness from Brenda, but she didn't want to get back together with him. Not long after their break-up Chuck killed himself, which sent Brenda into another tailspin. This young man was well-liked in the area and had many friends. Some of these friends were messaging Brenda privately, blaming her for his suicide, and saying things like, "I wish it was you who died instead of him."

She still struggles with the guilt of his suicide, feeling responsible for what he did to himself. Sometimes she wishes she would have died that day instead of Chuck. The pain from the suicide, combined with the pain some of her own friends were causing her, overwhelmed her. To this day she will cry instantly if you mention Chuck's name.

Shortly after the suicide Brenda received a job offer. To everyone close to Brenda this is what she needed to get her mind off Chuck. At work, Brenda met someone who was twenty years older than her. It didn't take long before this situation got out of hand and took a terrible turn. This man weaseled his way into sleeping with her, taking advantage of her sad state and need for acceptance. She was barely seventeen and he was thirty-six.

Shortly after they started dating she dropped out of school and moved in with him, against the wishes of her family. Soon after she moved in with him, when she was high, he talked her into doing a threesome with another girl so he could take pictures. The third person involved in this threesome was a self-proclaimed witch, another "wrong" person in her path—surely not a coincidence.

When word got out that she had done this for her boyfriend, another couple they knew started pressing her to do a threesome with them. Brenda turned this offer down and then these same friends revealed their fangs. They turned on her quickly, reminding her of what she had done to her last boyfriend.

Cycle With No End

Brenda and this man had three kids together by the time she was nineteen. He is a convicted felon and has been in and out of trouble his whole life. He has a drug problem as well and is not afraid to use in front of young kids. Once he even told Brenda that he wanted to rape her just to see what it was like. (Rape is in his family's past and I believe evil knew this.) She had told him no when he wanted sex one night and he got mad, blurting out the rape comment.

She has been awakened in the middle of the night numerous times with him on top of her, his hands choking her as he forced his way with her. Once she came close to passing out as he choked her. (There's an undeniable parallel here with how demons choke their victims on occasion.) She just recently had a baby and there is a good chance the child was conceived from an incident where he forced her to have sex against her will.

The few years she has spent with him have been filled with encounters as well. She describes the continuous sounds of kids running and laughing when no one is in the apartment. Several times these spirits have even touched her as she was lying on the couch. She has heard strange voices calling her own kids' names when no one else was in the house with her. Her children are plagued by night terrors, continuously waking through the night. Her three-year-old sometimes points underneath her crib as if something is lurking there.

As I write she is on the verge of leaving him for the second time. After an argument they had recently, as he walked away he put his hand to his head like a gun and pretended so shoot himself, knowing full well she still struggles with Chuck's suicide. As her relationship with this guy was unraveling, he would text her saying that if he loses her, he would end it.

Of Brenda's closest friends, one is a white witch and another was once a stripper. This is an example of how Satan keeps us close to those who will increase our chances of leading a life of destruction, keeping our quality of life as low as possible.

Perhaps some will conclude that Brenda is just someone who has made many bad choices in life and is paying for it. This is partly true. She has free will and was old enough to make different choices. But isn't it possible that evil has manipulated things to keep Brenda trapped in this lifestyle? I wish I had permission from some others to have written down more of what happened to this young woman. And I wish I had had the time and space to write down her hundreds of messages to me sharing the numerous encounters that she and her kids have had. I believe this woman has never lived a day of her life without evil present.

As of this writing, it seems that her three-year-old daughter may have a secret friend. A babysitter confirmed this. This babysitter also told Brenda that her younger son was talking to someone in his bedroom. So two of her children already have their own secret friends. This further supports my belief that families have a hard time shaking evil attachments, and this is one way that such attachments get passed down from one generation to the next.

Finding A Feeding Trough

Evil plays a role in all of this whether you believe it or not. Why else would the apostle Paul say that our struggles are not against flesh and blood, but against the spiritual forces of evil?

Let's personalize this for a moment: Assuming you believe evil exists and its proliferation is the primary task of Satan and his minions (demons), what do you think demons do day in and day out? Do you believe demons are sitting in some dark, musty basement with their feet propped up on the wood pile, reminiscing with other demons about the last house they haunted? No, they are constantly prowling the earth and harassing people. People like poor Brenda.

Stories like hers are common with those who have encounters. Most are not as bad, but they do happen more frequently to those who have encounters. This is largely due to the spiritual desert they live in. But part of evil's agenda is to make sure those they're oppressing stay locked in a life of uncertainty. I have case after case files like Brenda's where people have described how they can't seem to ever catch a break. If these spirits are around them, they surely aren't helping the situation.

It is well-documented and understood that evil feeds off our fears and despair. They make it a point to show up in the lives of those who have some of life's biggest struggles with the sole purpose of extending that misery for years to come. The times I have tried to show any amount of intervention with people like Brenda has brought on retaliation from them. That proves that evil is present, not wanting them to receive the help they need. They don't want anyone trying to take back what they believe they own.

The spiritual desert Brenda lives in will spawn more of the same. Her life will be a constant battle with many more wrong guys; many more bad situations. Struggles will be followed by more struggles until she makes the change and turns to God. That is the only way evil will hit a brick wall. Evil will run unabated and have free rein in her life until she wants to change it.

A late addition to this manuscript involves Brenda. She finally left her boyfriend and told me she wants to better her life. She moved into a friend's house—a family whose past includes many encounters. This grasp evil has on her is very difficult to break. I doubt this move to her friend's house was a coincidence. Evil had a hand in it, for sure.

This is the part of evil that most don't understand and will never come to grips with. They seek out people like Brenda and feast to no end. But they do it behind the scenes. They are not all knowing and have to be attached so they can continue the misery. That is the reason most people see these spirits. That is the reason that their house is haunted. That is why some people think Grandma is sitting at the end of their child's bed. I believe that chance and randomness are words that don't belong in the spirit vocabulary. They are organized and on the attack for any and all they can find.

When they are active in a family's life they have basically found a feeding trough. The food is limitless until that person or family makes the right choices to change what's in that trough. They will never leave, that is certain, until all the "garbage" is addressed. The grandkids will be the next on their target list unless something changes. Please, let this sink in.

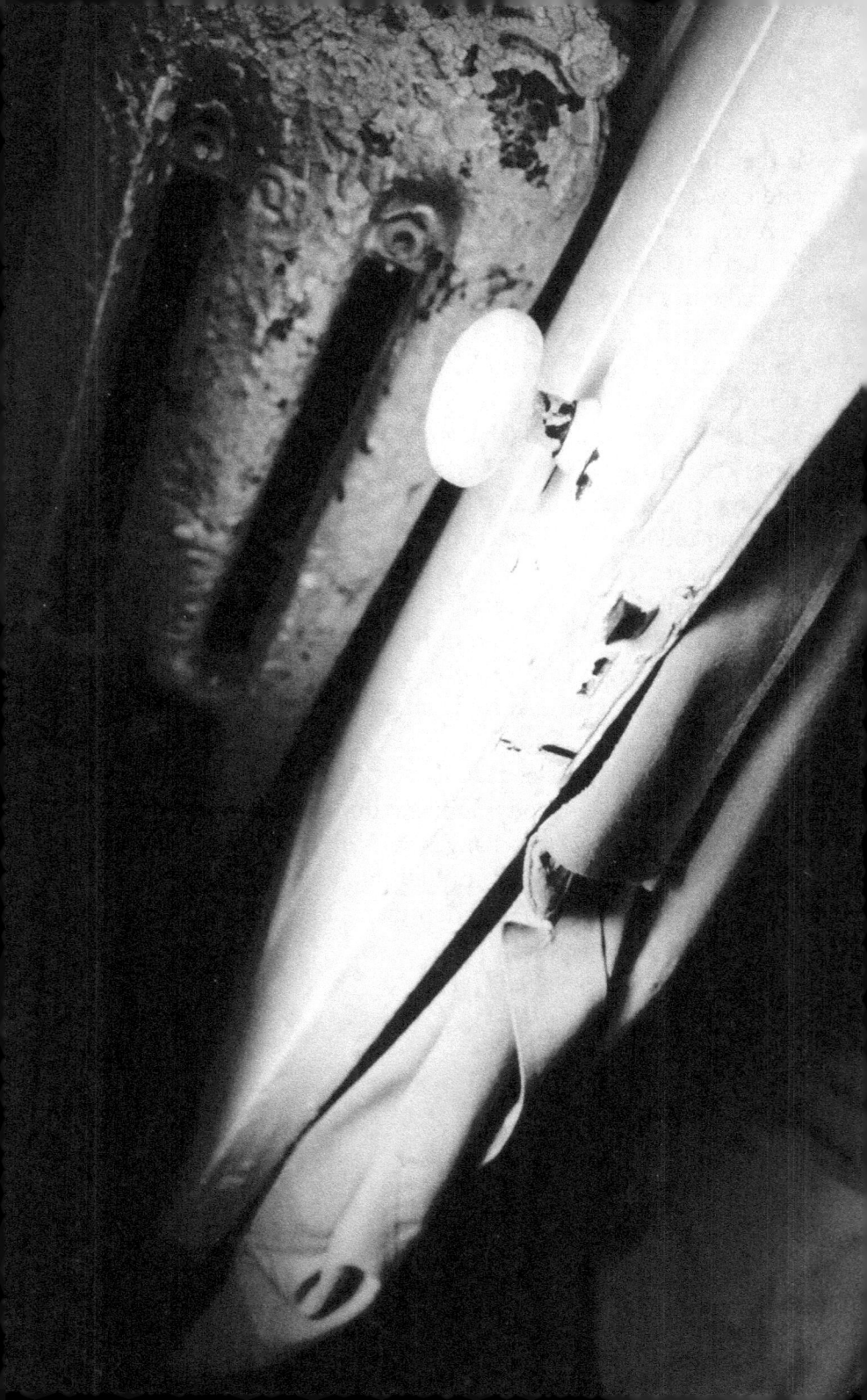

CHAPTER 14

The Big Three

Three things are the most common denominators in the lives of those who have encounters:

1. If the family has suffered through a divorce,
2. If the family has more girls than boys,
3. If the occult is in the family's past.

If these three are present, the activity rate is near 100 percent. I have investigated over 400 cases now and know how this works. And of all the families that meet my big three criteria, all but one family have activity, and I'm quite sure that family does have activity; they just refuse to tell me about it.

Divorce is an entry point that evil uses to get to many kids I have interviewed, partly because it is a traumatic event, especially in a young person's life. I've had countless kids tell me how activity picked up when their parents split. Kids feel like dad has abandoned them; that he doesn't love them anymore. Or a majority of the time, they feel they are to blame for what happened to their parents. That is a tremendous burden on their young minds. Evil wastes no time moving in to feed off of these feelings.

When a family has **more girls than boys** in it, evil seems to key in on that family. This was a surprising find for me as I talked to people. If divorce is added to this equation, it is even more inviting for evil—with no male figure around, evil has a feeding frenzy with families like this.

If the **occult** is in someone's family history there is a good chance it will be passed down to the generations to come. This is the generational curse, or generational bondage that many writers talk about. Most people don't even know they are entangled in this until they do some family research. This is the most common foothold evil has with anyone. When we dabble in the occult, we willingly choose to listen to demons instead of listening to God. He drops his protective hedge and grants our wish to let demonic beings roam around in our lives.

It has become blatantly obvious to me that if the "big three" are present in any family they will have the most encounters. In these families it is almost guaranteed that the future generations will have the exact same problems. The only time I have seen this broken was when someone accepted Christ as their personal Savior. The curse was broken and a hedge of protection went up around the family. The next generation of kids have been freed from seeing anything as well.

Sexual assaults are another foothold evil will use in someone's life that could easily be thrown in with the big three. I almost called this the "big four." But this is a subject most don't bring up and I very rarely ask anyone I'm talking to if this has happened. It's much too personal, so I let them divulge that type of information if they wish to do so.

Regardless, it does contribute to why women see more than men do. Incest is the darkest of darks, meaning the families that have experienced incest seem to have the worst of evil attached to them. My top five worst cases involve incest. This is betrayal at its worst, producing emotional damage that is hard to repair, and bringing terrible evil into a family's life.

Numbers Don't Lie

The best way to describe **my ten darkest cases** is to lump them together to see what they have in common, then see what conclusions emerge. [By the way, all ten were women.]

1. Broken homes. All ten came from some type of broken home. For any young child, their parents' divorce brings emotional overload, including feelings of abandonment, betrayal, guilt, and the perception of being unloved.

In one case, the woman met a new guy who, after a short time of their living together, started abusing her kids physically. Once she caught him outside peeking into a bedroom window where her daughter was changing. She did not know that he was a sex addict when they met. It seems to be a cycle from hell. There seems to be a playbook in the library of hell where this strategy gets taught to demons: Destroy the traditional family in order to create the perfect setting for evil to gain a foothold. Have no doubt: Evil has a plan—it's what God's Word calls "Satan's schemes." Once a woman is on her own, she becomes vulnerable and is easy prey for Satan to set his plan in motion.

Even if the mom meets someone who isn't abusive, the kids are still in a totally different mindset than they were when the family was together. Once dad is only around every other weekend, they change. In many cases they start doing things that wouldn't have happened if dad were in the picture—things like drugs, drinking, sex, staying out late, and getting into trouble. They look for acceptance in other ways. They do things in rebellion. Their normal way of life has been jolted. Satan moves in and works these poor kids over, starting in on the next generation—hoping that they end up in the same situation as their mom was in.

2. More females than males in the family. This finding surprised me at first, but perhaps it should have been obvious. These numbers are more meaningful than most will ever grasp. These ten women, plus their siblings, total thirty-one children. Of these, twenty-four of thirty-one were girls. The only family with more boys than girls in it was my own family, which had a deep involvement in the occult. When you exclude me and my four siblings from that total of thirty-one, twenty-three of the remaining twenty-six were girls.

3. The occult was present. Nine of these ten women had the occult present in their own lives or from a past family member. When the occult is present, demons are present as well. It ranged from deep involvement in the occult to just simply trying a Ouija board. I assume that the one person that didn't recall having the occult present had a past member of their family who dabbled in it, even if the person, herself, has no memory of it or they were never told it happened.

These women also had other things in common:

Rape or sexual assault. Nine of the ten women shared this history. It would appear that the trauma involved opens the door for evil to enter the picture. Five of the ten have been assaulted multiple times, intensifying each victim's already fragile emotional state. Typically, this haunts a woman for years if it isn't dealt with.

Seven of these assaults were incestuous in nature. [I consider a stepfather or "boyfriend" assaulting his partner's daughter to be incestuous.] One's home, and especially one's bedroom, should be a safe place. This is the ultimate betrayal by a loved one. One of these women was abused for over six years. The mother's boyfriend would attack her as soon as her mom left for work. She told me how he seemed to stretch it out, spending hours in her room attacking her, always telling her that she better keep quiet; or telling her that her mom wouldn't believe her if she said anything, anyway.

Apparitions. All ten have seen a dark figure or full-body apparition. Six of the ten have had instances where they saw multiple spirits at the same time. In several cases the spirits were possessive toward them and seemed to be almost holding them captive.

In the case of the girl who was sexually abused for six years by her mother's boyfriend, dark figures soon followed after the abuse began. They were always present in her room at night. As a result, she had to deal with two types of monsters through the course of each day. She even said her mom's boyfriend voice changed when he was assaulting her, turning noticeably evil. She remembers on several occasions that he seemed to be muttering something in a foreign language.

Generational curse. Seven of these ten women have children of their own. The collective total of kids they have is twenty. Of these, eighteen have had encounters themselves. The other two are so young that it is hard to tell if they have had problems. My guess is they do. If these younger two kids do see things, 100 percent will have followed in their mother's footsteps, demonstrating the generational curse.

What These Cases Show

It doesn't take a rocket scientist to see the similarities between the ten cases just summarized. The reasons these women (and others with similar histories) have encounters and see things has more to do with these commonalities than with any of the typical factors commonly cited in other writings:

- It's not that they are more sensitive to spirits.
- It has nothing to do with the house they live in.
- They don't have encounters because some spirit can't move on to the next world.
- They have encounters because a current family member is dabbling in the occult, or a family member from their past did so.
- Encounters happen because those involved have experienced some type of emotionally challenging time in their lives, and evil took advantage of their vulnerability. As the Scriptures say, evil was prowling around, latched onto them, and began the process of devouring them (and others within their sphere of influence).

Little Children

Tom is from my home town of Carney, Michigan. He is the youngest of three kids, having two older sisters. Their parents got divorced when he was young.

Tom told me that life for him as a young child was something he would never wish on anyone. He had a secret friend whom he called "Ted." Tom told me that Ted was always in his room, day and night. He remembers talking with his secret friend, but can't recall what was said between them. He does remember playing with his toys on his bedroom floor with Ted. What he remembers the most was when his secret friend got mad, he would show Tom his teeth. They were jagged and not human looking.

Fast forward some thirty years later: Tom now has a two-year-old son. One day Tom noticed something eerily familiar as he walked past his son's room. His son had his arm stretched out as if he was handing something to someone as he played on the floor. Tom told me he felt his heart sink as he realized what was taking place. His suspicions were confirmed when he asked his son who he was playing with. The son told his dad that it was his friend, whose name just so happened to be Ted. It is not possible that this little boy made this up.

For comparison with the ten women already mentioned, I want to examine the cases of ten kids who have secret or imaginary friends. My heart goes out to these young kids, and I am including their stories because of what my little sister had to go through when she was very young. While this list is more personal for me for that reason, I promise you I didn't make any of this up. A few of these children are close to my family to this day. I have prayed over some of them as they slept, knowing they suffer badly from night terrors.

1. Nine of the ten come from **broken homes**. The father of the tenth child spent a few years in jail. So there was a stretch of time where the house was broken. So you could easily say that all ten here came from broken homes.
2. Eight of the ten kids had families with **more girls than boys** in it. Six of the ten kids were the youngest child of the family and all of them were girls.
3. Eight of the ten kids had a parent or close relative who **practiced the occult**. These kids didn't practice it, but this shows again that when a family member practices it, the next generation pays.
4. All ten of these kids' mothers also had encounters. This supports my conclusion that the primary reason that children have encounters is more **generational** than anything else.

The fact that these two lists are almost identical supports my conclusion that the common denominators for those who have encounters can be tied to the "big three." Take away these three things from any family, and encounters are virtually non-existent.

Break It Down

As I was working on this very chapter of the book I received a call from someone who was babysitting her granddaughter (who just so happens to be included in the top ten secret friends list I just reviewed). I was already well aware of the some of the things this little girl had shared with her mom and grandmother. But my friend told me that if I wanted to talk to her myself, to come over.

I spent the first half an hour chatting with Tara's grandmother and noticed that Tara was slapping her own head and pulling her own hair a lot. Tara's grandmother told me that this was something that had just started up. I suspected that her secret friend had something to do with this change, so I asked her about it. She said that "Bob" told her to do it. Bob is her secret friend.

I then asked, "Does Bob pull your hair?" Tara said that he did. Next I asked her, "Does Bob hit you in the head?" Again she said yes. I turned it into a game of sorts, with me pointing to other parts of my own body to trip her up. She passed with flying colors. I pointed to my knee and asked if Bob hit her there. Then I asked her if Bob hits her in the arm, so forth and so forth. Every time I picked a different part of my own body and asked if Bob hit her there, she said no. All she would say yes to was the hair pulling and head slapping.

"Does Bob tell you to say bad words?" I asked.

"Yes," the little girl replied.

Tara's grandmother looked like she was going to cry when I asked the next question. "Is Bob mean to you?" Her exact words were, "He throws me on floor." That should shoot right through the heart of any parent. Here was an innocent three-year-old who couldn't protect herself. I also asked her if Bob was mean to her two-year-old brother. She said yes to that as well.

After a short break, we chatted some more. I asked her one more question, because Tara's grandmother has shared with me that on one occasion when she was changing Tara's diaper, there were some unusual marks on her backside. I asked her if Bob ever slapped her bottom. "Yes," she said. But then she added, "I slap Bob, too." Then Tara demonstrated how she slapped Bob. Her demonstration reminded me of how professional sports players slap a teammate's backside during a game. It also reminded me of another girl who told her dad that her secret friend pinches her backside.

Demonic Motives

I speculate that three things are happening when kids are visited by demonic creatures during the night. And I base this speculation on one underlying assumption—they must have a motive. They just don't cross over from the spiritual world and pop through their portal into a kid's bedroom by accident. In my opinion this is what is happening:

Because Satan rebelled against God and fell, he has one chief motivation—to keep us as far away from God as possible, in our minds, wills, and emotions. Satan wants our minds. That's why everything he is motivated to do is contrary to God and his Word. That is why Satan and his army of evil spirits concentrate on young kids. He knows that children in their earliest years are the most impressionable.

Both my sons went fishing with me early in their lives; now, both are avid fishermen. Both my sons learned to golf young in life. Now both are avid golfers; in fact, one of my sons went to college to pursue a career in golf management. They bowed their heads with us at supper time to thank God for our meal every night—even as they sat in their high chairs not totally understanding what we were doing or why we were doing it.

They're not perfect. My oldest son on occasion will let a curse word fly out of his mouth. I believe the reason for that is that he was two years old when I accepted Christ into my life. During his first two years I was in the Marines and I had a terrible military mouth. When I accepted Christ into my life my son already had his dose of potty mouth that unfortunately came from me. That cleared up quick for me and then, when my next son was born, he never heard me speak like that. To this day I have never heard my youngest son swear once. He is now eighteen years old and I am glad God cleaned up my military mouth for his sake.

Evil spirits are around young kids and they long to be part of the shaping process. They are evil sculptors and want to adversely affect a child early in life, trying to lock in their investment long-term, shaping them during their most impressionable years. Author Frank Hammond believes spirits go after kids with amazing intensity. In his book, *Pigs in the Parlor*, he says this about kids being attacked. "Evil spirits have no sense of fairness. They never hesitate to take full advantage of times of weaknesses in a person's life. Of course the weakest time in most lives is childhood. A child is completely dependent upon others for protection. Without question the majority of demons encountered through ministry have entered the person during childhood."

They (*evil*) seek to **manipulate impressionable young minds**. In many cases the children aren't even old enough to understand good and evil. Everything that demons do and how they do it is beyond me, but there sure is enough proof that they can even manipulate our dreams. We know they can get into our heads. When I think of small children being told to harm their siblings, it is obvious the forces of evil are at work.

I mentioned Aaron, earlier, and how his secret friend told him to kill himself. That type of thing is undeniable proof that sinister forces are at work, carrying out Satan's role as the thief who comes to steal, and kill, and destroy (that's the way Jesus described him in John 10:10). This is a long-term investment on the part of evil, teaching children wrong thinking, scaring them, filling their minds with dark and obscene things, hoping that they will hold on to these things all their lives.

Assuming that demonic forces do have motives, it seems logical that they are **scoping things out.** Think of it as an evil form of reconnaissance. Evangelist Billy Graham, in his book *Angels*, says, "Angels probably know things about us that we do not know about ourselves." What's true of good angels is also true of evil ones. They are not omniscient, so in order to know things about us they have to be near us. If they can gather intelligence they will know how to best attack and oppress us. They will know our weaknesses. This is a war and when war is being waged, knowing the opponent is crucial to influencing the outcome. They need an advantage so they mine us for information, starting earlier than most people would think possible.

They also want to **intimidate or scare us.** This was driven home for me when they retaliated against people I was trying to help break their bondage. When these people for the first time in their lives opened a Bible or said a prayer, evil demonstrated its power and abilities. The scaring element has a long-term effect on young children that leaves an emotional scar that will stay with them for many years to come. If you don't believe these encounters change a child, ask the parents of teenagers who still end up in their parents' bed at night because of what scared them in their own bedrooms.

One more reason could be given for them showing up, but I have to be cautious with this speculation. They are there, in some cases, **to harm these young kids.** For example, one young girl told her mom her secret friend throws her on the floor. One young boy had a slap mark on his face after spending time alone in his own bedroom.

Have no doubt: This is real. When a five-year-old boy names his secret friend, whom he has seen at the bottom of the stairs, then, ten years later, another little child names the same spirit to his mom, and describes an encounter at the bottom of the same staircase, it cannot be imaginary. If you blow off these secret friends as totally imaginary, you are ignoring something very sinister, and leaving your own child at their mercy to do what they want to them.

And you should never forget the story of Tom who had a secret friend named Ted. What are the chances that thirty years later his own son would have a secret friend named Ted? Zero. These simply cannot be a random set of coincidences. There can be no doubt that evil has paid attention to this family for a span of over thirty years.

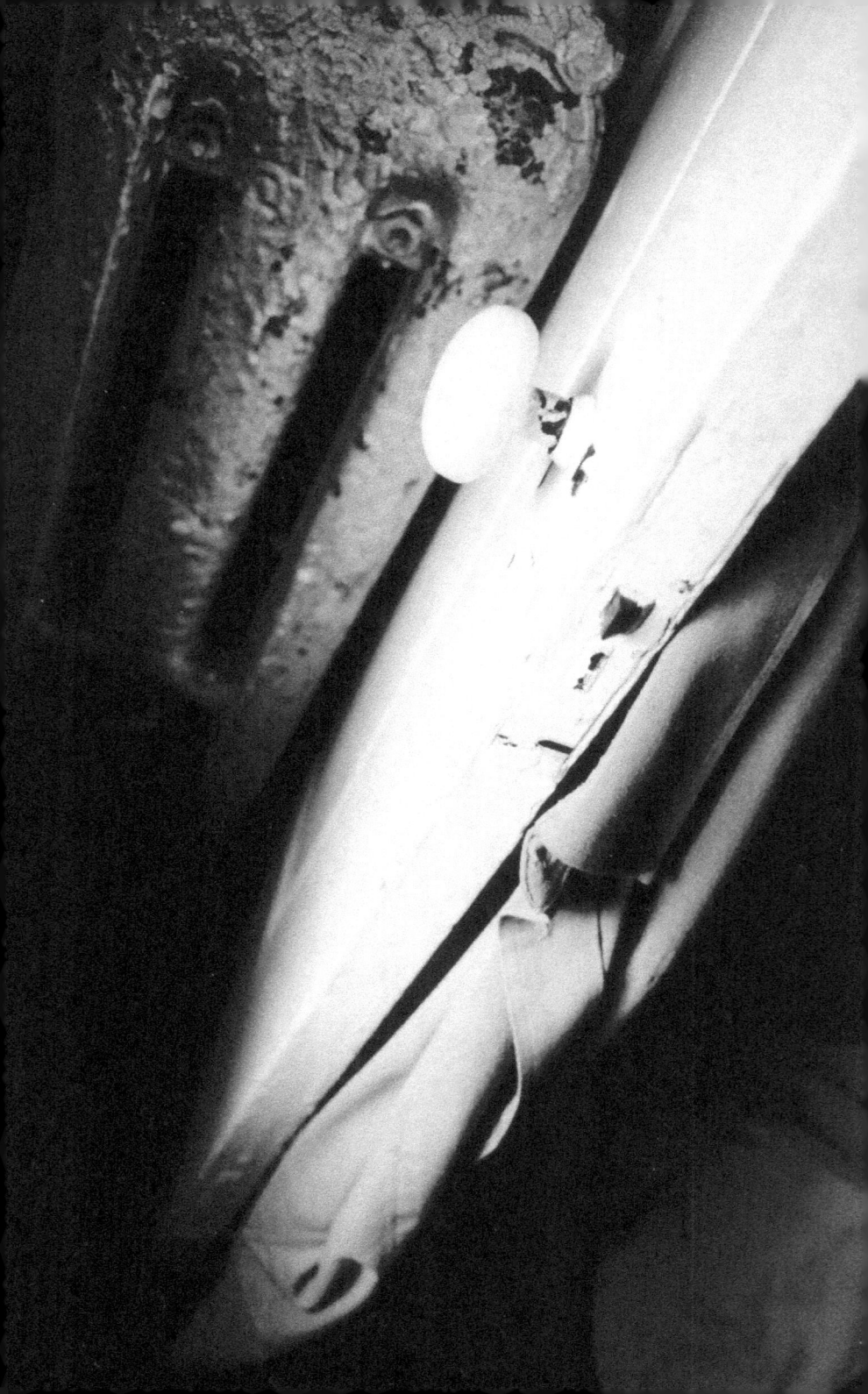

CHAPTER 15

Bumpy Ride Ahead

When I started this project, I knew that I might open a pretty big can of worms. I even had a local pastor tell me that I should back off. He was right about being careful, but I didn't agree with him on backing off.

I don't detect anywhere in Scripture where Jesus or his disciples backed away from evil. And judging from many self-professed Christians I have talked to, most pastors ought to address this subject more often from their pulpits. It is amazing and alarming to discover how ignorant believers are when it comes to how evil operates.

When I hear long-time Christians say that they have good spirits in their home, there is a problem. If the church or church leadership won't address this, understandably we will have helpless believers in the pews, ill equipped and uneducated when it comes to matters involving evil. Charles Kraft even brought this up in his book, *Defeating Dark Angels*. Right up front he said, "Sadly, many people have found no help in their churches or from psychologists and counselors." This isn't because their churches and counselors don't want to help. They just don't know how—or they are afraid of what they will find if they start digging into it.

Let me share two examples where church leadership was sought to help someone with their problems with evil, and they both backed off. One church leader hung up the phone on a guy and the other leader was afraid to walk into a particular home. Trust me, it's more prudent to realistically respect evil spirits than to pretend they don't exist. But as followers of Christ and as his representatives in this situation, we don't have to be afraid. More on this later.

Direct Retaliation

Let's return to Jeanie's case (Chapter 8) for a moment. Jeanie had moved to a different house and immediately had problems with spirits. One night, she invited my wife and me to come talk with her family about what was happening. I spent a good hour talking with her girls and at the same time, letting them pour their hearts out to me on what was going on with all of them. Each of them shared story after story, and I couldn't help but wonder what life is like for those who can't even get a good night's sleep. One of the daughters shared that sleep is something she never gets. I asked to go upstairs to see her room, the room everyone said gave them the creeps.

All of us went upstairs and nosed around. (Incidentally, my wife, Michelle, told me on our ride home that something was behind her on the stairs as we went upstairs.) After checking things out I asked Jeanie and Melody to stay upstairs while Michelle took the other girls downstairs. All three of us bowed our heads at the top of the stairs, just outside Melody's room and starting praying. (Remarkably, their dog started barking loudly when we did this.)

When I finished praying Jeanie said, "Something hit me in my back during the prayer." I then asked Melody to lift her mom's shirt up in the back to see if there were any scratch marks. Sure enough, there were three scratch marks going from shoulder blade to shoulder blade—direct retaliation in its truest form.

Melody starting pacing about on the top of the staircase and asked if we could go downstairs. She said something was next to her as we prayed. So we went downstairs and discovered that a spirit had manifested downstairs while we were praying upstairs. Katherine saw it in her bedroom while she was talking to Michelle in the living room. She said it was the same old man she was always seeing.

We didn't share with the younger girls what had happened upstairs—I left that to the mom's discretion. We did talk some more and decided to pray one more time before we left. We all stood and held hands in a circle in the living room. As soon as I started praying, the dog let loose barking again as if something was there. That of course, we weren't sure of. But after all that had happened that night, I expect that evil was watching and not at all happy about what we all were doing.

As of this writing we are all still engaged with addressing Jeanie's problems. The next few nights after the one just described brought more encounters for the family. Jeanie had her leg grabbed as she walked from the kitchen to the living room. Katherine has also been having problems. She said that someone was actually in bed with her two nights after our visit. She laid there and watched as her blankets were moving by themselves. And she said that items in her room were disappearing and reappearing quite often. She even messaged me, saying a strange hair brush had shown up on her sink one morning. It belongs to no one in the family.

Demonic Scare Tactics

Demonic retaliation is actually not what most people envision it being. I prefer to call it demonic scare tactics or showing off. When they don't like the way something is going or they see someone making the smallest of steps toward God, they manifest; in other words, they cross over from the spiritual side to our physical side. When someone shows the slightest hint of exploring what God has to say about all this they will make their presence known very quickly.

With my wife, Michelle, close by my side watching and listening to me interact with many people for this project, her viewpoint started changing. By that I mean for the first time in her life she realized that many of her own encounters may not have been good. She started understanding through Scripture, that the events were demonic. As her understanding shifted, her encounters diminished in number. The truth will set you free and that was very apparent in her case.

Michelle became eager to pass this understanding on to her children, to help them stop their own encounters. As her focus changed, she started talking to them about her new understanding. She actually became quite brazen with them and asked them how their relationship with God was. The scare tactics soon followed.

Ray

Ray is Michelle's twenty-one-year-old daughter. She is a very conscientious and at times can be quite mischievous. Her and her fiancé have a three-year-old girl and a five-year-old boy, and it is easy to tell that she loves them greatly. She is a very devoted mom and has a heart of gold. She is alone most of the time because her fiancé works out of state and is rarely home. She is a very open and honest person, admitting that sometimes her imagination may be playing tricks on her, especially when Jon is gone.

Like the rest of the family, she has a history of seeing things and hearing strange noises on a regular basis. When she was eight years old she awoke to find a young girl entering her bedroom through the wall with school books in hand. This spirit exited through another wall, simply vanishing. She remembers turning over very quickly and hiding under her blankets.

She has extremely vivid dreams and used to sleep walk. She was in an abusive relationship before she met Jon and it turned her into a recluse of sorts. She is content staying in her house and keeping away from the world. She told me the worst place she ever lived was in the apartments in Hermansville—where there were footsteps and running sounds coming from places where no one should be.

Michelle decided that since Jon was working out of state it would be safer for her to move closer to family. So in the transition of moving closer to us, Ray and the kids stayed in our home for a month. Ray was somewhat of an atheist, so talking to her about the unseen was relatively rare. Other than being forced to open a Bible at her Grandma's house, she admits she never really has read from the Bible. But one night the subject came up and we all started talking. Before we were done that evening, Ray did a little reading out of the Bible.

As the night ended, Ray was still sitting there reading, and for the first time in many years she was understanding things better. Her atheist mindset was starting to change. Maybe it was just a baby step, but it was an important step nonetheless. She had actually admitted to reading a little a few weeks prior to that, but it was more to appease us than anything else. But that night in our house she actually was letting it soak in. I could see her wheels spinning; it was obvious it was affecting her.

The next day Michelle and I had to run somewhere for a few

hours. When we got back to the house, Ray was crying and the others looked like they were close to crying. I had never seen her sob and shake like she was.

She explained that as she was sitting on the bed in Gina's room, she looked over at the doorway to see a tall dark shadowy figure walking away from her. It turned just as she caught a glimpse of it. All she saw was its back as it walked away. No one else had seen it. She actually thought someone had entered our home, so she grabbed a knife and started searching. There was no one in the house. Once she realized that what she had seen was not of this world, she broke down and started crying hysterically.

To me it was obvious that whatever this was, it didn't like the idea of her reading God's Word, especially now that what she was reading was sinking in. They knew it and they didn't like it. I believe it was a scare tactic of sorts. This figure had never showed up before to her. Then again, she'd never read the Bible with sincerity before, either.

Breanna

Michelle's next youngest daughter is Bre, a beautiful, petite little fireball that doesn't like to be backed into a corner. When I look into her eyes, I can't help but think that she wants to explode and live life.

When Bre lived in the same apartments her sister used to live in, she often saw little kids running around the apartment—kids that shouldn't have been there, especially seeing that the door was locked and no one could possibly get in. Little kids voices were commonly heard as well. One of these little kids even touched Bre's head while she was lying in bed. The sound of footsteps above them in the attic happened quite a bit.

Not long ago, Bre and her two kids stayed with us for a few nights just to visit. Just as with Ray, we started talking about some of the recent things that had happened. Bre's children, who are one and two years old, seem to have a problem sleeping. They cry a lot and have what I would even call night terrors. They have at times pointed or looked under the bed as they cried, like something was intentionally scaring them.

Anyway, we were all engaged in a very deep talk when Bre started reading from the gospel of John. I had suggested to her that for someone who is just opening the Bible for the first time (or young in the faith) it is the perfect place to start. She read that night and had an uneventful night while at our house. But things took a turn once she got home with the kids the next day.

The following night, Bre was back at her apartment in Hermansville. She was alone there with her kids, since her boyfriend was in Chicago selling Christmas trees. I told her before she left our house that if her kids woke up crying again in the middle of the night, that she should drop to her knees right there next to the crib and pray about it. "Why not give God a chance?" I suggested.

At midnight the next night, just like clockwork, the kids started screaming in their room. She went in to try to calm them down. She decided to stay in the room with them, sleeping on the floor. She also prayed for them and couldn't believe that the children slept the next four hours without waking. Then at 4 a.m. they (*evil*) made their presence known. The kids were crying once again. This time as she prayed for them next to the crib, a shelf came off the wall that was next to the crib. It landed on the floor next to her, almost hitting her in the leg. It is possible (though not likely) that the shelf came off the wall by itself. But what happened next couldn't be explained away as easily.

After the shelf came down, Bre went into the kitchen to fill a baby bottle. As she entered the kitchen, two soda cans flew out of the corner at her. They just didn't fall out of the corner they were in, *they came flying across the kitchen at her*. I inspected the corner these cans were in and they couldn't have just flown at her, somehow. In my opinion that shelf didn't just fall, somehow, either. The shelf and can episode happened just minutes apart, leaving me to conclude that they (*evil*) did not like Bre praying.

In his book, *Demons and Spiritual Warfare*, Ron Phillips mentions the Prominent German pastor, Kurt Koch. Rev. Koch and a German psychiatrist named Alfred Lechler researched demonization in Germany. They came to these four conclusions in regards to determining if actual demons were involved with a particular individual:

- resistance to the Bible,
- falling into a trance-like state,
- opposition to prayer, and,
- a negative reaction to Jesus' name.

Their research had more to do with finding out if people were actually possessed by evil, but the parallels are obvious in the cases just cited. In both Ray's and Bre's situations, prayer and the Bible were involved. Even though possession is not involved with these two young women, the findings of Koch and Lechler still apply. When these women did anything that showed a reliance on God, or when they turned to God via prayer or his Word, they (*evil*) showed their disapproval. When these brave young women took a step in the right spiritual direction, something didn't like it one bit.

Angelina

Gina is my wife, Michelle's, youngest daughter. She is tall, beautiful, full of life, and we pick on each other constantly. [I always tell her that picking on someone is a sign that you love them.] With her I have for the first time in my life understood why some dads stand on their porch with a shotgun when a new boyfriend comes to visit. I am very protective of her and yes, I do own a shotgun.

With Gina things are at a little higher level of activity. My research has shown that for some reason they (*evil*) prefer to pick on the youngest girl in the family the most. She was home alone a few years ago when she was paid a visit by a tall dark figure similar to what Ray saw more recently. [Gina and some friends also saw this dark figure another time as well. In that situation, though, five people verify seeing this figure.]

Gina sleep walks and occasionally wakes up not in her bed or in very strange positions in her bed. She has also had some dreams that have come true. These spirits like to mess with her cell phone once in a while as well. She has awakened to find her cell phone across the room with pictures on it that she never took. She heard a lot of unexplained noises when she was at her sister's apartment in Hermansville. She's told me that those were the worst years of her life in terms of dealing with the inexplicable ["paranormal"].

Recently, Gina was upstairs in her bedroom. She came downstairs and told us that she had heard footsteps upstairs, which prompted me to give Michelle a Bible to bring up there. It was opened to Psalm 18, which talks about God being our shield. Michelle brought it upstairs and set it next to Gina's bed. Seconds later, Gina was back downstairs saying that she heard something knocking on the door of her room. She was the only one up there. Once again we have one of Michelle's daughters doing something that they (*evil*) didn't like. They quickly showed their disapproval by scaring her. Granted, she had already heard the footsteps before the knocks, but I am sure the knocks happened because of the Bible's presence in her room.

These three examples could easily be written off as coincidence, spread out over the stretch of several months. Some people might even say that this family is just "sensitive" to the other side. This is something I have heard quite often since I started my research. I think that most people who say this either don't want to face the reality of evil all around us, or they are afraid to do so. With that in mind I want to share two more stories that are similar to the ones I just shared, the point being that the minute the enemy sees ground being taking back they will sometimes put on a real show.

Monica

I met Monica through a mutual friend. She is a Native American girl in her teens who has been through things that I wouldn't wish on my worst enemy, including physical abuse, a sexual assault, a terrible home life, and depression. And she is a cutter [i.e. she cuts herself]. She has endured so much that I sense that she wants it all over with. She told me that her best friend committed suicide while she was on the phone with him. I can only imagine the pain this poor young girl carries after something like that.

She also has a lot going on in her bedroom at night. Shortly before she was sexually assaulted, someone or something attacked her in her own bedroom. She came out of her bathroom and got tackled by this invisible entity. She said it felt like she was being choked during the attack (a very common tactic with demons). She also told me that she will never forget the bad odor in her room that night, another common effect when a demon is present.

She has awakened to blood and scratches on her body; she hears wind chimes and chains as well. She used to hear a little kid's voice when she was younger, but those encounters have since ended. She is plagued by constant dreams about her friend who took his own life. A lot of times he is standing there in her dreams looking at her with black stuff oozing out of his eyes.

Since we started corresponding, she has had new stories as well. She sent me a message a few weeks ago at three in the morning, a common time for demonic activity. She said she had been awakened by being choked again. She looked in the mirror later and saw scratches on her head. Whatever this was also spoke to her that night saying, "He will kill you." [Others have spoken of hearing such death threats. One woman told me that, the night after we talked, she heard a voice say, "We could hang her."]

Up until this point, I had not brought up anything about God to Monica. But recently, God did come up in our conversation. She keeps telling me she wants to change, but says point blank she doesn't want to be a Bible thumper. I reminded her that she had gone to see a priest some months earlier about these very issues she was having, even admitting to me that after her visit with him a few of her problems had improved. I told her that she could expect her problems to continue unless she wants to change, not just talk about it. I shared with her Matthew 10:39:

Whoever finds their life will lose it, and whoever loses their life for my sake will find it.

Her response to me after sharing that verse was, "Gah," which I took to mean she didn't want to be one of those types. When this conversation took place it was 5 a.m. She is a night owl and had been up all night. A lot of people I talk to who see things don't sleep well. That same day a revealing event in my own home proved that evil was paying attention to my conversations with Monica. It even shows how they may sometimes involve themselves in our dreams.

The Power Of The Enemy

Later that same night my wife awoke from a dream around 11 p.m. In her dream, she said I grabbed my Bible off the headboard and left our bedroom. She sat up because the dream seemed so real to her, and she looked over to find me still sleeping. Once she realized I was sound asleep she laid back down.

That same night, around 3:30 a.m., our daughter, Gina, dreamt that her brother was being dragged down the basement steps by something, but she couldn't really tell what had hold of him. Then, in her dream, she sat on our couch and lo and behold, a native girl entered her dream. Toward the end of this dream, the native girl was walking toward Gina with her arms extended out, crying. Imagine: Out of the millions of things someone can dream about, Gina dreamt about a native girl only a few hours after I had talked with Monica.

Gina awoke from this dream, troubled. As she lay there in bed, something started tapping on the wall in her bedroom. Her sister, Ray, and the kids were in the spare bedroom downstairs. So Gina went downstairs into Ray's room. Ray woke up when Gina crawled into the bed and immediately asked Gina why the bed was shaking. Whatever had scared Gina had followed her downstairs and was shaking the bed. Then it felt like someone kicked the side of the bed. Gina and Ray came across the hall and got Michelle, who went into the room with them. A few minutes after Michelle came back to our bed, at roughly 4 a.m., Ray's son said he saw a little boy by the doorway of their bedroom.

Then this experience took a very strange turn. After Ray's son saw the little boy in the doorway, Ray said I came in the room with my Bible in hand. She said it was about 4:30 when I did that. But I didn't even get out of bed that morning till after 5 a.m. And I never went into the spare bedroom. What are the chances of Ray seeing me walk into her room with a Bible in hand, and Michelle having a similar dream about me walking out of our room with a Bible?

My point is that, as it had been with Ray, Bre, and Gina, I had once again talked to someone about God and then the very same day something paranormal had happened. I had shared one Bible verse with Monica and touched briefly on how she needed to change her lifestyle. Evidently, that was enough to incite them to retaliate, and not only against me, against my whole family.

Simply put, they hate it when individuals whom they regard as "theirs" take even one small step toward God, so they act very quickly to put an end to it, using whatever scare tactics they can muster (and trust me, they have many in their arsenal).

Recap Of Their Power

When they retaliated against my family, they (*evil*) were showing us how they could involve five different lives in almost unbelievable fashion. Even though I was only involved indirectly, I was still a part of this amazing incident, which could not possibly have happened by coincidence. It must have happened by design. Let's recap the events of that twenty-four-hour period:

- That morning, around 5 a.m., I talk with the young native girl named Monica. I bring up God and share a Bible verse with her as well, and remind her of some past progress with the help of her priest.
- At approximately 11 p.m. that night, my wife, Michelle, dreams that I have taken the Bible off our headboard and left our bedroom with it in my hands. Around the same time she feels something pull on her foot while she is lying in bed.
- At about 3:30 a.m., Gina has a dream about a native girl crying. This wakes Gina. She is unaware that I had talked to a

native girl the previous morning. After she wakes, something scares her by tapping on her wall. Gina heads downstairs because she is frightened.
- Gina climbs into her sister, Ray's, bed and feels the bed shaking. Then it feels like someone is kicking the bed as well. Ray feels the shaking, too.
- Ray's four-year-old son wakes up around 4 a.m. and says there is a little boy standing in the doorway of the bedroom. Ray can't see this supposed child spirit.
- At 4:30 Ray sees me come in the bedroom with my Bible, just like in Michelle's dream five hours earlier. Ray rolls over, thinking that I have come in to pray about what had just happened.

I never went into the bedroom that morning. They (*evil*) were able to influence two separate dreams, both aligned with something that had actually happened. The more I think about the intricate details of that night the more I am left speechless.

This type of personal experience is something I would never think about sharing unless I had a good reason. Though I have been virtually clean of any activity for thirty years now, this had to be something like a shot across my bow (if I might use a nautical analogy). They (*evil*) didn't like me interfering in people's lives whom they had such a secure grip on. They must have viewed my efforts to help Monica as threatening, so they took retaliatory actions.

One of my favorite authors, Dr. Charles Kraft, stated that he is very careful when he is dealing with evil spirits. For example, when he is on the phone with someone who he feels has some kind of demonic presence around them, he says a prayer. The prayer usually centers around protection for the one he is counseling over the phone. He does this because he knows that evil is paying attention and he doesn't want his efforts thwarted. Having experienced even the level of retaliation I've just described, you may rest assured that prayer for protection for those I'm trying to help and those I love, is an even more crucial part of my own arsenal now than ever before.

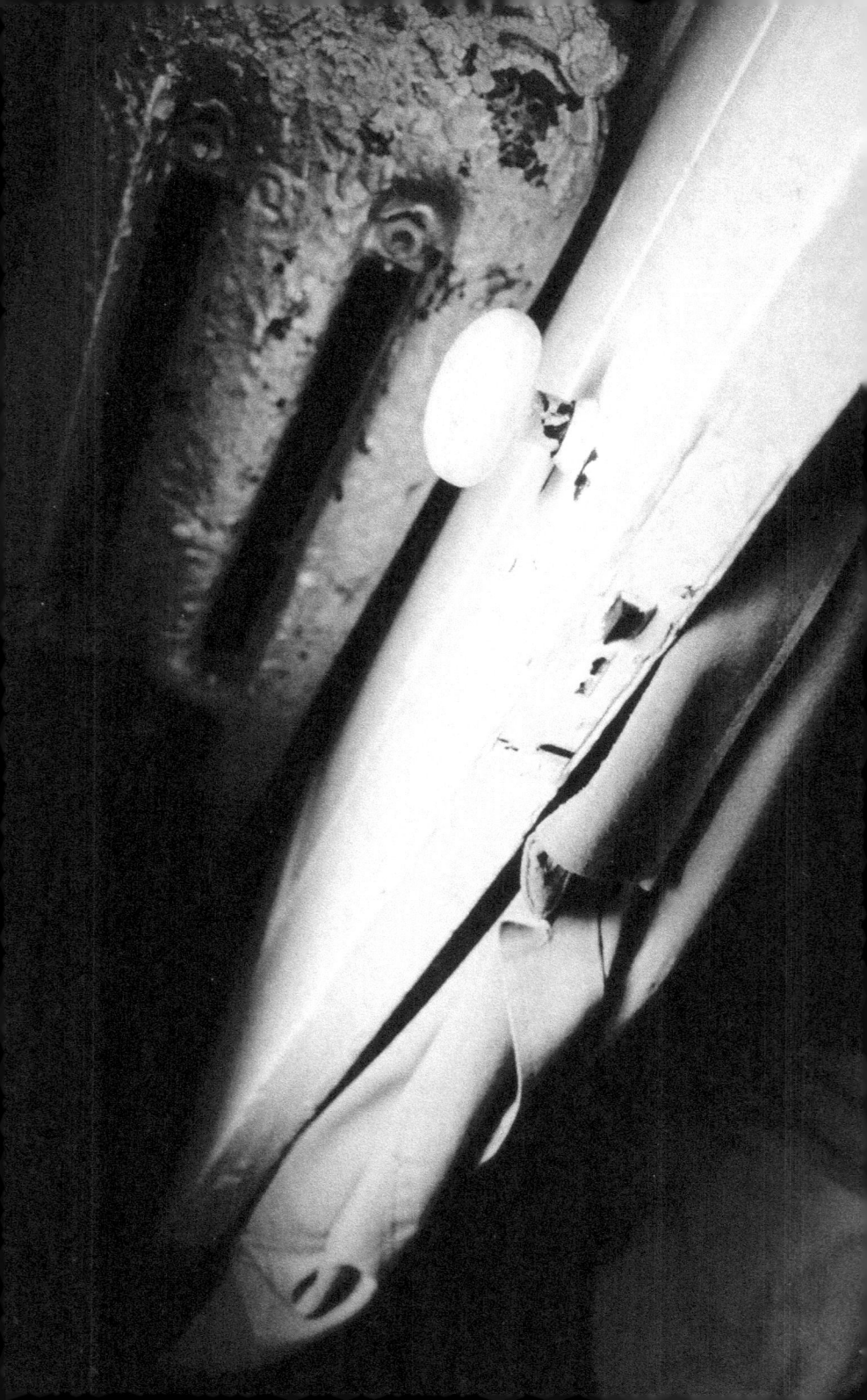

CHAPTER 16

What God Do You Worship?

Men like Dr. Charles Kraft, Neil T. Anderson, and Ron Philips, men who do battle with evil on a regular basis, all know and understand the importance of being right with God. If not, they would not stand a chance when dealing with these dark forces. We lay people have to understand this partnership with God as well. If God is absent in a person's life the battle with evil simply cannot be won. I feel one of the worst situations to be in is when someone "thinks" they are right with God but they aren't. It's like walking on two inches of ice when you think there are ten inches of ice below you. It's a false support system that you will only recognize when it's too late. This false sense of security became apparent with a few people I have dealt with in relation to demonic activity.

Amy grew up in a broken home, one of 261 broken homes I have come across so far in my personal research. Her stepmother physically abused Amy and her sister. Amy told me that the nights were the worst for them. Her real dad worked nights and it seemed that when he left for work her stepmother turned evil. Even the most minor of infractions led to some type of physical punishment. Amy told me that she would be lying in bed and could see her stepmom in the doorway to the bedroom staring at the girls as if she was brainstorming for a new way to hurt them. Amy remembers covering herself with the blankets hoping her stepmother would leave. But her stepmom wasn't the only one she had to worry about.

Amy and her sister were also sexually abused by an older family member. Amy said she was around six years old when this happened to her. But even that wasn't the end of it. There was one more monster lurking in the shadows of their bedroom.

She said that she and her sister were plagued by dark figures. They both spent many nights in their room watching these figures bounce around like they were racing each other from one wall to the other. And for some strange reason, they paid more attention to Amy's sister—something I've rarely heard of.

Amy's words to me were, "My sister finally quit fighting and learned to just do their bidding." This statement floored me. I asked her what she meant. Amy said that these spirits were sexually touching her sister. I know this is hard to believe but I've also heard it from others. Amy was only the second person to ever share something like this with me. I do have other cases where this sounds like it happened but it may be too painful and hard for these individuals to share with me.

For example, a number have said it felt like someone was lying on them while they were trying to go to sleep. Some of those told me that their blankets were moving while they felt this invisible heaviness. It is almost like they were being molested. I think that this unexplained heaviness so many experience is related to these spirits examining them or molesting them. Several women even told me that this spirit that was on them was hairy. How does a person imagine something invisible on top of them, yet know that it is hairy?

Getting back to Amy. She explained how the encounters continued for her into her teens. She even experienced what felt like a slap one time when no one was around her. She went and looked in the mirror and saw three scratch marks on her face. Demons tend to do things in threes for some reason. Some believe this to be a mockery of the holy trinity.

The Difference Should Be Christ

Amy told me that at age twelve she had accepted Christ into her life. That comment got my attention because as I interviewed hundreds of people, I was always hoping to hear about the change Christ can make in someone's life. She told me the attacks and encounters continued, though. In fact, she said, "The encounters actually got worse." That left me scratching my head, since Christ, and those who believe in him, have absolute authority over demons.

She became suicidal at age fourteen, continuing with that struggle until she was seventeen. She said that the suicidal thoughts seemed like real voices to her. [Hearing such voices is very common with others who have contemplated suicide.]

When she was nineteen she got married and soon after had two daughters. Shortly into the marriage, she learned that her husband was abusive. If he didn't get his way he would pin her against the wall, demanding she do what he wanted. When she started feeling scared for her life, she divorced him.

Having nowhere to go after the divorce, Amy moved in with family. It wasn't long after that when her kids were molested by a family member. Her one daughter now sees dark figures as well, though the daughter told me she does not want to talk about this.

Amy went on to marry two more times and is currently single. She told me she believed her most recent husband was possessed by his dead grandfather's spirit. He was also abusive, blaming the spirit possessing him for the abuse. That is when I began to think that she might not actually be a believer like she had claimed.

For one thing, the belief that a person can be possessed by a dead relative is unbiblical and has no chance of happening. Another reason I believe Satan still has some access to her life is that she still reads horoscopes. That is a sin in God's eyes. The last thing about her life that doesn't add up is that she still on occasion sees dark figures. She also shared with me that sometimes when she looks in the mirror she can see a set of piercing red-colored eyes looking back at her.

I am in no position to judge anyone and I also believe that I shouldn't try to do that. But in relation to seeing things and having encounters, I believe that if the hedge of God's protection is missing, then something may not be right in a person's spiritual life. Amy may also just not be spiritually mature enough, and therefore has allowed some footholds to remain in her life.

I believe that someone can be a believer and experience demonic oppression. They have attacked me as well. But I also believe that at age twelve she may not have really understood God's salvation plan. I think this happens to more people than most realize. Many believe they have trusted in Christ at a very young age; some even say they have been a believer their whole life. But at some point in their life any true believer must be spiritually mature enough to understand God's plan for salvation and what it really means to trust Christ for one's salvation (indeed, to entrust one's life to him). Of course there is nothing wrong with dedicating a child's life to God, as is practiced in many churches, and many have begun their walk with Christ a child at summer camp or Vacation Bible School, or in many other venues. But eventually each person must make or reaffirm a personal choice when he or she is mature enough to do so, and this is not a matter of age so much as spiritual discernment.

Satan's Crown Of Deception

What I'm saying is that a person may feel that God "has their back," when in reality, God may have withdrawn his protective hedge. That is why I call it Satan's crown of deception. Amy prays to God, yet she can't understand why it all continues. God is listening to her, but he is surely not pleased that she still relies on horoscopes for guidance. I don't say this being judgmental toward anyone. It is a cause for concern, though, when someone spiritually immature doesn't know what to do next or when they don't understand why things continue the wrong way for them. It may be simply that they think they are a believer when they are not.

A person may have given some footholds that allow evil to stick around and continue to harass them. Regardless of whether Amy is an immature Christian with footholds or not really a believer at all, Satan still has his claws in her to some degree and something needs to change in her life. If Satan has blinded her to his involvement in her life it unfortunately will go on with not much of a chance of things changing until she sees things as they truly are, spiritually speaking.

Dorothy

Dorothy's mother is someone I consider to be a devout Christian woman. I have sat across from her in many church committee meetings, been involved in youth programs with her, and witnessed her deep love for those around her. I mention these things because of where her daughter is today; specifically, where her mindset is today.

When Dorothy was six years old her father skipped town,

abandoning her and her mother. A few years later her mother remarried and tried to put their lives back together. It was shortly after they all moved in together that Dorothy's secret friend showed up. It reveals her emotional state of losing her dad and having a new one around. Evil feeds at this trough of instability, as has already been described.

Dorothy also mentioned that she was abused by her new stepfather, which haunted her for years. In terms of visitations, she described lying in bed and experiencing the heavy feeling that so many have happen to them. She remembers feeling suffocated, and that it felt like a literal person was lying on her.

Fast forward to the present: The language she uses to describe what happens to her today reveals that she is unaware that it could potentially be evil. She presently has a little girl (spirit) that lives in her house and Dorothy's granddaughter sees this same spirit as well. Her granddaughter, according to Dorothy, sees spirits no matter where she is. Sometimes Dorothy's television will change channels all by itself and turn on and off by itself as well.

She informs me that all this happens because she is in tune with the spirit world. On occasion she will hear voices in her house. These voices contribute to her mindset, causing her to believe she is just sensitive to the other side. She is unaware that the Bible clearly states that this is wrong and we are not to look on this as a gift, especially that it is a spiritual gift that God has bestowed on anyone.

You can't believe in God and his Word and still believe that all this activity in your house is from him or that it is good. The reason her house and loved ones experience all of this is because of a demonic foothold in their lives. In the same breath we can't pray to God as if he is the Lord of our lives and then ignorantly allow a demonic spirit to roam around. Whether you blame it on spiritual immaturity or not really being a believer, the bottom line is it is not right.

I will admit that with Dorothy's case it may be more of a generational curse. Even though Dorothy's mom is a devout Christian, this generational problem may be something that happened on her stepfather's side. I can say that with some confidence because I am aware of fifteen members of Dorothy's extended family on her stepfather's side who have issues seeing things as well. If this is not dealt with, the generational curse will continue for her future family members as well. So even though Dorothy has been involved with the church, her belief that her spirit guests are good is exactly where Satan wants her to believe.

Here is my point, in bold print: **If we claim to be followers of Jesus, and our home or a family member is visited by something from the other side, something in our lives has to be reexamined.** If God has removed his protective hedge, then something is amiss. Satan has us duped and knows we will continue to let it go on with no interest in stopping it. As long as we continue with the line of thinking that it may be something good, they (*evil*) have free access to roam our homes.

Angelic Protection

Are not all angels ministering spirits sent to serve those who will inherit salvation? **(Hebrews 1:14).**

Please look hard at this verse. It says that angels serve those who will *inherit salvation!* It does not say these angels are sent to just anyone. Clearly, angels are only sent as ministering spirits to those who are saved. I believe that one way they serve believers is that they are part of that protective hedge God puts around those who love him. I believe that angels protect us from Satan and his minions. If evil spirits are running rampant in someone's house then I question if they really are believers. While Christians can be oppressed, if someone truly has been born again they will have angelic protection, and the oppression will cease.

Part of the blame for the relative ignorance of some Christians in relation to doctrines related to hell, Satan, and his minions falls on the churches they have attended. Of course two people can hear the same teaching but take away different levels of understanding. But in some churches today, pastors tend to shy away from preaching on the "tough" subjects and doctrines. Pastors don't want to rock the boat and cause some to leave in search of someone not as likely to make them uncomfortable. In terms of teachings about Satan and demons, some don't want to scare their congregation. Of course, these are very difficult subjects to preach on, but that is still no excuse to avoid them. Pastors should take the time to better prepare their flock from the unavoidable collision with evil that happens to more people than most will ever understand.

God's Word Uncovers Darkness

My mother spent her latter years with a Bible in front of her on the living room table, which warmed my heart. I would go to visit her and loved seeing her reading glasses out on the end of her nose as she tore into God's Word. I even purchased a large print Bible for her as her eyes were getting bad due to her diabetes. I remember a lot of our conversations at the dining room table. One of the most common things I would hear my mother say was this, "I never knew that everything I used to do was wrong." She was slowly but surely seeing the error of her ways after all those years of practicing the occult. And during her last years, she accepted Christ as her personal Savior.

God worked in her heart those final years and I can only imagine what our lives as kids would have been like if that had been true earlier. If she had known from God's Word that she was putting us in harm's way, so much of our struggle would have been avoided. Granted, we could have still exercised our free will and gone down the wrong road in life. But we, at a much earlier age, would have been grounded in the truth.

Hebrews 4:12 says: ***For the word of God is alive and active. Sharper than any double-edged sword, it penetrates even to dividing soul and spirit, joints and marrow; it judges the thoughts and attitudes of the heart.*** When I think of this verse it reminds me of what could have been. Even though I know that hindsight is 20-20, I still wish someone had shown my mother back then that what she was doing was wrong. God's Word would have been alive and active in our family's life instead of evil spirits pulling the blankets off of my sister as she tried to fall asleep. Or when my mom spent time with friends and family, what would have happened if she had brought her Bible instead of that Ouija board? Would my cousin have been spared the encounter with her dark figure, the one that watched her from the end of her bed as a teenager?

Perhaps my cousin might not have killed himself had he grown up with a Bible in his hand. Of course I can only speculate on what could have been. This particular cousin spent a lot of time living with us and was more like a brother. Maybe things would have been different had he not been subjected to evil spirits being around. Only God knows that.

I believe my sister would not have had all those dark figures around her at her lowest point, the night she contemplated suicide. She probably wouldn't have even gotten to that point had she known God's love for her all of her life.

These and other questions never stop spinning in my mind. I believe that if God's Word had been present in our family's life growing up many of the other ills that plagued us would have been absent. Would all five of us kids have suffered through a divorce if God's Word would have been sown in our hearts at an early age?

Would all five of us kids have felt the effects of depression if God's Word and his love were fed to us instead of the influence of evil spirits? I am talking about my immediate family here, not all the rest of my extended family, though they can be included with the "what if's" as well. It's not productive to dwell on the "what if's" too much, but it sure makes my wheels spin to no end.

I have nine cousins who have suffered with seeing demonic beings as well. And I suspect that most of the others ones have, but they won't talk about it, so I have to assume that I'm correct. Depression, sexual abuse, divorce, kids out of wedlock, teenage pregnancy, encountering spirits, and a lot of the other ills of life plagued our entire extended family. I am not trying to say that my mom's actions caused all of this. I know my mother didn't make her extended family take the wrong fork in the road; that was ultimately their choice. But I would like to think that if she had focused on the Bible instead of that Ouija board, much of what I just mentioned might not have happened. Once the dark door is opened, evil moves right in and takes over entire families. No one seems to get spared. God has no choice but to remove his protective hedge when we as adults choose horoscopes, Ouija boards, tarot cards, and questionable lifestyles over his Word.

The More The Merrier

Let me summarize what can happen to families when they allow evil in. Our family, my parents and my four siblings, spent time with eighteen families over the years, by which I mean that these eighteen families are either close extended family or close friends —people that my parents made it a point to spend a lot of time with, all of whom lived in southern Wisconsin or Upper Michigan. Out of those eighteen families, sixteen of them have had issues with seeing spirits, I believe due to my mother's practices. Obviously this wasn't all my mother's fault, but she was a part of the problem and may have made things worse for these families.

The only two families that had no problems had one distinct difference from all the others mentioned. They are born again believers. The mother of one of these families was Kerri. When I contacted Kerri, she informed me that my mom had indeed broken out some tarot cards once at her house. But when Kerri told my mom flat out that it was wrong, my mom put them away. My parents continued to be friends with them, but Kerri refused to allow the Ouija board or tarot cards in her home. As a result, they have not had any problems with spirits in their home.

The other family with no problems is my aunt and uncle on my dad's side. They are believers, and I am convinced that, because of their faith, they didn't have issues either. Surely it is no coincidence that the only two families with no issues were Bible believing Christians.

Our only defense against this type of evil is to be grounded in God's Word. When we have his Word to direct our paths, evil runs into a brick wall. It cannot penetrate God's protective hedge around those who are his own. His Word helps us steer through life better equipped to handle whatever evil throws at us. Remember . . . each time Satan tempted Jesus in the wilderness, Jesus used Scripture to turn him away.

The two families I just mentioned were families that were already grounded in God's Word, families that never gave evil any type of foothold to work with. But even if a family has allowed evil into their lives, it's never too late. As the next chapter shows, even if a family's history is littered with encounter after encounter, when God enters the picture, evil has to flee, just like James 1:7 says: **Submit yourselves, then, to God. Resist the devil, and he will flee from you.**

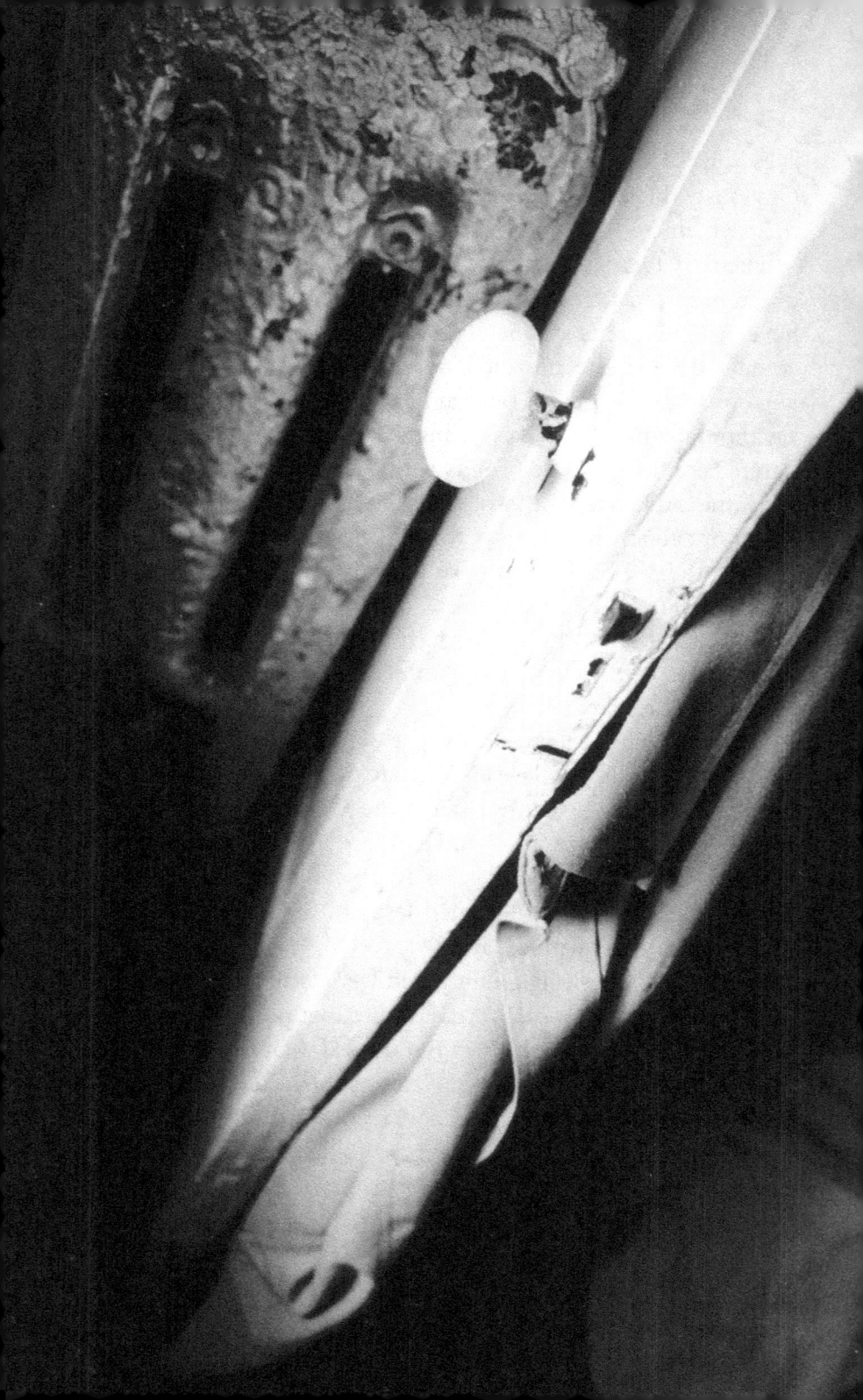

CHAPTER 17

Kicking Them Out

I met Harriet through a mutual friend and it didn't take me long to find out that she had faced many struggles. Her parents divorced when she was young and her father had a substance abuse problem that contributed to the break up. She came from a family with four girls in it (no brothers). She admitted that she had messed with a Ouija board a few times while she was in middle school. So Harriet had the three biggest contributors to evil activity in anyone's home—divorce, the occult, and more girls than boys in the family. This is one reason evil pounced upon her quickly.

She told me that she had always felt watched and also that she had felt darkness around her. This convinced me that something was attached to her as she grew up. She said that as far back as elementary school she could remember strange things happening to her. Harriet also confided in me that she was abused as a child; in fact, she and several of her sisters were sexually abused when they were younger.

Harriet also suffers from depression and anxiety attacks, which is quite common with people who see things—they seem to go hand in hand. She said that a couple of her aunts were into the occult, mostly tarot cards. This influence typically gets passed down to future generations, as it did in Harriet's case.

Like many other young girls who see dark figures, she had also experienced the strange heaviness, as if someone or something invisible was lying on her, when she was in bed. But she added a twist that I had never heard before. She said she was lying in bed when she was a teenager and felt something land on her. She said she froze and watched as her blankets were moving. Whatever had landed on her was now molesting her. An invisible intruder was taking advantage of her at a very young age.

Levitating Chairs

Roughly eight years ago Harriet decided to go see a local pastor, in hopes of it turning into counseling for her and her husband. She told me it didn't take long before the conversation with this pastor turned from her personal problems to the darkness in her life. As she shared her experiences with this pastor, he told her that they should probably spend some time in prayer about the evil rooted in her past. I wish this pastor was still in the area; we need more like him around.

They bowed their heads and started praying. In the middle of the prayer the pastor excused himself and left the room. He returned after a few minutes and continued the prayer. When they finished, Harriet asked him why he had left. The pastor said that during the prayer if felt like someone was trying to rip his chest open, and he actually felt his chair come off the floor. Clearly, whatever demonic entity was attached to Harriet attacked the pastor during his prayer. Evil doesn't like it when anyone tries to recapture ground that they have worked so hard to claim. I am thankful that there are still men out there who aren't afraid to do battle with Satan.

Since that day, Harriet has not had one episode with evil. She is an active participant in a local church and proof that this type of life can end for anyone that wants it to. It's worth noting that Harriet wasn't evil or a terrible person. She is a respected member of the community who never felt the need to discuss her past. She wasn't running into dark figures constantly. But she did recognize that things were not right in her life and she stepped forward to make a change. Thankfully, she was able to connect with a pastor who could help her.

Alicia

Several years ago, I met Alicia. As I began to do research for this book, she caught wind of it, and started sharing stories with me about things that happen to her during the dark of the night. Alicia lived with her mom in Hermansville, Michigan, a place I call "spook central," because of the approximately fifty stories I've garnered from folks living in or near that small town.

Alicia's mom, Mary, had some history with the occult because her mother occasionally did tarot cards and was adamant about reading her horoscope every day. Mary's encounters always seemed to happen in her bedroom, and she left the TV on all night long to drown out the common, unexplainable noises she heard nightly. Her encounters were always "friendly." For example, one night she claimed to have seen a woman holding a baby in her arms. She believed this to be Mary with the baby Jesus. Another encounter she had was with her own father. She woke to her hair being brushed aside, followed by a kiss on the forehead—something her dad would do to her when she was a little girl as he tucked her in for bed.

In her own bedroom no more than fifteen feet away, Alicia was battling her own set of problems. Her night life was as active as I have ever come across; specifically, her dream life often included dreams that would come true. Many nights these vivid dreams would wake her up. Once she dreamed about planes crashing into some tall buildings. This dream happened about a week before our country was attacked by terrorists who targeted the World Trade Center buildings in New York City. I believe it is safe to say she was dialed into the spirit world.

Alicia also had an ongoing problem with waking up in strange places. One particular morning she woke up clear across her bedroom, lying on the floor next to her bedroom door. All of her bedding was with her. Her pillow and blankets had come along for the ride. Some mornings she would wake up with her head at the wrong end of her bed. What was strange about these bedroom habits was that she could recall having horrible dreams the previous night—dreams of decaying faces and what she described to me as "zombie" looking figures were common the nights she moved around in her room.

Sleepwalking

What troubled Mary most was her daughter Alicia's sleepwalking. Many nights Mary would wake up to find Alicia standing over her bed just staring at her. Mary got the feeling that it wasn't even her daughter standing there, as if she had been taken over by something, especially since she was unresponsive the whole time she stood there. Then she would turn and go back to her own bed and lie down. Mary followed Alicia any time she was aware she was sleepwalking, fearing that Alicia would unlock the door and go outside.

As the three of us talked, I stated that nothing I was hearing, even the stories of Mary's dad showing up, sounded good to me. Of course this wasn't well received by Mary, who loved that her dad was checking up on her. But as I shared Scripture with her she began to understand it all a little better. Mary is a believer and she trusted in the Word of God. For the first time in her life she actually heard Scripture that proved we couldn't come back to earth when we passed on.

From that day forward the encounters for Mary and Alicia tapered off. Mary herself studied the Bible a little closer in regards to these spirits and finally came to an understanding that the encounters were demonic in nature. She actually became angry that evil spirits were mimicking her dad as she gained confidence that it wasn't him. She stopped using tarot cards and has not seen a full-bodied apparition since that day.

For Alicia things have tapered off as well. That she is aware of, she hasn't walked in her sleep for months. Mary told me recently that Alicia was sharing Bible verses with her boyfriend as they texted back and forth—certainly a promising sign of better things to come for Alicia.

My Own Life

Even in my own life I can see how God has set me free from anything remotely close to evil. I accepted Christ into my heart almost twenty-four years ago now and I have been free from anything happening all these years—until I started this book. I believe the generational curse has been broken as well, since my two sons have had no issues that I know of. My son's mother comes from a Christian family and my boys have very godly grandparents. So evil didn't have any footholds to work with in their lives.

Now that I've been writing on this subject, the activity has picked back up again. But that was expected. Just because I am a Christian doesn't mean I am immune from being attacked. It has been a quiet thirty years for me since that automatic writing session when I was sixteen, and I thank God for that. I also thank God for guiding me on this endeavor. I know I am doing God's will and putting a dent in the kingdom of evil, seeing that things have picked back up against me. That tells me they (*evil*) are not happy with me and are doing their best to derail this endeavor.

The rest of my siblings still struggle with different occult ties. I think most of them believe that all mom did was good, which has kept them from seeing the dark side of it, though none of them literally practice it that I am aware of.

My sister still claims she hears voices and sees stuff move around once in a while. It has tapered off for her as she has gotten older. I believe the dark figures have subsided, though she doesn't talk about them. She experienced some horrible things as a kid so I can understand why they (*evil*) still harass her with little things.

As far as my brothers, they haven't said much, so either they didn't have a lot happen to them to begin with, or they don't want to talk about it. I think one of my brothers had stuff happen, since he used to end up in my bed a lot because he was scared. He was only four years old at that time so it's likely that he can't remember a lot from that period. He did share with me that he was plagued with a reoccurring dream as a kid.

Another brother still brings up astral projections, but Mom told him to leave it alone, and thankfully, he listened to her. He has shared with me about a time when a dark figure appeared to him and approached him while he lay in bed. Over the years he has heard strange footsteps and unexplained noises. He also believes that a certain building is haunted where he works, because he has seen figures roaming about the place.

My last brother used to play "Dungeons and Dragons" a lot right after my father passed away. He has experienced some strange things, but feels he can explain them away. Perhaps he is in more of a denial state then the rest of us siblings.

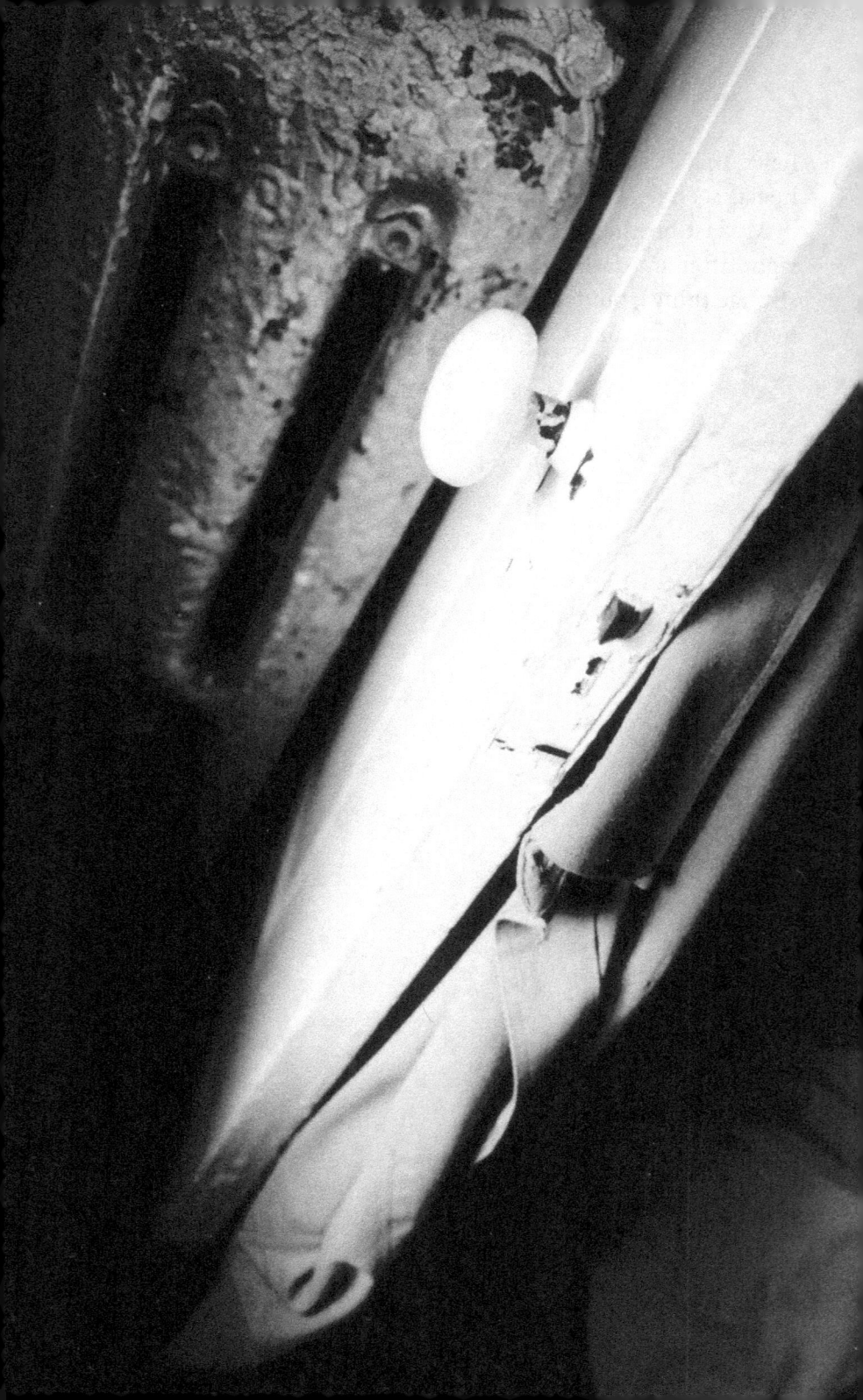

CHAPTER 18

Final Nudge

Common sense with all of this makes things so much easier to understand. For example, when I hear someone say a spirit is trapped in this world I respond, "You mean this spirit who can float through walls, appear out of nowhere in our kids' rooms, move objects supernaturally, and manipulate our dream life, can't figure out where to go next?"

If spirits took over my mom's hand supernaturally during her automatic writing sessions and wrote down amazing predictions of the future on a piece of paper, why didn't they just pick up the pen themselves and leave the family a note on the table saying, "Please help me move on to the next spiritual plane."

So many of today's horror movies end with a family finally at peace because they supposedly helped a spirit move on. The entire movie is plastered with scary encounter after scary encounter until the family discovers that this spirit's bones are buried in the basement. Why don't these spirits tape a note on the handle of a shovel, saying, "I'm down here, help me," instead of turning the light switches on and off when they need help or want our attention? Highly intelligent, out-of-this world spirits must lack common sense if you believe their antics are their way of trying to move on.

If these spirits want to show up in our kids' dark bedrooms just to say, "All is okay," why not deliver the message to the whole family in broad daylight at the supper table, instead of creeping around the house scaring everyone?

If these spirits are disembodied deceased relatives who were amazing people while on earth, why don't they like it when people read the Bible? I know hundreds of Christians who are loving, good hearted people. They are like that because of their love for God and because they read the Bible. If these spirits are "good," why do they react adversely to someone reading this same book that has shaped many people into amazing, loving human beings?

Why do these spirits act like Navy Seals, peeking around corners at people or staying in closets of kids' rooms? Why would they appear to young girls as reflections in the mirrors they are using? If they were dead relatives saying, "Hi," don't you think with all the power they have they would stay visible for a few more seconds so you could say hi back? Ninety-five percent of the time people only catch a fleeting glimpse of these spirits.

"Come on," we would say, "you just appeared in my room with the door shut, so that means you came through the wall or just materialized out of thin air. Stick around for a moment longer and let me say hi back. Why vanish on me?" Or is it that they really don't want you to see them long enough to see that it isn't a dead relative?

What about the supposed child spirits so many see? In Luke 16 it says that angels carried a beggar to heaven when he died. That's evidence that we get an escort to heaven when we die. Why would God allow these "child spirits" to remain on earth when his own angels carried an adult's spirit to heaven? Common sense suggests that these same angels would escort these precious young kids to heaven as well, especially since Jesus said that "their angels [i.e. the angels of little children] do always behold the face of my Father . . ." (Matthew 18:10, KVJ). This is where the concept of the "guardian angel" comes from. While we can't be sure that all believing adults have an angel or several of them assigned to them, we can know from the Lord's own words that this does apply to children.

Allow me to use my mother in another common sense scenario. Let's look at her automatic writing session with Sir Isaac Newton [mentioned earlier in the book]. If he by chance is one of these lost spirits who can't find his way home, why is he trapped in the Upper Peninsula of Michigan? He died in 1727, that's nearly 300 years of his lost spirit roaming around Upper Michigan. From what I read on him, he was a pretty smart chap. If a smart chap like Mr. Newton can't move on to the light and is trapped here in Upper Michigan, we are all doomed when we die.

When you really take the time to tear apart claims that are made about these encounters, it's easy to see the deception involved. Ignore the movies and TV shows that embed deceptive ideas in people's minds about what is really going on, and decide for yourself, using the Word of God as a guide and your own common sense as the filter.

Made For TV

In my 400-plus interviews, I have heard countless stories of spirits audibly contacting people, most often within the confines of their bedrooms late at night. These spirits tell people things like, "All is okay. It will be all right. Do not be afraid." When little kids tell stories of having secret friends they always have a name to go with the story. So obviously, these secret friends are telling these kids their names.

Why is it then that TV "ghost hunters" and paranormal teams have such a hard time getting spirits to talk to them—the same ghost hunters then have to resort to placing a recording device on a table so they can catch a spirit talking. In paranormal circles this is an electronic voice phenomenon (EVP). The group sits around being very quiet, while recording for half an hour or so. Then they play the recording back and listen intently. Lo and behold, they catch a spirit's voice none of them heard with their human hears during the actual recording session.

More times than not, the recording they capture is scratchy and barely understandable, with the spirits evidently straining to speak audible words. Are these spirits' vocal cords under too much strain with cameras and recorders present? They can speak fine to little kids late at night when they invade their rooms, but they have a hard time speaking clearly with cameras around. Really?

These same spirits that have all these supernatural abilities they put on display for us day in and day out can't pick it up a notch when cameras are rolling and recorders are recording? This made for TV stuff is deception pure and simple.

On one such show a spirit came across a baby monitor and said, "Get out or die." They seem to be able to verbally contact us when they want to do so, so don't be fooled by their sudden inability to murmur even one barely audible word to these paranormal teams equipped with their extremely sensitive recording devices.

Many families who invite paranormal teams to their home sit down with them at the beginning of the show, sharing what they have been seeing. Having watched many shows, I find it odd that the spirits being described are usually dressed in clothes from the turn of the 20th Century. Why doesn't anyone ever see spirits dressed in parachute pants from the 80s, or bell bottoms from the 70s? Perhaps this turn of the century style of dress adds allure and mystique. Or perhaps it's to convince the audience that the spirits are ancient and come from a long time ago.

When I lump everything they do together, including all the stories I have heard and those I've shared in this book, their (*evil*) actions prove to me they are in the business of deception, just like God's Word warns us: ". . . for Satan himself masquerades as an angel of light. It is not surprising, then, if his servants also masquerade as servants of righteousness" (2 Corinthians 11: 14-15).

Bottom line: These evil spirits have mastered a universal smoke and mirrors show.

A Simple Dream

Sharon's life has been littered with encounter after encounter. Her dream life really caught my attention as we spoke, because she has an ability that I have only come across one other time. Some of her dreams have actually come true. Exposing evil's part in this is a little trickier when things like this happen.

One of her dreams was quite simple. Her parents are divorced so her dad was seeing someone who lived in another town not far away. In her dream, her dad's girlfriend was climbing up a ladder. As she neared the top of the ladder, she fell off. That's all that Sharon remembers from her dream. Well, two days later, Sharon's dad called her from a hospital to say that his girlfriend had been cleaning the leaves out of her rain gutters when she fell off a ladder, breaking her leg.

There are obviously two sides to this story. Is there a chance that God was using Sharon to maybe warn her dad's friend? That is very possible, but highly unlikely. At the time of the dream, Sharon wanted nothing to do with God. She never read the Bible or took time to pray. That is why I question if this dream came from God.

On the flip side, evil encounters had been part of Sharon's life from a very young age. Her mom had dabbled in the occult and all her siblings have stories of encounters with things not of this world. My conclusion: Evil orchestrated this whole sequence of events—Sharon's dream as well as her dad's friend falling (or was she pushed?) off the ladder. Evil spirits were present in Sharon's room to plant a dream in her mind. Then some of their evil cohorts knocked her father's girlfriend off the ladder. It's that simple. Only God knows the future; evil spirits don't.

My mother's out-of-body abilities were not a gift, either. She made claims of going off to faraway places to help find lost children. Why couldn't these supposedly loving, caring spirits just go take care of this themselves? Why go through the supernatural effort to convince my mom to leave her body and use that same supernatural power to go help find those lost children? It was not a gift; it was a demonic illusion. My mom used these supposed loving spirits one minute to help people with her "gift," then hung a cross in my bedroom for protection the next. That kind of "math" doesn't add up for me, and it shouldn't for you, either.

Likewise, my mother's automatic writing sessions were not a gift. When she allowed evil spirits to take over her hand, she was not practicing something heavenly. The Bible says that gifts will be bestowed on believers, but these gifts don't include the ability to make contact with the dead. God did not dispatch Sir Isaac Newton to earth to tell my family our dog's puppy count before the puppies were born.

If you want to expose all of this for what it really is, it is very easy to do. The problem is that most people don't feel the need or have the desire to do so. As far as they are concerned, you can call it a gift, or call it being sensitive to the spirit world, *just don't call it demonic*. They refuse to call it demonic because of the implications that label would have about what is really going on in their home at night.

Evil must be exposed for what it really is, a strategic course of action filled with deception and deceit. Their goal is to keep an individual or family connected with their side of the supernatural their entire lives, so that over time the family members may even come to believe that these entities have good intentions. These "good intentions" are a false front that blinds many to who these pretenders really are, and therefore hold them captive to their deceit.

Spirit Meter

I was really hoping that by the end of this book, I'd have a formula or at least some suggestions about how to evaluate and deal with demonic influences in a person's life. But the truth is: One family has an occasionally light switch turn on or off by itself, while another family has to deal with their daughter being pinned down in her bed at night by some invisible evil force. Indeed, the creativity of Satan's minions to match their methods to individuals seems almost limitless. If only there were a paranormal tool or "spirit meter" to really gauge with certainty what was going on in a particular house.

The closest I can come to a tool like that is God's Word, which has quite a lot to say on this subject. For example, Job 1:8-9 reads:

> **Then the Lord said to Satan, "Have you considered my servant Job? There is no one on earth like him; he is blameless and upright, a man who fears God and shuns evil."**
>
> **"Does Job fear God for nothing?" Satan replied. "Have you not put a hedge around him and his household and everything he has?"**

That protective hedge I've mentioned several times throughout this book is a type of spirit meter, an indication of where you stand with God. I believe that hedge has different heights and strengths depending on how closely you are walking with God. Job walked so closely with God that his entire life was blessed by God. Job's children were even blessed by how closely Job walked with God. Satan was aware of this and complained to God about it.

Alongside my driveway I planted some spruce trees years ago with one purpose in mind—to protect my driveway from the blowing snow we often get here in northern Michigan. I planted the trees to the west of my driveway as a hedge (commonly called a "snow fence" here). The idea is that the wind-driven snow will hit that hedge, tumble over it into a drift, and not reach the driveway.

The first few years the hedge provided minimal protection, because the hedge hadn't grown high enough yet. But with time, it proved a worthwhile investment on my part as the snow piled up behind that hedge winter after winter.

With time your hedge can grow and become stronger as well. The way to make that hedge similar to Job's is by first believing that Jesus is the Son of God, who died on the cross for your sins. Then as you read God's Word and grow in your walk with him, that hedge will grow as well. The only time I have seen anyone mentioned in this book stop evil in its tracks was when they believed that Jesus was their Savior, and the Word of God was a part of their everyday lives. They had "planted" a hedge of faith against the schemes of the evil one, and its protective power came from God.

Wicked Meter

Wickedness can be measured to a certain degree through Scripture as well. For example, Jesus said: *"When an evil spirit comes out of a man, it goes through arid places seeking rest and does not find it. Then it says, 'I will return to the house I left.' When it arrives, it finds the house swept clean and put in order. Then it goes and takes seven other spirits more wicked than itself, and they go in and live there. And the final condition of that man is worse than the first"* (Matthew 12:43-45).

This passage is saying that evil spirits have different levels of wickedness. This particular evil spirit needed "backup." It had to go and find other evil spirits to help him torment this man – demons even more wicked than itself. At the least, this teaching suggests that there is a hierarchy of evil spirits, some more powerful and wicked than others.

To apply this today, maybe the families that have a TV turn on all by itself or a light switch with a mind of its own have weaker evil spirits around. And perhaps those who get pinned down on their beds and feel like they are being choked have more wicked evil spirits around.

There may be certain reasons why the more wicked ones are present within certain families. My research suggested that the individuals who have endured the most trauma are the ones who have the most wicked spirits around. For example, incest and a deep involvement in the occult bring on very dark spirits.

Many who stated that they were sexually assaulted at some point in their lives have also shared stories of being physically contacted by these evil spirits; for example, being pushed, lay upon, scratched, pinned down in their own bed, or even being choked by an invisible spirit.

Involvement with the occult brings on darker evil as well. The spirits may view their hold on certain families as a generational right. Clues to this are when kids at a very young age are having night terrors, are scared of being alone in their rooms, and may even have secret friends. They are being harassed because a parent or a grandparent dabbled into the occult. If the occult is a factor, it is likely that some of the more wicked demons will move in. The children won't be spared. And once these spirits attach to someone they are very hard to get rid of, perhaps because they don't like to lose what they worked so hard to gain access to.

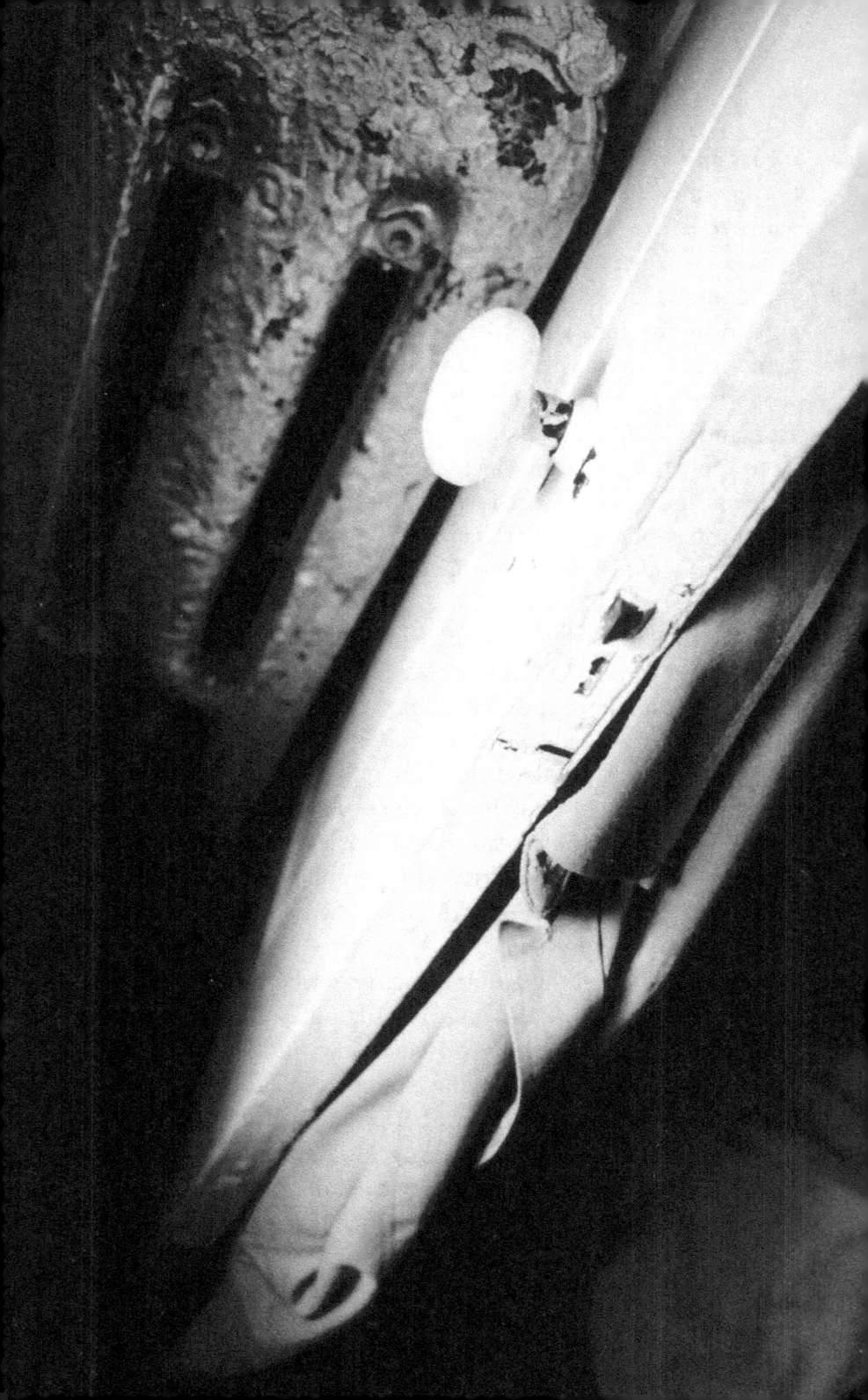

CHAPTER 19

All I Know

Julia has a young son who apparently sees half a spirit in his bedroom at night. He's told his mom that the spirit is cut in half, at the waist. He can only see the upper half of this spirit and it is constantly seen by him floating around in his room. It scares this little boy enough that very rarely will he make it through the night sleeping in his own room.

Julia's house has quite a bit of activity in addition to this apparition, including the sound of footsteps upstairs, and voices and other sounds with no explanation. The craziest night for the family involved dishes flying out of their kitchen cabinets landing on the floor and breaking into many pieces. As the family ran into the kitchen from the living room, they found all of the cabinet doors swung open as if someone had ransacked their kitchen.

One remarkable incident occurred when Julia was driving away from her work place one day all alone, like she normally does day in and day out. As it happened on this particular afternoon, one of Julia's co-workers was following behind her in her own car going home as well. She noticed someone sitting next to Julia and thought it was strange for her to be giving someone a ride home, since their place of business only has a few employees. The next morning at work she asked Julia who she was giving a ride home the afternoon before. Julia said to her, "There was no one in my car with me yesterday."

Was this a guardian angel in the seat next to her, assuming a role as her protector? Or was it an evil spirit showing off to the co-worker in the car behind, revealing itself to her but not to Julia? That answer will come, but not in our lifetime.

Some Day We Will Know It All

As much as I hate to say this, we simply don't have all the answers to such things right now. Even the apostle Paul admitted that we as human beings just don't know it all

> *For we know in part and we prophesy in part, but when perfection comes, the imperfect disappears. When I was a child, I talked like a child, I thought like a child, I reasoned like a child. When I became a man, I put childish ways behind me. Now we see but a poor reflection as in a mirror; then we shall see face to face. Now I know in part; then I shall know fully, even as I am fully known* (1 Corinthians 13:9-12).

There will be a time in the future when we will be given all the answers to life's mysteries. Until that time, we have to do our best to understand and comprehend things laid out before us, with our limited human knowledge, discernment, and wisdom.

But relying on human logic has its own inherent dangers, whether it's our own logic or someone else's, or even the result of the pooled logic of an entire group. Reliance on human logic alone has produced millions of ideas and opinions on what people are seeing or running into from the other side. If you "Google" paranormal books online, you'll get over twenty million hits. So you can pick and choose what you want to believe and what direction you want to take with this.

In 2 Corinthians 12, the apostle Paul describes being caught up to the third heaven where he heard inexpressible things, things that a man is not permitted to tell. In the book of Revelation, the apostle John talks about being on the verge of writing down what the seven thunders said, only to be told to not do it and seal up that announcement so no man would know what was said until the appointed time in the future.

There are simply things that God does not want us to know right now. Not everything in the spiritual realm has been revealed to us. This opens up the door for many to speculate about who and what they are seeing. Our limited understanding of this has allowed many theories and beliefs to develop through the years. But don't let that stop you from using the Scriptures to guide your perspective and actions, because it is possible to find enough biblically backed answers to the most fundamental questions. We owe it to ourselves, and more importantly, we owe it to the small children who rely on us to help and protect them.

Don't Jump On Bandwagons

You ultimately have to weigh the risks involved when allowing your child to continue to talk to some spirit in their bedroom. You as a parent have to decide to do nothing if your child tells you someone sat on their bed last night, or that someone whispered in their ear as they were trying to go to sleep. If you want to accept such things as your family's status quo, that is totally your right as a parent. But you must also live with the consequences of ignoring what is going on, or pretending it's not all that important.

Kate and three of her friends wanted to test out a Ouija board they had, so they decided to meet at a local cemetery and ask the board some questions. They chose this cemetery to make their test as scary as possible. They all pulled up to the cemetery and walked from their car in the dark to the first headstone they could see. Using their cell phones as light, they proceeded to lay the board out and start their night of experimenting.

They sat in the grass with the board between them. Before they even asked the first question they all heard the giggles of little children. It scared all of them so bad that the four of them bolted out of there, not even picking up the board. They just left it on the ground by the headstone, jumped in the car and left.

The next day, when it was light out, Kate and one of her friends went back to get the board. As they walked up to retrieve their board, they noticed the markings on the headstone closest to the board. It had the names of three girls on it. They had all died on the same day and were all under the age of eleven. Kate told me that she researched these three little girls and discovered that they had all died in a house fire in the area.

In light of what Jesus says about the angels of young children, is it rational to believe that God would allow the spirits of these three souls to stay back here on earth, roaming around? Or would God's angels escort an adult beggar to heaven but leave these little souls here on earth to roam around? Kate and her friends were tricked that night by demons pretending to be these girls. At the risk of repeating myself, I urge you to trust me. If something is in your child's room at night, there is a good chance it is not something good.

In the book of Revelation, John talks about what heaven is like, and the difference between existence there as compared to what it is like while here on earth. Revelation 21:4 says:

He will wipe every tear from their eyes. There will be no more death or mourning or crying or pain, for the old order of things has passed away.

Imagine for a minute these three little girls from Kate's cemetery encounter. If these poor souls were lost and confused, still roaming the earth as some might believe, doesn't that contradict a passage like Revelation 21:4? Being "lost" in my understanding of the word, will bring about feelings of sadness and despair. How can people who have died, no matter how tragically, still have to worry about being lost or confused? How can they still be hurting? The promises found in God's Word seem to get thrown out the window when I listen to people tell me why they think that children like this are still roaming around, visiting children who are still alive.

Over three thousand years ago Job described what would happen at his own death: *"The eye that now sees me will see me no longer; you will look for me, but I will be no more. As a cloud vanishes and is gone, so one who goes down to the grave does not return. He will never come to his house again; his place will know him no more"* (Job 7:8-10).

So if your child tells you that Grandma sat on the end of their bed, or that Grandma's in their closet, I urge you to remember these words. **It is not Grandma.** Even if your daughter smells Grandma's perfume, the scent of her hair spray, or her chocolate chip cookies baking in the oven, **it is not her**, it is a deception.

My Dad

The Bible is loaded with Scriptures that tell us that when we pass on there are only two destinations, heaven or hell. Job tells us we can't come back. The Old Testament King David said that while his deceased infant son could not return to him, that he would go to him, someday. Luke tells us that there are fixed barriers in place that won't allow world jumping. Jesus himself tells us that no one has gone to heaven and came back to talk about it.

When my father was a few months away from dying I asked him if he believed that Jesus Christ was his Savior. He told me, "Don't worry, Danny. I believe in Jesus." He knew it was weighing on my mind as he neared the end. Then a few short months later, he passed away in the hospital with his whole family around him. He even held on long enough for my brother to get home from Germany before he passed, which I felt was a gift from above. I placed my Bible on his chest when he had passed on. With the family surrounding him, I read John 14:1-3:

> ***Do not let your hearts be troubled. Trust in God, trust also in me. In my father's house are many rooms; if it were not so, I would have told you. I am going there to prepare a place for you. And if I go and prepare a place for you, I will come back and take you to be with me that you also may be where I am.***

Jesus Christ himself said that he would be preparing a place for us, a place that it is not on this earth, but in "his Father's house." It is a reserved spot in heaven for those who have trusted in Jesus. If it was important enough for Jesus himself to be so specific about the fact that we have a pre-determined place somewhere other than this earth when we die, then it is a promise I hold on to dearly. It is a hope I have that I will see my dad again. I will know right where to look for him the day I am lifted upwards. And I'm reminded of this (and comforted by it) whenever I read those verses.

I won't have to frantically search for him when I get there. The promise and hope I hold on to is that God's Word promises me he will be there. As I walk through the gates of heaven, there is no doubt in my mind that I will see my dad. His spirit won't be stuck on earth like some think can happen. He won't be taking care of unfinished business on earth, either. He is resting peacefully in his heavenly home. He is there no longer struggling with depression, fear, sorrow, or confusion. There are very few things in life that make me tear up, but the thought of seeing dad in heaven is one that gets to me every time. They are joyous tears because of God's promise, Titus 1:2 says: *"... a faith and knowledge resting on the hope of eternal life, which God, who does not lie, promised before the beginning of time...."*

To even think that he won't be there when I get there is unimaginable for me. To think that his soul or spirit is lost on this planet somewhere is also unimaginable for me. To believe that he has gone from being my father to a ball of energy floating around this planet haunting someone or some house is not even a possibility.

He is not ministering to me quietly behind the scenes as a "friendly" spirit, God already has that job covered by his mighty angels. His last moments on this planet were with his family, that is for sure. And after that the laws of this physical world no longer applied to him and he went to a place where he was introduced to a new set of laws that only apply in heaven.

Lack Of Hope

While researching this book, I have heard story after story of encounters with things not of this world, things that I had a hard time believing ever happened in and around the small community where I live, and things about my own mother that made me shake my head in disbelief.

It wasn't the spookiness of the stories that caught my attention, but certain denominators that surfaced as I listened. Words like spooky, creepy, scared, terrifying, and a host of other words never made me sit back in my chair. It was words like despair, hopelessness, sorrow, low self-esteem, divorce, loneliness, abuse, fatherless, and depression that made me sit back in that chair.

These are words that go hand in hand with many who have spirits around them on a regular basis. The ills of life or a generational curse are the two ingredients to blame for spirit activity within someone's home. I have witnessed this far too often for it to be coincidental.

Many people have accepted the lie that these evil spirits are around for other reasons, perhaps even good reasons. Nothing could be further from the truth. They picked up on the scent of hopelessness and followed it to their front door. When they got to the door, they checked and found there was no protective hedge around that family, so they came in with lightning speed.

You need to plant that protective hedge of faith in Christ, for when you are his, nothing in heaven or earth or anywhere else can separate you from the love of God.

Our Hope

Those words of despair, hopelessness, and depression can disappear if you choose to take these unwanted houseguests head on. But you have to take a chance and rely on God's power to help you. Nothing the world tells you to do about them can help you. You have to admit that they are not your loved ones stopping in for a visit. You have to dig down and get righteously angry about what is going on. You have to turn to God in faith, for anything else you try will be futile.

Someone I know is trying to help a girl who is being attacked in her bed at night by an unseen spirit. They have tried the traditional worldly approaches to solving this and nothing seems to be working. There is only one way to take these evil spirits on and that is in the power of Jesus Christ.

You have to repent of all that you have held on to so dearly for most of your life. You have to stop reading horoscopes, stop going to see mediums, stop messing with Ouija boards, and stop relying on spirits whose sole objective is to trick you into relying on them for guidance. You have to admit that they are in this with one thing in mind, to lead you astray and keep you as far away from God as they possibly can.

My first twenty-four years on this planet were filled with everything I've included in this book. No, I am not exaggerating. My first sixteen years included the company of demonic beings. They were in my bedroom as a kid growing up. I was present when loved ones made contact with them. And I saw things that can't be explained with human logic.

I also lived a life of despair. My parents moved us fifteen times and we never had money for anything. Our entire family wrestled with depression and hopelessness. It was an unending cycle of never catching a break, and I believe with all my heart these demonic beings amplified this cycle of despair in order to make us want more of their company. My parents ultimately made their own choices in life, but evil compounded those problems.

Then in 1989, at the age of twenty-two, I was honorably discharged from the Marines with a drinking problem that threatened my marriage. We had moved back to Michigan from California and I brought that terrible problem back home with me. After drinking one night I came home and got in a fight with my wife. I struck her for the first time in our marriage. That's when I knew that I needed to change or my world was going to crumble right before my eyes. I needed to change or I would lose her and my son, who would have grown up in a broken home like so many I've described in this book, harassed by demonic beings and feeling trapped in their darkness.

A pastor reached out and "took me under his wing," with the result in 1990 I accepted Christ as my Lord and Savior. I was forever changed as I knew for the first time in my life what the word hope meant. The evil spirits that had plagued me vanished. The words despair and hopelessness were no longer in my vocabulary, either. This broke the generational curse as well. My sons never saw a spirit in our home. They always slept through the night soundly and without interference.

As I pen these last words of the first draft of this book, it is Easter Sunday, a day Christians all around the world celebrate because Jesus Christ died on the cross for our sins, then rose from the grave by the power of God three days later. That same power that God used to raise Christ from the grave is the power you can have as a believer in Christ. The demonic world shudders at anyone who has this power. Why do they shudder? Because they know they have to obey that power; they know that they don't stand a chance when faced with it.

You ultimately have the choice regarding whether or not to allow demonic beings access to your life and your family. With that choice comes great responsibility, because this is not just about you; it's about your children as well. This is a choice you will have to live with as your child crawls into bed with you during the night because of what's in their bedroom, under their bed, or in the closet. And rest assured that God keeps a close eye on kids and what we as parents and adults do to them. Jesus said, **"But if anyone causes one of these little ones who believe in me to sin, it would be better for him to have a large millstone hung around his neck and to be drowned in the depths of the sea"** (Matthew 18:6).

The Invite

Don't let your preconceived idea of who or what these beings are influence your actions. They are not haunting your house; they are there because someone opened the door. You are not more "sensitive" to these spirits and therefore you see them; they are there because they have been invited. If you have unique "gifts" like my mother had, they are not gifts at all. Evil spirits make them seem like gifts because they know this is what you want to believe.

There is only one invitation that will end all of this for you. You have to invite Jesus Christ into your heart and accept him as your Lord and Savior. You have to repent of your sins and demolish all of their strongholds (incorrect thinking patterns). Trust in what God says in his Word and believe in the good news as described by the apostle Paul in 1 Corinthians 15:3-4: *For what I received I passed on to you as of first importance: that Christ died for our sins according to the Scriptures, that he was buried, that he was raised on the third day according to the Scriptures. . . .*

Instead of inviting evil into your life, invite Jesus in, for he wants to have fellowship with you, like friends around a dining room table. In Revelation 3:20 we find this invitation from the Lord: *Behold, I stand at the door and knock. If anyone hears My voice and opens the door, I will come in to him and dine with him, and he with Me* (NKJV).

Accept that invitation and evil will flee. Your child will sleep through the night, instead of having night terrors. Any generational bondage that plagues your family will be broken. That feeding trough they (*evil*) have been feeding from will be emptied and washed clean, and they will move on.

Perhaps you've heard this very simple explanation of how to proceed: *For God so loved the world that he gave his one and only Son, that whoever believes in him shall not perish but have eternal life* (John 3:16).

Seek out a pastor who is willing to allow his chair to levitate off the floor or to let something evil paw at his chest in order to help you. Make evil hit a brick wall for you and your future loved ones—those you have now and those to come. What is the best time to turn your life heavenward, and allow Jesus to be Lord and Savior of your life? Now, of course. For now is all you have.

List Of Resources Consulted

CHAPTER 2

Ghost Hunters: True Stories From the World's Most Famous Demonologists (St. Martin's Press, 1989)

Cornwell, Peter, dir. "Haunting in Connecticut." Lion's Gate Entertainment, 2009

CHAPTER 3

Wan, James, dir. "The Conjuring." Warner Bros. Picture, 2013

CHAPTER 5

Zucker, Jerry, dir. 'Ghost.' Paramount Pictures, 1990

Miller, Joel. (2012, Oct. 21) Do you believe in angels? www.foxnews.com/opinion.2012/10/21/do-believe-in-angels/

Jones, Susan. (2013, Dec. 17) Poll: American's Belief in God is Strong–But Declining

cnsnews.com/news/article/susan-jones/poll-americans-belief-God-strong-declining/

CHAPTER 6

"Unholy Communion: The Fourth Kind Unveiled." Joseph Jordan and Guy Malone (2013, June 21) Retrieved from https://www.youtube.com/watch?v=f7qy9oYOcRw

Shyamalan, M. Night, dir. "Signs." Touchstone Pictures, 2002

CHAPTER 7

Dickason, C. Fred, *Angels Elect & Evil*, The Moody Bible Institute of Chicago, 1975

Phillips, Ron, *Everyone's Guide to Demons & Spiritual Warfare*, Charisma House, 2010

Unger, Merril F., *What Demons Can Do To Saints*, The Moody Bible Institute of Chicago, 1991

CHAPTER 8

Wan, James, dir. "The Conjuring." Warner Bros. Picture, 2013

Perron, Andrea, *House of Darkness House of Light*, AuthorHouse, 2011

Toods, Keven, dir. "The Haunted." Discovery Communications, 2009-2011

Kraft, Charles, "Panel Discussion," retrieved from Roberta Winter Institute, Posted June, 4, 2013

CHAPTER 9

Amiel, Jon, dir. "Sommersby." Warner Brothers, 1993

CHAPTER 13

Ramis, Harold, dir. "Groundhog Day." Columbia Pictures, 1993

Lewis, C.S., The Screwtape Letters, Macmillan Publishing Company, 1982

CHAPTER 14

Hammond, Frank and Ida Mae, *Pigs In The Parlor*, Impact Christian Books, Inc., 2008

Graham, Billy, *Angels*, Word Publishing, 1994

CHAPTER 15

Kraft, Charles, *Defeating Dark Angels*, Regal, 2011

Appendix 1

Attachments Often Related To Demonic Activity

The feelings, emotions, or even environments listed below are experienced by most human beings at some time in their lives. With an "attachment," a person feels this way constantly. When there is no reasonable explanation for why these feelings surface continually, the person needs to explore if they are dealing with an attachment. For example:

Depressive issues can plague an individual – including hopelessness, despair, suicide, death wish, or despondency.

Bitterness is common – including rage, resentment, retaliation, unforgiveness, and jealousy.

Insecurity can exhibit as self-pity, inadequacy, fear of failing, rejection, constant panic, worthlessness, and extreme fear of things including: snakes, heights, an intruder breaking in to your home, etc.

Sexual issues are prevalent with spirits as well. Symptoms include: fantasies, pornography, lust, masturbation, rape, homosexual feelings, spouse swapping, and incest. (Even thoughts of sex with animals and close relatives happens to those who have attachments).

Guilty feelings plague most who have attachments. Shame, unworthiness, lying spirits, self-condemnation, and when someone is constantly saying they are sorry for no worthy reason.

Control – including domination, spouse snapping all the time, spouse feeling like a prisoner, suspicion, distrust, fear of accusation, and contention top this list.

Forgetfulness is followed by constant frustration, confusion, procrastination, losing items all the time, and putting items in places where they don't belong—for example, putting the mouthwash in the refrigerator.

Bursts of anger are very common with those who have attachments. Rage, murderous thoughts, suicidal thoughts, acts of violence, self-harm, blame, hurtful remarks to those you love, and occasionally, harm to animals is a red flag especially in children.

There are also things that I have noticed throughout my interviewing that may reveal that darkness is close by on a regular basis. The things listed below aren't always the case, but more times than not I feel they are. They include:

Dressing Gothic, household items disappearing and reappearing, house always feeling cold, isolation to bedroom, nose and lip piercing, extreme tattoos, tattoos honoring the dead, overboard with cats, fascination with imaginary characters (Harry Potter, fairies, mystical figures, etc.), continuous money problems, appliances always breaking down, homosexuality, pets changing demeanor suddenly, sleep walking, vivid dream life, constant feelings of being watched, being watched in the shower as well, and someone in and out of terrible relationships, constantly moving and losing job after job, waking up with bruises the size of fingertips or waking up with scratch marks, sometimes in threes, waking up with pain in shoulder or chest, kids never sleeping through the night (they often wake up crying or screaming), talking with a secret friend, never listening to parents, saying words they shouldn't know, and trying to hurt their siblings.

---

[1] This list is copyrighted, and cannot be reproduced without permission of the author.

About The Author

Dan Langenfeld was born in Racine, Wisconsin and has lived most of his life in Michigan's Upper Peninsula. He grew up under the influence of the occult and has spent the past twenty-five years studying the occult and demonology. Over the past few years he has interviewed more than 400 people with paranormal problems in their lives. The information from these interviews is the basis for this book.

Dan is a veteran of the United States Marine Corp, honorably discharged in 1989. He has been actively involved with programs for kids over the years, including coaching little league for ten years, teaching Sunday school for teenagers as well as adults, while serving as Director for his local Awana program.

Dan and his wife, Michelle, currently reside in Carney, Michigan where Dan owns and has been operating his own small business for fourteen years now. Please feel free to contact Dan at: *swordofthespirit66@yahoo.com*, or you can reach him on his Facebook page, "Upper Michigan Paranormal Truth Seekers."

Peak Publishing
Arvada, Colorado

PEAK PUBLISHING promotes healthier living and wholesome values by publishing resources for the reader's enjoyment, education, or inspiration. We help authors share their stories through memoirs, fiction, biographies, family histories, children's literature, how-to-do-it manuals, educational materials, and more.

Fulfill your dream. Write that book. We can help you reach the world in print and eBook formats. Contact us at:

1-877-331-2766 | *peakpublishinginfo@gmail.com*

www.ingramcontent.com/pod-product-compliance
Lightning Source LLC
Chambersburg PA
CBHW071601080526
44588CB00010B/976